Garth Cartwright, New Zealand born, oft' wandering, is an award winning journalist, sometime World Service broadcaster and the author of *Princes Amongst Men: Journeys with Gypsy Musicians* (Serpent's Tail).

Praise for *Princes Amongst Men*

'Roma music is redolent with Gypsy lore, language, passion and personality. [Cartwright] found a vibrant, living musical tradition that is central to pan-European culture' *The Times*

'A valuable chronicle of their personal histories [Roma Gypsies] and musical development... He writes lyrically and builds steadily to create a sense of anticipation' *Times Literary Supplement*

'Funny, revealing and frequently moving' *Observer Music Monthly*

'Excellent survey of Roma musicians in the Balkans... What distinguishes Cartwright is his style, his verve and his wholehearted engagement with his subject' *Guardian*

'As Bulgaria and Romania creep on to the travel and property pages, this book about Balkan gypsy music could become an essential alternative guide... For anyone interested in the reality of Roma culture, or planning a holiday in the region, this is the perfect offbeat companion' Sue Steward, *Daily Telegraph*

'Insightful, energised and empathetic' *Time Out*

'Reminiscent of Jack Kerouac or Hunter S Thompson...the prose is carefully written and keenly observed' *New Internationalist*

'You don't have to be a fan of gypsy music to appreciate Cartwright's book... Part travelogue, part musical history, it's full of picaresque tales told in an appealingly off-beat and impressionistic style' *Uncut*

MORE MILES THAN MONEY

Journeys Through American Music

GARTH CARTWRIGHT

A complete catalogue record for this book can be
obtained from the British Library on request

First published in 2009 by Serpent's Tail,
an imprint of Profile Books Ltd
3A Exmouth House
Pine Street
London EC1R OJH
website: www.serpentstail.com

ISBN 978 1 84668 687 0

Designed and typeset by folio at Neuadd Bwll, Llanwrtyd Wells

Printed and bound in Great Britain by Clays, Bungay, Suffolk

10   9   8   7   6   5   4   3   2   1

The paper this book is printed on is certified by the © 1996 Forest
Stewardship Council A.C. (FSC). It is ancient-forest friendly.
The printer holds FSC chain of custody SGS-COC-2061

FSC
Mixed Sources
Product group from well-managed
forests and other controlled sources
Cert no. SGS-COC-2061
www.fsc.org
© 1996 Forest Stewardship Council

To: Charlie Gillett, Chris Strachwitz
and the indomitable spirit of Curtis
Mayfield; three who, each in their own
way, helped shape how I heard America

Contents

Acknowledgements

A road trip such as this relies, to a large degree, on connections. Whether they provided information, contacts, food, music, transport, company, even a sofa to sleep on, I'm indebted to all of the following: Roger Armstrong (Ace Records), Chris Strachwitz (Arhoolie Records), Kathy Norris (Canyon Records), Greg Butensky, Jim Kelly, Sharon Schanzer, Elijah Wald, Luis Rodriguez, Radmilla Cody, Leo Dodd, Andria Lisle, Scott Bomar, Tim Sampson, Diana Jones, Lenka Romanova, Bruce Iglauer, Michael Frank, Jimmy Castor, Mickey McGill, Charles Wright, Ian Hancock. Back in the UK my friend and editor John Williams and my friend and agent Hannah Westland both helped shape the sprawling notes that became this book. Gracias, amigos! Pete Ayrton and Andrew Franklin at Serpent's Tail/Profile are passionate, hands-on publishers. Ian Anderson at *fRoots* provided space for reports from the American road. Shout outs to: Bernard MacMahon, Allison McGourty, Adrienne Conners, Neil Scaplehorn, Gareth Evans, Conrad Heine, Marc Gengel, Florence Halfon, Steve Bunyon, Henry and Helmut at Asphalt Tango Records, Orville Saunders, Leon Parker, Rob Hackman, R. Crumb, Rupert Orton, Pete Z, the Jones-Benally family, Errol and Adam, Joe Cushley, Michael Dregni, Niamh Murray, Nita@ Goldstar.

Certain photos for this book were provided by Dave Peabody, Alan Balfour, Colin Escott, Tony Russell, Heather Scaplehorn, Elijah Wald, Canyon Records, Alligator Records, Arhoolie Records and the Soulsville Foundation – their help and generosity are appreciated.

To friends international: many blessings!

To my parents, who gave me my first taste of America with Mark Twain and westerns, your support – no matter how crazy my quests may seem – is always appreciated.

Last but not least: to Florence Arpin and Alexander and Ariane, who always make returning to South London a pleasure.

Since we don't know each other, I want to give you a complete picture of myself, why I'm interested in America, why I'm always occupying myself with America: because in America, there's the whole world. In Italy there's Italy, and in France there's France. The problems of America are the problems of the whole world: the contradictions, the fantasies, the poetry. The minute you touch down on America, you touch on universal themes. For better or worse, that's the way it is.

Sergio Leone

I always thought it was our America as much as anybody else's – circus people and carnival freaks, prisoners and music makers, troubadours, minstrels, hobos and poets and such, we can't let the goddamn country go down to politicians and corporate madmen and media people and college professors, run it over and ruin it all. It's ours, our goddamn country. We built the midway, didn't we? And we make the music that goes on the midway, from sea to shining sea. You know, goddamn, Ronald Reagan died recently and they flew the flag half-mast. Well, did they fly it at half-mast for Ray Charles? For Johnny Cash? Declare a national holiday? Yet these people, Ray Charles, Johnny Cash, Hank Williams, they moved and changed the daily lives more than any politician who are just grifters and scum. Wouldn't even let them in the goddamn midway. So let us now praise the real American heroes, the ones with heart and soul who changed things for the good.

Little Jack Horton

Gambling on a future: dice men, Mississippi, 1939

Prologue: Last Call at Lee's Unleaded

No moon illuminates our journey and the stars, why, they fear to shine. A damp Saturday night. October's cruel winds now wane but something ominous, witchy even, remains in the atmosphere. I try and explain this to the driver. He nods, says, 'Uh-huh, urban voodoo.' Well, I think, that explains everything. Silence envelops us as we continue through Chicago's West Side. Considering this neighbourhood is dense with public housing the quiet is eerie, almost unnerving. I stare into the gloom: few street lamps and little sign of human activity. Get the sense of a city under siege; doors bolted, lights dimmed, movement suspended. At traffic lights a jeep pulls alongside, all eyes on us, driver and passenger, pale-skinned outsiders. The Cherokee trembles, subsonic bass patterns reverberating through its chassis, bass like a war dance, and I – *as ever* – recognise in the rhymes Atlanta's Goodie Mob.

> *I'm tired of lyin'*
> *I'm sick of glorifyin' dyin'*
> *I'm sick of not tryin'*

I'm tired too. Bone weary and exhausted from pursuing an insane American quest. Lights change, jeep roars off, all fuel-injected rush. Our car splutters, barely idling. Pray silently: *please don't break down here.* A burnt-out tenement looms on our left, all shadows and ash, ash and shadows. Damn, how *did* I end up so deep in an urban cityscape few voluntarily venture into? I've felt more at home, safer, in North Africa, Pakistan even, than I do on these streets where we share a common language and culture. Chicago's urban decay reminds me of Guatemala City... edgy, broken, *hostile.* Feel a twitch in my limbs. *Getting jumpy.* Strange how foreign one can feel in a cityscape that is very familiar. Mentally I've walked these streets across the decades: certain sounds from vinyl, images offered up in films, the sights and smells conjured by books, offered me what bluesman Big Bill Broonzy called 'the key to the highway'. This mythic key unlocking an America that exists beyond the McUSA we consume daily, allowing those who possess it to, as Americans say, cross the tracks. But who in their right mind wanders into black ghettos and Mexican barrios? Enduring eighteen chafing hours on a Greyhound bus just to get to Nashville? The red-eye exhaustion from driving for days on end solely to party in a honky-tonk? Or dancing in a Nevada desert sandstorm hoping for – *what!?!* – don't know... a 'vision', I guess. For near on two months now I've been constantly moving through America, an endurance test that recalls doomed Texan troubadour Townes Van Zandt singing

> *Livin' on the road my friend*
> *Was gonna keep you free and clean*
> *Now you wear your skin like iron*
> *And your breath is hard as kerosene.*

To be as desperate and free as old Texan outlaws appeared attractive from a distance but, by now, I'm too weary, too beat, to get tripped up on romantic conceits. Restless. That's how I explain myself to others. 'Restless: 1. unable to stay still or quiet. 2. ceaselessly active or moving: the restless wind. 3. worried; anxious; uneasy.' *Collins English Dictionary* has my number. What else explains an adult life spent fleeing convention and regulation?

Growing up in Auckland, New Zealand, surely contributed to my sense of rootless unease. Aware you're existing at the bottom of the world, this sense of isolation enforced by most of the media we consumed: once heralded as Little England, post-WW2 NZ swapped British colonial influence for the embrace of everything American. Go to a movie, switch on the TV, tune into a radio station... we were sold American and, as fledglings, gobbled and gobbled. Tennessee held greater mythic appeal than Taranaki while California appeared the promised land. The Americans colonised my subconscious and, in April 1990, I landed on US soil, whippet thin and naive as only a Kiwi youth could be, determined to follow Huck Finn's example and light out for the territory. Whatever that territory was. For six months a rusty $600 Buick carried me through a land of some beauty and much disappointment, the imaginary America I inhabited in Auckland rarely coming in sight. After an extended sojourn in San Francisco I fled to London, a city so grey and unwelcoming my life till then appeared to have been lived in Technicolor. *Key to the highway?* First I needed to unlock my mind.

Tucked away in South London tower blocks across the nineties I realised how British politics and pop culture were immeasurably shaped by the USA – often by its worst elements – and felt no desire to return; Europe and Asia provided new sources of fascination. Instead, when American neocons ranted about 'Old Europe' refusing to join their 'war on terror' I despaired at what had become of the nation that once enchanted me. But after writing up a year in the Balkans among Romany Gypsy musicians, one replete with references to blues music and Beat poets, it became obvious I needed to look anew at the USA. Time, then, to try once again and find a key to American highways.

I returned to the USA unsure of what I would find. From London the rhetoric of Cheney and Rumsfeld suggested 'freedom' was twisted into covering for fear and repression while New Orleans, fabled city of song, now existed as an emblem for American decline and neglect. George Bush Sr was president when I was last here and now his namesake occupies the role; American military were in Iraq then and are again now. *The more things change the more they stay the same?* Let's find out.

I found out: kept finding and finding until the road heading south from San Francisco ran out in Chicago. South and West Chicago's bleak streets once served as a port of call for generations arriving from the Deep South; here almost a century ago the likes of

Louis Armstrong and Memphis Minnie made music that would prove a gash in Western consciousness. Many followed and their Chicago creations remain among the twentieth century's most influential: Mahalia Jackson developed a form of gospel vocal that now dominates popular song; Muddy Waters plugged in and the resulting electric shock can still be felt; Chuck Berry cranked out what came to be called rock 'n' roll music (*'it's got a backbeat/you can't lose it'*). These artists were teachers in the Sufi sense of the word, their wisdom travelling farther than simply that of musical influence.

The final night of this pilgrim's quest. And I'm so tired, so tired, so tired… haven't slept right since I don't know when. What better to do, then, than get in a ride and roll through Chicago's West and South Side? Here we are now, in search of destinations that may no longer exist, streets offering only abandoned buildings and the eerie quiet surrounding communities in collapse. We pull over, parking close to neighbourhood bars, and quickly exit the night into rooms full of sound and light where bands play on the floor or upon makeshift stages, small ensembles conjuring up the grooves that built Chi-town, singers talking in tongues, slippery rhythm sections, guitarists feeling for colour, music still capable of casting spells. Locals check us, two white men, but the driver's a familiar face and the focus rapidly returns to music and drinks and laughter, keeping the spirit flowing. We join the party, shot glasses held high, hips moving to the music. Again and again we do this, partying until instinct suggests we move on, casting long shadows beneath street lamps, slipping into darkness.

Last stop: Lee's Unleaded Blues Bar, way deep in the South Side. Shag carpet, heavy velvet curtains, fake marble bar, claret-coloured walls; Lee's offers *Superfly* chic, a loud, tough interior, hustler's paradise. Chicago is full of blues bars steeped in nostalgia but Lee's is unconcerned about tourist fantasies, no posters of Howlin' Wolf or Robert Johnson on these walls. Johnny Drummer leads the house band, a dapper, smiling man, his sound the Southern soul-groove black America now considers 'blues'. I order whiskey. A glass is placed in front of me but, as I turn to observe Drummer, my drink gets lifted. On the South Side this is a minor affront, not something to make an issue of.

Order more whiskey and, this time, hold glass close. Johnny Drummer exits the stage and lush locals begin taking turns on the mic. A small, plump man in a fluffy Kangol hat, features impressively ugly, wrists heavy with gold, diamond-studded crucifix hanging round his neck – ghetto fabulous, indeed – starts singing of how all the girls love his hot dog. The tune's generic, limpid chorus and slick innuendoes fitting the post-midnight club vibe. 'Little Scotty!' someone shouts and many applaud. I've heard of Scotty; one-time pimp, sometime Sancho Panza to Jesse Jackson and Louis Farrakhan, noted South Side soul-blues singer. Scotty acknowledges his audience, wraps what appears to be a badly burnt hand around the mic, begins to sing, musicians locking behind him, and I fall back to philosophising: *could it be that right here, right now, I'm witnessing a requiem for American music?*

American music has done more for US standing than any politician or policy, touching lives, inspiring dreams. A crippled French Gypsy banjo player called Django, upon hearing Louis Armstrong for the first time, muttered 'Ach moune' (Romany for 'my brother'). The Rolling Stones, when arriving in the USA in 1964, were asked what they wanted to see in the country. 'Muddy Waters and Bo Diddley,' they answered ('Where's that?' replied the credulous interviewer). Saharan nomads and Algerian rai singers, Soweto township dwellers through to Palestinian youths, all took inspiration from American music to carry their own native tongues forward. Zulus played jazz, Maoris sang soul, Japanese women mastered Ike Turner tunes, Slim Dusty employed a Texas twang when singing about an Australian town with no beer. And every nation has an Elvis impersonator. Even suburban brats raised on thousands of hours of junk US TV sensed in American music a mystery and longing that made the world infinitely more interesting. *Am-er-I-ca!* We loved that land even though we'd never set foot in it.

There's little popular American music today that spells out *Am-er-I-ca!* in all its eccentric, offbeat brilliance; instead contemporary American music has more in common with the

Mc franchises on every high street: heavy-metal crybabies, moronic rappers, over-emoting R & B divas, freeze-dried country singers, scholarly jazzers, indie-rock entropy... music, once so much a part of a community's character, is now shrill and banal, a tinny squeak of sound. I'm generalising, sure, but one thing is certain when listening to twenty-first-century American music: the thrill is gone. 'The buying and selling of music, what they've done to it, is a disaster on the scale of cutting down the rainforest,' cartoonist R. Crumb once suggested to me as we sat hypnotised by the sounds emanating from his 78s of the earliest American music. A musical rainforest that helped the world to artistically breathe and now deforestation is almost complete... better be careful or I'll end up crying into my whiskey. After thousands and thousands of miles cutting across the USA, was I, tired and emotional at journey's end, sensing a music, a *culture*, I had loved for so long now turning to dust before my eyes and ears? Such thoughts. The kind that carry their own psychic blues weight.

Johnny Drummer introduces himself, a gracious man, happy to talk about being raised in Alligator, Mississippi, right smack on Highway 61, enlisting in the services, cutting a blues 78 for Sam Phillips but getting recalled to the navy for Korea before he could build a Southern rep, resettling in Chicago and 'What a city Chicago once was! My *God*, son!' Playing drums in countless South Side bands over the decades, a pro until his house burnt down and car got stolen in the same week, then working a nine-to-five for the District School Board, occasionally releasing 45s on obscure labels, switching to keyboards because they are easier on you than drums ('as you get older'), Johnny's perseverance establishing him as a South Side veteran. He pauses, looks at whoever's tripping up on stage, the crowd getting messy, catcalling and laughing, says, 'Two things you couldn't give me: land in Mississippi and a bar in Chicago.'

'Lee's used to be such a fine place,' he adds. 'Back in the seventies you had Junior Wells, Son Seals, a lot of good people played here. Now, well, look what we got.' *Look indeed*: the latest singer to take the stage, Yard Dog, is missing a leg so balances on crutches while singing 'Slip Away'. A buxom black woman in a copper-coloured wig stands close, smiling and caressing him. Yard Dog, perhaps enjoying her attention too much, wanders off key. Still, he sings with feeling, giving the song a darker blues feeling than surely was originally intended, nodding and muttering 'uh-huh' as people shout affirmation. Gripping crutches, Yard Dog hobbles off stage. Copper Wig takes control of the mic, starts delivering a freak song, challenging every man in Lee's with each salacious line. Johnny, whose theme song is 'I Want to Get into Your Head Before I Get into Your Bed', shakes his head – tiny, pendulum gestures – and focuses back on me.

'I hear you been roamin' 'round America?'

'That's it, listening out for good music and trying to take freedom's pulse.'

'You find it?'

'The music or the freedom?'

'I know 'bout the damn music. How's the freedom?'

'If constant movement registers as being free, sure.'

'Uh-huh, that's a very American kind of freedom.'

'Travel?'

'Naw. Restlessness. Thinkin' you'll find someplace better down the line apiece.'

Down the line apiece: I found ruin and beauty, openness and intolerance, despair and hope. All encountered across a territory they call America. Johnny's watching me carefully, maybe expecting some smart-ass, white-boy answer. Me, an outsider just passing through, and him, a man who's spent a lifetime learning exactly what America has to offer. The night fades. Copper Wig's still singing about breaking bedsprings while church is only a few hours away. Sirens flood the air, lending a brief frisson to Lee's, an edge to everyone's lush consciousness, one that fades as police or paramedics rush past. I glance at Johnny and shrug, tongue too thick to offer any real insights right now upon my two score and ten American days and nights. He looks at me, gives another of those polite, sad shakes of his head, says, 'This is it, son – end of the line.'

Sound and vision: Ed Lee Natay and Canyon records
founder Ray Boley, Phoenix, AZ, 1951

INTO THE SOUTH-WEST

San Francisco, Reno, Black Rock Desert, Las Vegas, Tucson, Phoenix

When you say 'America' you refer to the territory stretching between the icecaps to the two poles. So to hell with your barriers and border guards!

Diego Rivera

And I, to whom so great a vision was given in my youth – you see me now a pitiful old man who has done nothing, for the nation's hoop is broken and scattered. There is no center any longer, and the sacred tree is dead.

Black Elk

Lighting out for the territory:
sharecroppers stalled on the way to
California, 1937

chapter 1

San Francisco: A Baptism in Sound

'Everything cool?' asks the Bishop. I glance up at the towering figure in long purple robes, features fierce yet benevolent, and answer yes, thank you, all is cool. Considering this is St John's African Orthodox Church and the man addressing me is Ramakrishna King Haqq, aka Bishop King, founder of the only temple on earth dedicated to the worship of John Coltrane as a latter-day saint, things are most ricky-tick.

'You know, I'm about to start a journey,' I say to the Bishop, choosing words carefully, 'a long journey, across a lot of the US. I can't explain exactly what the journey is about 'cos it's a quest of sorts. All I know is that I'm guided by music and, y'know, I want to search out the American music I love. But I'm scared of what I'll find 'cos America is losing this music and... well, I think maybe losing its soul.'

'I hear you,' says Bishop King.

'So what I'm trying to say is, I think I made the right decision to come here today.'

'That's the spirit calling, son.'

The spirit calling. Why, yes, indeed.

San Francisco, Sunday morning, and I woke feeling ragged, suffering from both jetlag and a Golden Gate Bridge-sized hangover. Do the right thing, go to church. But not just any church; the congregation of St John's once worshipped Coltrane as God incarnate. I wonder what JC, being a humble type, would have made of this? In 1981 Alice Coltrane sued the church for the sum of $7.5 million ('Widow Of "God" Sues Church', read a newspaper headline) owing to its apparent misappropriation of her husband's image. Alice's lawsuit went nowhere but the resulting publicity helped attract attention: the African Orthodox Church – a popular storefront church in black neighbourhoods – approached King about joining the fold. This meant recognising Coltrane as a saint (not God) and adhering to the Scriptures instead of the psychedelic mish-mash of chants and prayers the One Mind Temple (as St John's was then called) recited. King took the leap, studying for a Doctor of Divinity degree in Chicago and, in 1984, set up St John's African Orthodox Church. St John's never became simply another outlet for Bible thumping: I last caught the church in 1991, a wild and woolly mix of homeless centre, impromptu jam session and black gospel church. All of which made some kind of sense in Haight Ashbury, the messianic preacher with a massive afro and saxophone recalling a time when the likes of Charles Manson and Jim Jones also courted followers from the 'hood's poor, lost and disaffected. The playing was raw – one cacophony had me thinking 'uh ohhh, punk jazz' – but big fun, life-enhancing, the kind of thing that gave the Haight its loose, wild vibe.

Rising rents evicted St John's at the end of the nineties. Yet anyone possessed with the conviction driving Bishop King wasn't going to fade away and I found St John's residing in a Lower Pacific Heights church. This nondescript neighbourhood of warehouses, office buildings, used-car lots and shapeless apartment blocks – the kind of place you might choose to live if only to deny your very existence – appears anathema to St John's spirit and I can only guess the congregation have been lent this violet-coloured temple. Upon entering I noted Coltrane's version of 'My Favourite Things' playing through the speakers. A tall black man in purple robes greeted me. The hair's greyer, shorter but, unmistakably, it's Bishop King.

'You came from London to be here?' He sounded pleasantly surprised. 'See, this proves my point that jazz is the ambassador for the United States. It calls people from all over the world to America and they come to us because John Coltrane has moved something in them. So someone like you comes here to give praise and thanks. That's good. That's the spirit calling.'

Well, maybe. A long time's passed since I last attended a church service. Yet music expresses the transcendental, articulates stuff beyond words. Which, I guess, is what I've come to worship. So how did the Bishop develop the Coltrane cosmology?

'In 1965 my wife and I had to decide where to go to see some jazz. Back then there were a lot of jazz clubs in town. A lot. We decided to go to the Jazz Workshop in North Beach. Playing that night was the John Coltrane Quartet. The room was small, crowded, very smoky, and what I heard there I like to call a 'baptism in sound'. I grew up attending Pentecostal churches and the experience in the Jazz Workshop was comparable to what happened at church when the music and preaching built to such a level the congregation felt a direct connection with God. The old folks called it 'the Holy Ghost falling on the people'. It manifested in different people in different forms. Some people would dance, some people would cry, some people would rejoice, some people would speak in other tongues. But for that moment, that period, time was arrested, so to speak. You were obeying the Holy Spirit. And, son, that's the feeling I got that night listening to the Coltrane Quartet. They played with a intensity beyond entertainment. A intensity that went beyond jazz musicians trying to push the envelope.

'Jimmy Garrison, he was the Quartet's double bassist, played a solo and it was like nothing I've ever heard. The man was lost in the music and where it was taking him. So much so, drool was hanging out of his mouth. He was gone with the music, way, way out there! I realised right then the music of John Coltrane was representative beyond culture. He was making music that wasn't just a cultural or ethnic thing. There was a higher calling to his art. I began to see God in the sound. This was a point of revelation. Not that I immediately went away and set up the church. More Coltrane's music allowed an evolution, or a transition, to begin. The consciousness level began opening, evolving. You understand now what I say about a baptism in sound?'

Uh-huh. At least, I think so. Not that I've ever felt a particularly religious impulse towards anything. But a baptism in sound… well, sure. Music talks in tongues I don't try to understand, speaking to the intuitive and primal, one of humanity's greatest resources to share and communicate with. Bishop King looked on as I mentally chewed this through. 'Everything cool?' he asked.

I'm early so kick back in a pew, thinking about JC, while the Bishop and his musicians set up. *The sound of John Coltrane*: thick yet swift and tending to coil and coil until exploding with power and tension. Not the warmest of saxophone tones – when my teenage self first heard Coltrane playing alongside Cannonball Adderley on Miles Davis's *Kind of Blue* I preferred Adderley, his soulful blues tone more appealing than Coltrane's mercurial solos – but one that's come to signify an unswerving artistic discipline, Coltrane being to post-war jazz what Che Guevara was to Latino revolution. Indeed, JC came to represent a jazz pilgrim's progress: the saxophonist as seeker of spiritual and musical enlightenment. Coltrane was a romantic modernist, believing art must forever be an act of radical renewal, that creativity enabled communion with the cosmos. His excessive appetite for drugs and alcohol ended after Miles Davis fired him (and punched 'Trane out: for nodding off on the bandstand) and he turned to the disciplined pursuit of nirvana as practised by Hindu ascetics. The kind of intensity that goes with such beliefs energised Coltrane across the sixties, his music constantly evolving, challenging all others to challenge themselves, reaching apotheosis on 1965's *A Love Supreme*, the album's expansive title and sonic rush hinting at what a generation of seekers were searching for. Coltrane seemed to channel the decade's *zeitgeist*, an icon to Black Power and psychedelic rockers. Today Coltrane's sound still casts giant shadows across a very tame jazz scene but, just as agitprop and lysergic guitar solos failed to usher in a post-Woodstock utopia, the sheets of sound JC pushed forth post *A Love Supreme* register only as skronk. Coltrane belatedly realised this and hoped to

Meditation: Coltrane
contemplates his tools

collaborate with sitar minimalist Ravi Shankar but liver cancer
stole him away in July 1967.

I think of how Cannonball Adderley went on to pioneer soul-
jazz and enjoy pop success, unhindered by Coltrane's excesses.
I think of Miles asking JC why he soloed excessively, the reply
being he didn't know how to stop, Miles saying 'you take the
horn out of your mouth, John.' I think of Alice Coltrane's *Journey
in Satchidananda* and how she turned the harp into a fluid
instrument for surfing the jazz cosmos. I think abou— 'We serve
food after the service but please make yourself at home,' says a
young black woman who I hadn't even noticed approaching me.
Food? OK, she's thinking I'm homeless and have come for the free
food they serve after the ceremony. Only away from London two
days and already considered a hobo. Bloodshot eyes and drawn
features, I guess.

By 11 a.m. people are trickling in: smartly dressed black families,
a smattering of fellow tourists, two youths with long hair and

instruments and several homeless men (who sit way down back). Bishop King begins the service with a Bible reading that he intersperses with thoughts on America today, at one point favourably quoting Black Muslim leader Louis Farrakhan. A long, silent prayer meditation follows. Several women start singing a psalm, loose and gospel-flavoured. Then the band kick in – keyboards, electric bass, drums, two saxophones, clarinet – the sound strong and full, rhythm section locking, keyboards providing a melodic bed, Bishop King blowing big, fat Coltrane-notes out of his saxophone while the clarinet player dances around him, looping notes like he's lacing shoes. Other members of the congregation start banging tambourines, the female choir wailing and howling. Two black kids, dressed for church, try to find some space to join in on trumpet. Not easy as the Bishop and a dreadlocked sax player are ripping great solos, but the boys' stifled squalls suit the atmosphere, slipping bum notes into proceedings, hungry to engage with this big loud ritual. A man carrying a pair of bongos arrives, sits, finds a rhythm, joins the jam. The rockers in the congregation clutch saxophones and listen intently until one starts to blow. Ouch! He stops, breathes, blows again. *Parpppp!* A little girl, obviously bored by proceedings, looks on with disgust: *the adults get to have fun but no one plays with me!* A homeless guy, hair sprouting in every direction, ambles forward, pulling notes out of his harmonica, dancing a little shuffle. He's not in the same key, maybe not even in the same dimension, as the band. But spiritually, sure, he's continuing the Haight vibe.

'John Col-*trane*': I recall proto-rappers the Last Poets snapping those three syllables over a beat while offering praise to a musician they considered a fellow militant, and this gets me imagining Bishop King, back in the day, surely positing JC as a proto-Black Panther, sax in one hand, shotgun in another, *A Love Supreme*'s scratched vinyl blasting through huge speakers, brain on fire with revolutionary dreams. Not that there's any sense of violent uprising in the air this morning; no, today's ceremony is about spiritual uplift via galvanic musical overload. I mean, this place is jumping as people dance and sing and play and throw themselves into Coltrane's cosmic blues. Just like they did when jazz first announced its miscegenated self to America and the world around a century ago. Myself, I date the twentieth century's birth to 26 February 1917, when the Original Dixieland Jass Band entered Victor studios in New York to cut the first jazz recordings. The ODJB weren't particularly talented – five white New Orleans musicans who'd copped licks from playing alongside their black neighbours (soon to become a familiar story) – but once Americans (and then the rest of the world) got to hear their primitive riffing and barnyard stomp the century caught fire: this wild Southern sonic hybrid, a new music shaped in Louisiana and Mississippi, Texas and Tennessee, kin to what was developing in Cuba and Haiti, Brazil and Jamaica, a blend of African and Spanish, Jewish and Gypsy (and African), Anglo-Irish and French (and African), sent a rush of blood to everyone's head. And would continue to for most of the century. In St John's it still does: the joint is rockin', hot jazz, music that starts in the groin, demands the hips shake, engages the soul, *hoo-doo voo-doo*. The congregation's fired up, spirit calling, responding.

Jazz today: too often bloodless and cerebral, seemingly comfortable as a quasi-classical music. Witnessing Wayne Shorter, a sax-playing descendant of Coltrane, in London a few years past, I had to flee the concert hall, so stuffy and precious was the playing. Some might say Shorter was playing jazz but I only heard noodling. Coltrane's finest music has an earthiness – *native bloodlines* – that establishes it as among the USA's most potent twentieth-century musical creations. And there's very little in this world that rewards engagement quite like great American music. Sure, Pablo Picasso was no asshole, a great movie engages many senses, certain poems and novels resonate and many a life-enhancing invention, from combustion engines to instant noodles, has lead humanity forward. But American music, specifically the stuff made by the nation's most marginal citizens, celebrates the twentieth century's inclusive genius, the people's spirit, like nothing else. In 1977 the USA sent the Voyager spaceship to the farthest reaches of the universe and on

9

it, alongside Bach's Brandenburg Concerto, Senegalese percussion and Indonesian gamelan, is Blind Willie Johnson's 'Dark Was The Night' and Chuck Berry's 'Johnny B. Goode'. Lucky ET.

Yakety-yak! A sax is chattering and St John's jumps and the whole place is convulsive with sound and sweat and good vibes and if a noise approximating a field holler (or maybe it's just a hungry drunk) arises from the back pews, well, why not? All around the honkers and shouters push things forward, building a trance state. And I'm feeling fresh; a Coltrane blast clearing my hangover. The music continues to build, atmosphere casual but intense, Bishop King blowing serpentine sounds that caress and tease and murmur about places, experiences, full of colour and light, of humanity, how we rise and fall, blues and good news, mercurial stuff, not easy but startling, asking only absolute concentration, and the dread picks up a clarinet, starts blowing thin, beautiful shrieks while a sax player jumps on drums (the drummer now settled on keyboards) and the bassist, a young woman with a bright smile, keeps thumping that tough, liquid rhythm out, no drool but Jimmy Garrison's spirit lives, and the sound… loose, free-form (but not free jazz), churning, choir shrieking and shaking, congregation shouting encouragement, kids dancing, rockers and bongo and harmonica all throwing themselves in deep, chasing 'Trane's wild, mercurial sound far, far out. *Bam! Bam!* Recall Ralph Gleason writing of Cannonball Adderley's live North Beach set 'at times the atmosphere of the Jazz Workshop resembled a church as much as jazz club', and think, *yes!* Legend has Buddy Bolden, mythic New Orleans jazz pioneer, putting trumpet to lips and 'calling the children home'. Bishop King's blowing, music calling us to this temple of sound in the Frisco wastelands. The right place to start my American music quest? *Everything cool!*

San Francisco, golden city of utopian dreamers, is where my previous American sojourn finished in early 1991. I always imagined I'd make it back some day and after ruining my health riding ancient Balkan roads the idea of the New World held a lot of appeal. When Greg, a Frisco friend and fellow musical traveller, mentioned joining his posse to attend the annual Burning Man festival in the Nevada desert I got to thinking about what else America might have on offer. One festival, no matter how unique, couldn't justify a US visit. But to use Burning Man as a springboard to follow up a lifelong passion for American music, music created by communities in specific locations? Well, as the Arabs say, I could feel the breeze beneath my nostrils. Before fleeing the USA for Europe last century I lived in Haight Ashbury, working menial jobs – digging ditches, washing plates, care work – available to those who didn't hold Green Cards. The pay was lousy but the Haight offered cheap rent, cheaper drugs and plentiful live music. A good time could be had, yes indeed. Even if I never fell for the Grateful Dead tie-dye and acid culture many of my neighbours embraced I liked the 'hood's vibe, the sense that the Haight remained an outpost of American outlaw culture. Fifteen years on and the dotcom boom has flattened San Francisco. Capitalism takes no prisoners and the Haight I wandered post-church was, while little changed architecturally, a place transformed. Only the addition of Amoeba Records, a vast second-hand music emporium, wins approval. Once-plentiful live music venues have vanished. As has the grungy character that fired the neighbourhood's raw brio. A few youths in Dead T-shirts linger, hoping for some hint of halcyon days, but the spirit is long gone, replaced by Gap, Starbucks and the chain stores that take the high out of high streets everywhere.

I wander along Upper Haight – still home to a few second-hand soul-record shacks and a majority black populace – but even here things are in flux: the 'Californian master race' Bay Area punk icon Jello Biafra once jested about making their presence felt with vegan organic cafés. I grab a bus uptown to North Beach. Italian cafés serving huge latte bowls and expensive cheesecake sit alongside City Lights, publishers of Ginsberg's *Howl* and the finest bookshop on the planet. The climate's humid, overcast, seagulls buzz overhead and a certain kind of tension hangs in the breeze. Can't put my finger on it, some uneasy energy still lingers. Yet for what? The restless, intuitive vibe that once inspired Jacks London and Kerouac, Lenny Bruce and the finest West Coast jazz clubs, to take up North Beach residences is long extinguished. It's not just jazz that's faded, San Francisco's music scene has been a flatliner for many years – Counting Crows, a band who serve microwaved 'classic rock', and Green Day (ditto for 'classic punk') are the last Bay Area acts to gain real prominence. The city's musical energies have decamped north to Portland, Oregon, a college town where grungy alt.rock dominates. Cartoonist Joe Sacco – a Portland resident – has satirised his home town's preening musical narcissists, youths wilfully oblivious to the waning creative (if not commercial) energies now generated by rock.

Taking a Bart train across the Bay to El Cerrito, I arrive at Down Home Music, a vast emporium of American roots music and base for Arhoolie Records, the independent label founded in 1960 to record and reissue regional American music forms. Arhoolie founder Chris Strachwitz is responsible for uncovering a fabulous wealth of American and Mexican vernacular music; I figured I'd soak Chris for advice on my forthcoming journey but he groans when I mention Burning Man – his former documentary-making partner Les Blank is, apparently, now focusing on filming the festival's 'art cars' (neo hot rods) – and shrugs as to what I might expect to find across a USA where he once uncovered the likes of bluesman Lightnin' Hopkins and zydeco king Clifton Chenier.

'After World War II this raw energy was out there and the working class got factory jobs and pretty good money and they could support bands out of that. You didn't have the huge difference between rich and poor, people made good wages, unions were strong. Now... now it's almost like slavery, it's disgusting, people working so hard just to earn a living wage and they've got them hooked on all this crap they want to sell them. And that kills music. The Anglo world is totally the same everywhere. San Francisco and Chicago are still unique because people live in them but Houston and Dallas and cities like that are awful, completely deserted, people go and huddle in their yuppie areas and eat the same dog burgers and drink the same wine and listen to New Age crap. It's completely soulless.'

Understood. But what if I emulate Chris by leaving Anglo America behind and crossing the tracks?

'I hate to put it like this but with the end of segregation a lot of black music has ended. Back then blacks lived in self-contained areas, almost ghettos a lot of it, and they had their own community support systems which included plenty of clubs offering music, everything from downhome blues dives to sophisticated supper clubs. Now all that's left in those communities are the poorest people who can't move out. In other areas you still have strong regional traditions – Mexican banda brass is really popular with the immigrants. In Texas there's tejano which is for the bilingual Mexicans who were born in the US. Cajun and zydeco keep going in rural parts of Louisiana, although they hardly ever speak French any more. And in real poor parts of the Appalachians you'll find people keep their fiddle traditions. But a lot of vernacular music is dead. I went to Preservation Hall in New Orleans two years ago and it was a parody. This all-black jazz band were playing but the leader had to play up his Louis Armstrong mannerisms to get a rise out of the audience. It used to be a dancing audience and now it's a sit-down audience that want to hear "When the Saints Go Marching In". You'll find out for yourself. Getting on the road and meeting the musicians is the way to do it.'

I mention I'm staying in the Mission district, a Mexican barrio located close to downtown, and Chris says to look out for mariachi bands playing Mission bars. I ride the Bart back across the Bay, ascending at 16th Street and Mission, where I'm surrounded by a tsunami of piss stink, cheap wine and crack fumes as the local crazies beg for change and holler at one another. Living in Peckham, I'm familiar with miscreants, although America has more of 'em. And they're louder and smellier. But, for the most part, harmless and spirited: a vagrant digging through trash turns, locks eyes and gleefully says, 'I got everything I need an' then some!' While the Haight's been homogenised, the Mission retains a scruffy identity, adult emporiums advertise Video Latino, grocery stores sell bleeding Jesus trinkets, offer to cash cheques and send money south, bars have signs declaring 'No Drogas. No Pistolas Permitir', customised Cadillac Coup de Ville's roll past pumping sweet-and-sour snatches of Sinaloan horns, shops sell shirts emblazoned with the Virgin of Guadalupe, mariachi and ranchera CDs are stacked high and murals depict Aztec rituals and regeneration, all dense purple and yellow tones. Lively? Like a carnival!

The Mission's hectic energies stand in contrast to much of the Bay Area, San Francisco having the lowest US adult/child ratio yet the highest adult/designer dog one. What this says about the city I'm unsure, but if they removed the Mission from the city's statistics the curve would only widen: returning here I feel visible relief 'cos kids are everywhere (and so are women: don't see many females in some parts of SF) and dogs are barrio dogs, skinny and undomesticated, and a sense of joy, of yah-yah-yah abandon drifts through the 'hood. 'Mo' money,' sing-shouts a Mayan-looking youth dancing on the sidewalk to a messy hip-hop groove, 'mo' money!' In the twenty-first century the Mission's something of an urban reservation; here the city's nighthawks and losers, hustlers and dreamers, gather in a last stand against encroaching gentrification. Walking up Mission Street, music blaring from cars and bars and people spilling on to the streets, I sense Frisco's tough old soul still scraping itself off the sidewalk to go another round. Then I think of how New York's East Village has been swallowed whole into glitzy Manhattan – 'Disneyland for college kids,' sneered Iggy Pop when I once asked him why he fled the East Village for Miami – and wonder: for how much longer can the Mission resist the tidal wave of wealth that has suffocated San Franciscan culture?

I take a seat in a neighbouring bar, order 'una cerveza' and the barmaid answers in Spanish. Got it right on that one: not too much English spoken here. Frayed-looking Mexican men shoot eight-ball or loll beneath paintings of naked women with impossibly pneumatic breasts while the jukebox plays low-rider faves by the Dells and War. Chris suggested mariachis in the Mission sometimes turn up at local bars and play tunes for tips. Here's hoping! The locals ignore me, the sole gringo, while I observe them, squat and black-haired and moustache-wearing, creased features, faces out of Peckinpah movies. Thinking of crazy Sam reminds me of how the first Chicano icon, nineteenth-century bandit Joaquin Murrieta (1829–53), ended up in Frisco: his preserved head on display in a local museum. Murrieta was killed by Californian Rangers, his notoriety so great that his head toured California for decades with citizens paying $1 to see it and the hand of his partner in crime, Three Fingered Jack. The city lost Murrieta's head (and Jack's three fingers) in the San Franciscan earthquake of 1906 but any mariachi worth his sombrero should still be able to sing Murrieta *corridos*, his legend weaving injustice, race, poverty, corruption, guns and violence, a real American death trip. To the Spanish-speaking populace – thousands having remained in California after the state was annexed by the USA following the Mexican–American War (1846–48) – Murrieta was a hero, the inspiration for Zorro, a man who stood up against Anglo-American cultural and economic domination. That's the myth. More prosaically, most of the men Murrieta robbed (and murdered) were Chinese mineworkers – for decades Chinese played out roles not too dissimilar to those of Africans in the South, literal beasts of burden, their legacy San Francisco's Chinatown. Today it's Murrieta's descendants, Latino migrants, who occupy this role. With no accordion-toting musicians appearing, I feed the jukebox a dollar and punch in a Charles Wright tune. The opening bars of 'Express Yourself' jab across the bar then cut out when a Murrieta lookalike pulls the plug and begins DJ-ing techno-banda at maximum volume. I take this as my 'hasta la vista, baby' moment and exit back on to Mission Street.

Sunday night and the streets are dense with heavy traffic, air full of cool Pacific draughts. Hearing a slapped bass, I enter a pitch-black corridor, finding a pumping hillbilly band rocking a basement bar. 'Who is it?' I ask the cashier. 'Wayne "the Train" Hancock,' she replies. Imagine finding the Texan wildcat playing in the Mission! Wayne's beating out the rhythm on a Martin acoustic, his three-piece band snap strings and boogie and he sings of thunderstorms and neon signs, of juke-joint daddies and Hank Williams's railroad rides. Rockabilly kids – boys dressed in tight suits and string ties, girls in polka-dot dresses that billow as they dance – spin across the floor. When the Train takes a break, gasping 'thank yuhs' in a drawl even more nasal than that he sings in, I figure enough Texas for now; I'll be in that huge state soon enough.

On the sidewalk and a trio of young Latinos, two guys and a girl, crash into me, tipsy as, everyone apologising, then they're bumming cigarettes, offering shots of Night Train – *Dios mio!* – suck it an' spit, nasty shit. Where, I ask, is the music at? They laugh, shrug and say no good music ever comes out of the Mission. But Carlos Santana, I say, grew up here. This attracts open-mouthed disbelief – that anyone as wealthy as Carlos ever walked these filthy streets! – and they ask 1) do I know Santana? 2) is that what I wanna hear? I offer double negatives. I mean, the Mission's most famous son now churns out corporate bilge but please don't take this as criticism of your 'hood. 'Nah, nah,' says one who by now I've worked out is called Jorge, 'he's just for *patos*. An' you don't look like a *pato*, bro.' Gee, thanks. Then Maria, I think that's her name, says, 'How you know this guy ain't a *pato*, Jorge? Look at his shirt,' and starts pointing at my Polynesian print shirt, which, I guess, compared to their uniform of basketball tops, looks very un-urban. I try to explain the shirt's a Tongan design and I'm from New Zealand and Maria, as if to apologise, says, 'You sure speak good English for a foreigner!' I enquire about mariachis and they laugh – 'a gringo who likes the music of our *abuelos*!' – and we swallow some more Night Train and smoke another Spirit and they say, 'Hey, bro, hang with us. Maybe we'll meet some friends, score a little weed.' I consider but, no, no, far too old to be getting down with the kids. Getting down with their grandparents is more my style these days. Our goodbye involves lots of weird handshakes I can't get the hang of and they say 'mind how you roll, bro' and I say 'take care, chicos' and off we wander into our Mission nights.

Hours later, having finally given up on coming across a mariachi troupe, I find myself in some ragged drinking hole where James Brown tunes are strained through blown speakers and no one dances – damn, no one even twitches. San Francisco, what's happened to your beautiful blue soul? Doesn't this city feel the need to go out and engage a little? Or is everyone locked into the dance clubs? Nodding to slippery electronic beats, minds swollen with MDMA. Either that or they're tucked in bed with laptops, working out ways of earning mo' money... mo' money... mo' money. Ponder my Mission blues while waves of exhaustion wash across me and a tequila shot is lined up. The bar is held together by duct tape and the barmaid's drunker than any of her solitary customers and a song about coming to Frisco and wearing flowers in your hair starts looping through my skull, just the chorus, seemingly sung horribly slow and mournful with a dulcimer twanging away in the background... *Saaaannn Fraaaaan... cissss-co... wear some flow-uhs in yer hair...* and think how stupid that tune must now sound. How stupid it always sounded, an anthem for those who bled the Haight dry. I can imagine dealers humming it as they drugged and raped the teenage runaways who arrived expecting nirvana. Slam my tequila. The barmaid cheers, pours another. I reach for it but jetlag overrides, insisting I sleep. *Right here. Right now.* Except the bouncer, who helps me on to the sidewalk, disagrees. Disoriented, I stumble into the night. Sad ole Frisco, no song in its heart, no flowers in its hair.

Burning all illusions tonight: Black Rock Desert, Nevada, 2006

chapter 2

Black Rock Desert: Ghost Dancing

Monday morning I wake to people flushing and brushing, ready to seize the day, but all I want is to sleep off the tequila hound blues. No such luck: marching orders are shouted, sofa reclaimed. OK, let the quest begin. Grab coffee and wonder why I'm about to attend a week-long festival in the desert, especially one without a musical focus. Excuses rather than answers spring to mind: Burning Man's often described as a continuation of the Haight Ashbury 'freak' vibe that once made this city famous. Also, it gets me into the South-west, a territory for centuries considered empty wasteland but now where twenty-first-century America is being spun. And, as a tower-block dweller, the idea of a week in the desert holds a strange appeal, especially after yesterday's sermon at St John's; biblical prophecy and desert pilgrimages often going together.

Our van fully loaded – nothing but coffee and ice is for sale at Burning Man, everything else must be taken in – we roll out into a silent 20th Street. Cruising along Upper Mission, I note a bar from last night and my hangover throbs harder. A street mural, dense with Mexican Catholic iconography, whispers border tales. Roll down the window and the dawn tastes of unknown pleasures. Take a last glance at the Mission, aware I'm heading into the wild, wild West. Who'd have imagined a more perfect launch pad for the journey I'm about to embark upon? *Vamos? Vamonos!*

As we cross the Bay Bridge grey clouds peel back, revealing Pacific Ocean blue. Traffic's dense but moving and as we scramble through radio stations searching for news a public broadcaster carries a report on how the number of Americans living below the poverty line continues to increase. Jim and Greg, veteran 'burners' I've hooked up with, are bemused by my travel plans: running around America in search of the last surviving outposts of vernacular music? Like... *why?* Not that they're averse to music, just American roots music appears pretty hokey to them. Jim asks how I aim to travel and I suggest Greyhound buses and he shakes his head, saying he's never ever ridden in one. They're for poor people, he adds. Jim and Greg are East Coast-raised computer whizzes who shifted to San Francisco and tapped into software gold mines. They both like to travel internationally but shudder at the thought of Texas, Tennessee and Mississippi: red states where guns and Bibles are culture and liberals are considered traitors. Music is my muse, I try and explain, and the more messed up America is the better the sounds tend to be. 'Consider New Orleans, guys, before Katrina it had a remarkable musical culture alongside extreme poverty, racism and the highest murder rate in the US.' They laugh warmly at my enthusiasm for places they couldn't be paid to go to. Greg says, 'You are one loco Kiwi.' Indeed, crazy times ahead.

Leaving the Bay Area, we circle Sacramento – Governor Schwarzenegger's fiefdom – then begin climbing the Sierra mountains. As we cross the Donner Pass my imagination goes to work. Inconsequential as the pass appears today, its name reflects the fate of an 1846 wagon train from Illinois that, while attempting to reach the promised land of San Francisco, got stuck in early snowfall in the Sierra Nevada, leading to starvation, insanity, cannibalism... true American Gothic. Everyone from Joan Didion to Stephen King has employed the Donner tragedy as supine metaphor for California nightmare, and our smooth trek over the pass gets me dwelling on the horrific events that engulfed the pioneers, noting that, yes, very bad things can happen to the unwary or unlucky traveller in the USA.

Entering Nevada we stop in Reno – ugly duckling to Las Vegas's high-rolling peacock – for bad food, beer and 40 gallons of water. Reno's a dusty frontier town whose time has passed, decaying casinos offering cheap accommodation for distant ski fields. Yet Reno was once dubbed 'the centre of the universe' for

Rumble in Reno: Johnson vs
Jeffries, Nevada, 1910

an event that determined Nevada's future: on 4 July 1910, Jack
Johnson fought Jim Jeffries for the heavyweight boxing title.
Jack London coined the term 'the Great White Hope' for Jeffries.
Johnson's victory here unleashed a racial Armageddon: scores of
blacks were assaulted, maimed and murdered by vengeful white
mobs in the days to follow, the first event ever to launch coast-
to-coast race riots (the second was the murder of Martin Luther
King). A ragtime tune that followed Johnson's victory went

> *The Yankees hold the play,*
> *The white man pull the trigger*
> *But it makes no difference what the white man say,*
> *The world champion's still a nigger.*

The decline in boxing's status as social event today means no
one sings anything about whoever's champ. I mean, who is world
champion today? I think we're in that rare era where a white hope
may genuinely hold the heavyweight title. Admittedly, some giant

from the former Soviet bloc. But his name and face are hazy while Jack Johnson hovers totemic and timeless, an American icon.

Outside Reno the road opens up and Jim puts his foot down, pushing the van farther, faster. Everything feels right: blue sky above, black tarmac below, arid surrounding vista, miles slipping past. I'm riding the American highway, hungry for experience, a thousand songs swirling though my skull, thinking yes-yes-yes. Double yellow lines curve into the horizon while heat waves shimmer and morph. The landscape is lunar, centuries of sand-heavy desert winds chewing upon rock, rolling-scrubby-barren: no sheep roam, no hawks arc, no roadkill. Water, how precious water must be to all who live among the desert landscape. We stop for gas at Pyramid Lake Reservation services, flat plains surrounded by rolling hills, a land so dry that tawny browns are just about the only colour going. A handwritten sign stuck to the gas-station door announces a meeting to combat police brutality against Paiutes. What goes on, I wonder, in this empty territory? The Paiute have lived off these infertile lands for centuries, and as burners pass through their reservation they gather along the roadside, children waving and laughing, teens selling 'Indian Tacos', adults eyeing all with contemptuous caution, elders aware nothing new will be seen under the sun, watching our motorcade ripple into their desert. The surrounding hills morph, shift shape, pink and black, unforgiving. Onwards, through salt flats, onwards, past fields of volcanic rock, onwards, under cerulean skies, onwards.

This fierce landscape kindles more memories of American death trips – did the pioneer settlers who opened up the Applegate-Lassen Emigrant Trail in the 1840s tramp through this same wasteland? Considering the abundant aridity, they may have: in 1848 Peter Lassen acted as guide to a covered wagon train from Missouri bound for California. Crossing the land we now know as Nevada, they found the terrain barely passable, struggling through desert after desert – all suffered terribly and many died. Such folly didn't stop the route becoming the first highway to San Francisco a year later when the California gold rush unleashed a human frenzy. Soon water was sold for up to $100 a glass by speculators who realised easier money was to be made from human folly than mining for gold. The hapless mining migrants who couldn't pay the price demanded were often left to endure a terrible death, tongues black and swollen, eyes bursting from skull. And now we party on these killing fields of old American dreams. Strange days are upon us.

As we arrive at Empire the gas station and general store announces 'Last Gas/Shops for 97 miles'. We buy ice creams and drive on, soon entering the ephemeral city of Black Rock. First indication of what lies ahead comes as we pass a sound system where burners bounce in various states of undress. A copper-coloured muscleman, naked except for sunglasses, pumps to the beat, phallus cutting a fleshy arc through the air. Well, I think, well, well.

Dust, drugs and techno. Six days into Burning Man and DDT defines the burners and their annual ritual. Tomorrow is day seven. And on day seven I have a lift out of this godforsaken place where no plant or animal life can survive. Having tallied the days stuck here I'm now calculating the hours till I leave. And here comes another reason to flee: desert twisters. At a distance tornadoes pack a surreal beauty, but as they begin to spin across the vast playa (desert basin) Burning Man occupies, the sky gets turbulent with debris, forces of nature adding chaos to the mix.

I stand still, digging these dust devils, admiring how they turn up to gatecrash the party, rip shit up, pondering on what lore comes riding their tails: nomads who once sailed Saharan sands on camel trains conjured tales of genies from desert storms; what do the revellers here, awash on Ecstasy and LSD and the tightly woven dreams from always knowing only plenty, make of this ferocious wind? A tsunami of sand and grit blasts over me. Let's store that one as Thought for the Day; right now, restlessness having caught me out, I'm in the middle of the playa, stranded hundreds of metres from both our campsite and the nearest large enclosed event tent. Burning Man is laid out on a clock principle:

I'd left our campsite (ten o'clock) aiming to get to a DJ tent (five o'clock); rather than cycling around a track following the circular clock pattern I'd attempted to cut across the desert diagonally. When the atmosphere is calm this is a difficult-if-possible cycle through thick desert sand. When dust devils fill the air cycling is impossible. Now I'm reduced to pushing bicycle, concerned more with survival tactics than myth. In the distance I can see the Man. The Man is a towering wooden structure, ever more totemic as sands whip around it, situated at the centre, the heart, of the site. There, I think, I will go. Shelter, yes, is a given beneath the Man.

Wearing a T-shirt as face mask and pushing a bicycle through a maelstrom makes for uneasy movement. And the desert storm, one of considerable natural ferocity, shows no sign of relenting. Cursing hoarsely, straining against the cotton weave covering my eyes, I feel a wave of self-pity sweep over me – *'this isn't fun!'* – then chasten myself as I think of those individuals facing a Desert Storm in Iraq, one involving not only sand and wind but all manner of calculated violence. Stumble as a twister rips past then regain balance and trudge forward. Feel like dumping my bike but, inevitably, I'll need it later. Push it, as the song goes, push it good.

By the time I reach the Man I'm dusty, sweaty, weary, my skin stinging from these fierce, alkaline sands. But I've made it, safe in the sanctuary of the Man, the festival's wooden womb upon which stands the ultimate pagan cyber icon. I gulp water (Survival Rule No. 1: never, ever leave your campsite without water), sit in the shade and wait for the storm to ride out. Dig out Mark Twain's *Roughing It*, appropriate text for the festival – neither running water nor fresh food is available, I'm caked in grey, powdery dust – and begin to read. Twain hadn't developed his mature style when he wrote *Roughing It* (1872) so tries too hard to make big points and raise guffaws. Still, his writing on crossing the deserts of Utah–Nevada – then known as the Great American Desert – is memorable: *'From one extremity of this desert to the other, the road was white with the bones of oxen and horses. And the log chains, wagon tires, and rotting wrecks of vehicles were almost as thick as the bones.'* The pioneers who survived the crossing and made it to San Francisco never, I'm thinking, wore flowers in their hair. And today's heavy weather, does it make burners bond deeper, the festival more ritualistic? Possibly. Next thought: what would Twain make of the burners, these pampered descendants of his pioneers, and their Nevada party? The folly of youth, trust funds and contemporary Californian culture would surely draw a barbed Twain aphorism. Final thought: fundamentalist American evangelical Christians often like to ask 'what would Jesus do?'; well, what would he?

Burning Man has its share of fundamentalist burners who tend to claim the festival's a quasi-utopian event, the portal to a brave new world of sorts. Admittedly, Burning Man is a brash, hedonistic alternative to mainstream USA: many burners promenade naked with every kind of body, from the grossly obese to the surgically perfected, on display, Ken Kesey's Merry Prankster ethos is revived and some of the art-cars and free-standing sculptures are genuinely inspired. The biggest alternative to McAmerica involves the absence of anything for sale and no branding. But

Players on the playa: burners let it all hang out, Nevada, 2006

there's another visible absence – that of almost anyone from California's burgeoning African American, Latino and Asian populaces while no Natives from the nearby Paiute Reservation have made it down. This and the unceasing soundtrack of techno and trance (or trance and techno) emphasise how monocultural the festival's vision is. The $200 entry fee, rules on speed limits (5 mph), weapons and dogs (banned), filming (don't even think about it: the festival is copyright conscious) imply Burning Man's moved far from the frontier spirit that first made it famous in the early nineties – veteran burners recall a genuinely wild, no-rules, anarcho happening – and evolved into an 'alt.corp' event. That pretty much everyone I meet here works either in computing or entertainment suggests the playa exists as a playground (a giant sandpit) for wealthy Californians to annually get in contact with their inner hippy. Think about it: if Steven Spielberg and Bill Gates danced past painted Day-Glo no one would bat an eye. BM's that kind of party.

Hiding beneath the Man pondering such ignites me to venture back on to the playa. *Ugh! No! The elements spit sand in my face!* I retreat back beneath podium, the inner pioneer in me staying well hidden. *What would Jesus do?* Keep his ass tight, f'sure. Among those also seeking refuge here is a large, masked transvestite. He leans over and passes me a card. 'For your travels,' he says. On the card is printed a demonic face and the message 'Get Out Of Hell Free'.

That evening we gather at our Black Rock campsite, sandblasted and sunburned, a motley crew. As the sun slips away all rise and walk towards the Man. Across the playa people trek towards the Man. The evening air is clear and calm and the Man, built of simple, sharp angles, around seven metres in height and mounted on a circular podium base that gives him another four metres, stands totemic, a South-west effigy. The podium base – where I sheltered – is now closed off, packed with incendiaries, and a hushed tone has settled across the playa; art-cars parked, sound systems silenced, people reserving energy, ritual under way.

Bonfires start sparking as the desert cools and Saturday night descends. A neon skeleton flashes along the Man's limbs. Drummers beat a tattoo. A fire dance performed by dozens of women in black – cheerleaders from hell – begins and the burners, some thirty thousand, roar appreciation, their appetite for destruction roused. Fireworks spiral from the Man's feet, smearing colours across a big, black sky, and the burning begins. A collective roar, almost orgasmic, a week of dust and rough storms and hard partying while waiting for this release, the destruction of a man who symbolises... what? Nothing. Anything. The effigy as everyman.

The Man burns. First slowly, then quickly. A huge tongue of flame rises and curls and licks the structure and his spine cracks and the Man falls to earth with a solid boooooom! Feverish burners rush forward, leaping at the outer edges of the flames, trampling embers. *That's it*: the Man burned. More accurately, that's the start of it, the burning signals party time, and tens of thousands of pedestrians and cyclists and art-cars (decorated as giant eyes, missiles, purple people eaters, spaceships) spill across the desert. The playa lights up with sculptures, some breathing diesel flames, others kinetic, while dozens of sound systems pump beats to twitchy ravers. Party *on*. But I'm off, fleeing way out into desert darkness until the fires are dots in the night and the sound systems just a distant pulse. Running from a party full of semi-naked women surely signifies I'm Geek No. 1 but I can't stand a minute more of electronic bleep-bleep beats. Torture by techno? Something like that. Plonk my ass in the sand, stare at the stars and wonder what Wovoka, the Paiute shaman and holy man who inspired the last Native resistance to Anglo America, would make of this spectacle.

Wovoka lived near Pyramid Lake but I'm sure he knew Black Rock Desert – isolated, harsh environments always appealing to mystics – and initiated the Ghost Dance after a powerful dream on New Year's Day, 1889. Suggesting God had spoken to him and if the Indians followed his instructions a new world would be created, Wovoka inspired the most powerful dance of nineteenth-century America, a dance celebrating peace and renewal, a dance that would spread from the South-west through tribe after tribe until, more than a thousand miles away, it reached the Lakota (Sioux) who Ghost Danced with such fury, calling down spirits to save them from the white man's dominance, that, in 1890, their great leader Sitting Bull would be gunned down. To finally crush the dance, the US Army massacred over two hundred men, women and children on the snowy wastelands of Wounded Knee.

Stranded in the Nevada desert at an expensive rave isn't the best place for contemplating subjects as complex as Native emancipation and the spirit of dance. I mean, people are here for many reasons yet music is what makes the night come alive. But the music is lousy. My America's one largely shaped through music, music rooted in a community and its values and struggles. Here the sounds are techno and trance's loveless thud, electronic junk. If Burning Man ever links with Mali's Festival in the Desert (imagine Tinariwen striking up their guitars and singing those ancient Tuareg blues!) or invites Bishop King's congregation to celebrate Coltrane in the desert or employs a Paiute powwow troupe, well, souls might just be moved, minds fed. Like those of the Grateful Dead – who started out as the Haight's house band then devolved into stadium-rock fodder – Burning Man's values have diminished as its worth has increased. No surprise: contemporary American culture gets co-opted by commerce very quickly, moving from underground to overground in a flash; the futurism of BM already feels old, its values shallow, all of it based (literally) on sand. Six desert days down and very much time for me to get back on the road, see whether any roots still hold and, if so, do they nourish a new America or offer only a semblance of what once made this nation great? Heavy thoughts. Sometimes I wish I could just switch my mind off and enjoy what gets the masses moving. I mean, shivering in the desert is no fun at all: time to re-engage with the main event.

Back among the party people and Erin, a willowy, dark-eyed woman who is part of our camp, says, 'Whassup, star-sailor?' I speak my mind and Erin asks, 'So why did you come to Burning Man? No musicians here. Just DJs.'

'San Francisco was once Gonzo Central. I thought this might be a continuation of that spirit.'

'Yeah, this is mild. You want wild things come with me to a Rainbow Gathering.'

'What I really want is to see if I can find that raw, primitive America where the spirit's not yet tamed.'

Erin laughs and talks of growing up raw and primitive in rural California. 'When we saw roadkill we'd jump out and check how warm it was. A dead deer put a lot of meat in our freezer. That might sound weird if you've never lived hand to mouth but, for us, it was essential.'

OK, a real frontier girl: 'Want to join me on the road?'

'Thanks but I'm saving to travel in India.'

India: I once wandered that huge, fragrant nation for six months, even trekked up to wintry Dharamsala where Richard Gere sat among backpackers listening to the Dalai Lama lecture in Tibetan. Instead of pondering on universal wisdom I wondered why Richard hadn't bought Cindy Crawford along. *Doh!* Then I managed to get a very unholy dose of amoebic dysentery. *Oh, India!* Oh, holy fool I was!

'Reckon you can find enlightenment,' asks Erin, 'in the good ole USA?'

'In the sense of becoming enlightened as to my understanding of America, sure.'

'Want to go to Big Sur and meet a guru?'

'Personally, I'd rather go to Hollywood and meet Jessica Alba.'

'*Jessica Alba?*'

'Don't they say America's where you come to realise your dreams?'

Erin laughs loud and hearty as techno mugs the desert dawn. Salmon-pink skies, dust-covered dancers, burnt sculptures, diesel's corrosive stench... the rave at the end of the universe... that's how this place feels. 'Gimme a beer, dude,' begs a fat girl, all manky dreads and Celtic tattoos. 'Gimme a butt,' she whines.

Enough. I'm now brutally weary of California's New Age party people. 'These burners,' I say, 'pod people, ya know?' Erin honks – a woman with a laugh like that would make for a fine travelling companion – and announces she's off to find our camp's pod people. Techno so loud the desert appears to tremble. My journey's just beginning and I'm in Nevada wasteland surrounded by a rehash of European rave culture. Jesus! It's bitterly cold. I'm shivering with desert chill and doubt. *Christ!* Am leaving in a few hours' time – count every minute – just need to relax and ride out this electronic storm. Time to recall Robert Frost's dictum: '*the best way out is always through.*'

Downtown and downtrodden: Las Vegas, 2006

chapter 3

Las Vegas: Genuine, Justifiable Hope

Less than three kilometres from where the lights sparkle brighter than anywhere else on earth squat Las Vegas's cheap motels. Everything exudes a sour sense of loss and despair, twilight lending the flickering neon attempts at ALL RO MS V and M T L a pathetic ambience. And almost everyone on the street is black. Just my luck, I've landed in the Vegas ghetto. A black girl – and I mean girl, surely no older than fourteen – in very short shorts starts calling out to me, saying, 'Honey, yuh wanna good time?' Thanks, but I'm exhausted by Burning Man's 'good time'. I hurry into the nearest motel. At the desk there's a fried-looking white woman with a crazy grin revealing several missing teeth. Daily and weekly rates are available; I take a room for $30 unseen, just asking one question: 'Is it going to be quiet 'cos I'm shattered?' She laughs, a weird cackle, says, 'Should be, Sunday night normally is. But you should of seen the chaos last night!' and cackles again. The room is functional – bed, TV, toilet, shower – cigarette burns in the carpet and the sickly scent of air freshener emphasising a flatliner in this city of hotel spectacle. I shower for an eternity, scouring Black Rock dust from my skin. Was up all last night and today endured a day-long journey from Black Rock to Vegas in a vehicle driven by a motivational speaker. As we drove the 305 south – a red road, a desert highway – through small towns with names like Neil Young songs (Battle Mountain, Tonopah, Round Mountain, Indian Springs), he spoke as if on autopilot, Captain Upbeat, treating me as the captive audience. I scanned raw land for the Basque shepherds who apparently ply their trade in this wilderness, corralling sheep and speaking Euskadi, but they and everything else remained hidden, perhaps wary of being subjected to Captain Upbeat's motivational mantras. American optimism can appear very attractive after British cynicism but about thirty minutes into our seven-hour journey I felt like screaming. Now, so fresh and so clean, I really should sleep but, uh-uh, I need to take on Vegas.

Stepping out, I find the neighbourhood quiet, uneasily so. Walk fast – *the ghetto shuffle* – past gun dealers and liquor stores. At the top of Fremont Street I come across the Fremont Street Experience, an open-air pedestrian mall that stretches for five blocks and is designed to drag tourists from the Strip to downtown. Entering, I find everyone staring upwards as the Experience unfolds. This involves watching a 90-foot-high-barrel-vault canopy where an alien invasion of earth is powered by two million light bulbs. The Experience's sub-*Independence Day* shtick appears aimed at six-year-olds but the mall is packed with adults – heads back, jaws open, oohing and ahhhing at this colossal waste of electricity. Spectacle over, America's rich tapestry mingles: the Fremont Street Experience is packed with fat Asians, slick Latinas, tattooed homeboys, sombrero-wearing Mexicans, chunky college kids, hip-hop honeys and their strutting partners, militant Christians who wave placards announcing gambling's a sin (and sinners burn) and burly drunks who laugh and throw abuse at the Christians and laugh some more. Essayist Dave Hickey lives in Vegas and champions it as '*a town that can serve as the heart's destination*'. People come to Vegas, writes Hickey, dreaming of riches and escaping the monotony of much of America. '*Vegas cheats you fair – unlike the rest of America (and Washington in particular), the payoffs are posted and the odds easily calculable.*'

Next to the Experience stands the Golden Nugget, one of the few surviving casinos from Vegas's Rat Pack heyday. Gambling holds no appeal for me, especially casino gambling, such dowdy places to drop your wages, but the Nugget serves a buffet and the past week's privations have provided me with a serious appetite. Reaching the buffet involves walking through an acre of slot machines and craps tables attended to by herds of squat troglodytes sucking on cheap drinks, smoking, shrieking, groaning, forever engaging in the mechanics of the game. Easy money, that's what Vegas seems to offer, and the Nugget's heavy with the psychic sweat of those hunting easy money. Where the likes of Philadelphia and Boston were founded upon a dedication to God, Vegas got built upon the lure of filthy lucre. In Madrid there's a statue of Lucifer falling from heaven – they should recast it in Vegas, a city that celebrates sin. The sin I'm currently tempted by is gluttony and $10 lets me at it: *good eating!*

Forty minutes later I waddle out through the gaming room and off to where a shuttle bus runs from downtown to the Strip. The bus arrives and fills with penurious visitors who want to see the Strip but can't afford to stay there. We cruise down Las Vegas Boulevard, a wasteland populated only by pawn shops, porn shops, titty bars, liquor stores and bleak-looking condos. The multimillion-dollar fairy dust sprinkled on Fremont Street not yet spreading to link up with the Strip. The bus empties out amid a neon blizzard, sidewalk heaving with several thousand of the city's annual forty million visitors. In 1963 Elvis Presley cut 'Viva Las Vegas', his hymn to the city that would later relaunch him as a live performer then initiated his decline, unaware lyricist Doc Pomus had never ventured west of Newark, New Jersey. Back in '63 Vegas may have possessed an outlaw vibe, something loose and fast and illicit, but such spirit has long been crushed – today Vegas feels like being stuck in a second-rate theme park: wading through crowds I witness dancing fountains, battling pirate boats, a volcano that pops, and – worst of all – sub-Disney recreations of New York, Paris and ancient Egypt. What a crock of crap.

Vegas has no culture to speak of – the likes of Elvis and Sinatra heading here once their creative energies were expended focused only on raking in dollars – but many American entertainers long to play here, a stint at a Vegas casino suggesting some kind of plateau. Or, if not to perform, then to be seen, Vegas being celebrity heaven. Standing at the intersection of Las Vegas Boulevard and Flamingo Road I think, '*Yeeeeee, ain't this where Tupac got snuffed?*' To be exact I walk a block east, crossing from Caesar's Palace past Bally's down to the corner of East Flamingo and Koval, a site marked only by traffic lights and a *USA Today* vending machine. Here a white Cadillac opened fire on two black males riding in a black BMW sedan on 7 September 1996. The driver of the BMW, Suge Knight, was scratched by shattered glass but his passenger, Tupac Shakur, took four bullets and would die without having regained consciousness five days later. The duo were in town for one of Mike Tyson's farcical post-prison bouts and Tupac, being Tupac, had earlier stomped an LA Crip gang member he saw in a casino. No one has ever been arrested for Tupac's murder but considering his volatile nature the list of suspects must be very long. Fittingly, Tupac died a brutal public death, body shattered like those of Bonnie and Clyde decades before. I've little time for Tupac, his staccato rapping (a mix of bragging and sentimentality) cast in undernourished arrangements. But as an icon Shakur's everywhere: the subject of at least a dozen books and a similar number of DVDs while his estate keep releasing albums of 'new' material. For Tupac's legacy is defined by his actions: *seek out fame no matter what it costs, be loud, aggressive and photogenic* – Tupac lived life as if starring in his own gangsta rap movie and many now consider him a tatt'd, bullet-torn martyr. A martyr to the thug life he espoused? Or America's treatment of young black men? Or capitalism? Or rap? A Black Studies lecturer or *Vibe* magazine hack is guaranteed to be penning a book on one or all of the above.

Back on the Strip I wander into Caesar's Palace and find bars pumping house music. A rave in a casino, *whoo!* I pitch up at a bar where piped muzak floats out – *how has music, once an occasional pleasure, come to dominate so many of our public spaces?* – and order a margarita from a waitress in a toga. She has the cool manner of someone in service too long, eyes glazing (I'm so obviously not a high roller, not even a low roller), asking me for ID. How over-regulated can the land of the free be when they still insist on checking those who shed their youth way back? Then I notice the ever-present supervisor, watching her, watching me, watching the bar. What a depressing environment to work in: constant surveillance, musical pap and the endless ringing of slots. Surely this combines to drive you insane? Or maybe it crushes your soul, my waitress having become a Vegas zombie.

Several margaritas in and the waitress still offers only a glimmer of a smile. I'd love to ask her where she's from, why Vegas appeared so attractive – every year tens of thousands of Americans flock to Vegas seeking new beginnings: the South-west having experienced a 5.2 per cent population increase between 2000 and 2003 – is it the city or something personal lending a sour twist to her features? Jobs, climate and, I guess, a degree of personal freedom lend this city of spectacle an allure. Many of the employees and gamblers are Asian, part of the new America being shaped in the desert. Vegas has, over recent years, become home to a large Ethiopian community – surely the desert climate and work opportunities, not the gambling, draws them here – but Amharic faces aren't visible tonight; I imagine they're sweating in kitchens and cleaning. I wander through the epic nothingness of Caesar's and back on to the shuttle bus to Fremont Street, where the ceiling is now silent. Walking towards my motel, I'm attracted by Western Hotel on Fremont, its glaring yellow light beckoning poor gamblers into a sizeable cancer palace of 25c, 10c, 5c and 1c slot machines. The atmosphere's American gothic, a set from a lost David Lynch film – hunched bodies focus on losing their coins, carpet worn, walls discoloured, a stand sells Pepsi – Miller – Hot Dogs, employees look as weary as the gamblers, no pretence at glamour or sophistication. Hickey wrote of Vegas gambling, *'win or lose, you always have that instant of genuine, justifiable hope.'* Looking at the faces gazing at slots, 'hope' appears in short supply here. The Western Hotel is Vegas Raw, the stench of cigarette smoke, disinfectant and desperation mingling. No hint of easy money at the last-chance saloon.

'I do so much stuff it's amazing. Prince and me, we're the only ones who do everything.'

No false modesty surrounds Jimmy Castor, a musician who boasts of being 'the only link between doo-wop and hip-hop'.

THE JIMMY CASTOR BUNCH

Jimmy Castor and his funky Bunch
1976

Born and raised in a Harlem tenement, Castor relocated to a house in the hills above Vegas in 1997.

'Ain't nowhere in the world like Vegas,' says Jimmy, who doesn't gamble or drink and has been married to his congenial wife Sandy for a considerable number of years. 'We came out here after the worst snowstorm in New York history. I wanted somewhere warmer, somewhere I could ride my motorbikes and I'd had my eye on Vegas for a long time.'

In this sense Castor is the typical East Coast retiree relocating to the South-west for year-round warmth. Born in 1943, Castor, like many others of his generation who have shifted west, lives off the fruits of his labours – specifically, the samples utilised by rap and pop producers from Jimmy's back catalogue.

'I've been sampled over three thousand times,' says Castor, his slim torso pulsing with energy. 'First up were the Beastie Boys. They thought they could rape my music so I went to court over it. Luke Skywalker and a lot of other rappers were the same. They don't know that Jimmy Castor's from the ghetto, from the street, that he's going to fight to protect his music. Well, they know now. You sample me you better damn sure pay me.'

Jimmy has a long, long list of who has sampled him; top of the list are the Spice Girls who bit the sax riff from Castor's anthem

'It's Just Begun' for 'If You Can't Dance', the last song on their debut album *Spice* (20 million sales): Jimmy got a royalty on every sale.

'I wouldn't say this is the house that Spice built,' says Castor, 'but, yeah, they helped with the down payment.'

Is Jimmy retired?

'No way! I still make music. Still put the Bunch together for concerts. Just not often.'

Ever play Vegas?

'I've played Vegas. I should be on the Strip. I wanna be on the Strip. Why's Barry Manilow on the Strip and not Jimmy Castor? It's racism. Racism! My plan is to go to Europe, get a war chest, and then come and storm the Strip. It's difficult 'cos what they love here is fakes. And,' adds Jimmy, 'I'm the real deal.'

Small of stature but big of presence, Jimmy Castor's one of the great characters in post-war black American music. Castor's music, full of novelty and inventiveness, good humour and sparkle, would ideally light up a casino. But Vegas music is Celine Dion and Elton John, square sounds. Also – and Jimmy doesn't admit this – although he's been involved in hits in every decade from the fifties to the noughties, he's had only a handful under his own name. Barry Manilow may be abysmal but he's sold zillions as Bazza; Castor Mansions were built by Jimmy being vigilant over his publishing royalties.

Born on 2 June 1943, in Harlem's Sugar Hill district, and raised by his mother and grandmother, Castor shined shoes and sold papers to help make ends meet. Learning violin, saxophone, piano and studying theory, he was accepted for the Music & Art High School ('full of rich kids arriving in limousines with lots of talent but strung out on Valium') but back in Harlem he ran through the Projects with the Cobras and the Falcons ('baseball teams but really gangs'). Doo-wop was the East Coast's answer to the rock 'n' roll explosion and teenage males could be found harmonising on streets, in stairwells and bathrooms. Aged twelve he formed Jimmy Castor & the Juniors and, in 1956, their song 'I Promise' (written by Castor) was turned into a Top 10 R & B hit by the hottest doo-wop band in America: Frankie Lymon & The Teenagers.

'Our block was always full of girls wanting to see The Teenagers – I lived on 165th Street, Frankie on 166th, Sherman [Garnes, The Teenagers' basso voice] on 165, The Ronnettes on 168 – and I remember "Fools Fall in Love" becoming this huge hit, making them the first supergroup of colour, them getting on big buses and going off to tour. Seeing all that I knew music was what I wanted to do. When Frankie covered "I Promise" my first cheque was for $2,500! Man, my family shifted straight out of the ghetto! No more living among roaches and rats!'

Castor's vocal similarity to Lymon meant he was often employed to sub for the wayward Frankie. Touring the USA with Sam Cooke, Little Richard and The Platters, he learned early on what life on the road costs: down South in the 1950s a state trooper got on the bus and racially harangued the musicians. Sam Cooke steps up and asks the officer to mind his language. The trooper goes for his gun, Sam sucker-punches him, removing his gun and dumping the unconscious Nazi at the side of the road. 'That's how I came up,' says Castor firmly, 'treat me with respect. Don't mess with me.' Even as a teenager Jimmy never got fooled, making sure he was paid in cash while Lymon accepted toys, booze and drugs in lieu of royalties.

'Frankie was at the back of the bus drinking Southern Comfort, smoking weed, with women. He'd say to me, "Try some of this" and I'd refuse and he'd call me names. Call me a sissy. But I never messed with that stuff for three reasons: my mom, it's wrong in the eyes of God and I wanted *more*. Later on I saw Frankie opening cab doors for a quarter outside clubs I was working... begging. Then one day the word comes that he's OD'd at his gran'ma's. We rush up there and he's dead behind the toilet, all bent up, turned orange. What a waste. A great natural singer dead at twenty-five.'

The doo-wop phenomenon was short lived and Castor completed high school. Upon graduating he became a full-time musician. The sixties were happening and Castor worked hard ('I paid a lot of dues. Playing all the bloody razors. Doing weddings, bar mitzvahs. Seven dollars a night between the whole band, that's what we had to split'), meeting Malcolm X ('he told me "I'm a dead man" when I last spoke to him. A week after his murder we had to play the Audubon Ballroom, bullet holes everywhere') and helped pioneer Latin Soul.

'I'd started playing timbales 'cos I loved what Tito Puente was doing with *Dance Mania*. Growing up in Harlem there were lots of cats from Puerto Rico around so we heard their music and they heard ours and that's how the Latin Soul sound came about.'

Like doo-wop, Latin Soul was a New York street music phenomenon; Joe Bataan, Joe Cuba and the Salsoul label arose from it. Jimmy scored his first big hit in 1967 with 'Hey, Leroy, Your Mama's Callin' You', a crazy block-party favourite that became an anthem across Harlem and the Bronx. Castor went out on the road with The Temptations – 'they were so hot, "Ain't Too Proud To Beg" was a huge hit, but David Ruffin was a mean guy, hooked on cocaine and beating on Tammi Terrell. No surprise he died in a crack house' – and Motown boss Berry Gordy Jr tried to sign him but Castor refused to give up his publishing. Castor's sound kept developing, a powerful New York hybrid bearing comparison to Jimi Hendrix and Sly Stone.

'I met Jimi when he was playing with Curtis Knight. Nice guy. We'd jam, me blowing my sax, Jimi playing with his teeth and making all kinds of noise. I'd say, "Man, you need your own band!" We stayed friends and would cover one another's songs – he cut "Hey Leroy" and I cut "Purple Haze". Sly I knew 'cos we were playing the same clubs in the sixties. He had a great, great band. One of the best I've ever seen. But they were doing a lot of drugs before they even got really popular. Not smart. I saw what drugs did to Jimi and Sly close up. Last time I saw Jimi he gave me a ride across Manhattan, crazy driver, running every red light, he was so unhappy, messed up on drugs and bad management and all the hangers-on that he didn't know how to handle. I've known so many people who have died or gone to jail or ended up homeless addicts. And not just musicians – one time I'm back in New York and this guy I used to be friends with approaches me and he's a wreck, his hands all swollen and ruined from injecting shit into them.'

Castor kept working, developing the Jimmy Castor Bunch, whose proto-funk would prove hugely popular in the early seventies as songs such as 'Troglodyte', 'Bertha Butt' and 'King Kong' became both R & B and pop hits while the title track of 1972's *It's Just Begun* became a dance anthem for the B-Boys, who were inventing hip-hop culture in the Bronx. Jimmy's seventies albums convey the Castor aesthetic as a mix of futuristic funk, novelty dance tunes and offbeat covers – 'First Time Ever I Saw Your Face', 'You Light Up My Life', 'Whiter Shade of Pale' – that often found Jimmy stretching out on sax. Hired to open for Parliament, the JC Bunch were audience favourites: George Clinton threw them off the Mothership tour for upstaging Parliament's stoned groove. 'I never rated Parliament,' says Castor, 'their lame-ass groove, Gary in his nappy, Clinton acting the fool... more a mess than a band.' Ferociously independent, nobody's fool, Castor signed to then fell out with both RCA and Atlantic. 'I found I had to sell my records myself, the companies weren't interested in making an effort. I'd go for a record signing and find no Castor Bunch records in the bin! Once Ben E. King and I got off on the wrong floor in the Atlantic building and everywhere there were posters and campaigns for Abba, Genesis, Led Zeppelin, but nowhere any black music promotion. We never got no support.' He pauses, fists balled, then breathes deeply and continues: 'Sandy says I should be grateful that things have turned out well for us. Our kids are all doing great. I do well from looking after my publishing. The music still commands respect. But... but I don't feel that I've got my dues.'

Jimmy's verbal flow calms then revs up again when he recalls seventies highs and lows. The JC Bunch toured a lot, burning up the stage coast to coast, then disco sideswiped funk, leading to a downturn in bookings. Jimmy began accepting bookings in Latin America, the Caribbean, Saudi Arabia. 'Trinidad... man, we were number one there with "Loves Theme" for a year! Get off the plane and the minister of labour greets us with a crowd of three thousand people! Same in Panama. "Whiter Shade of Pale" was number one there for six months. Gas was two cents a gallon in Saudi and gold was cheap so I bought lots of it and put it in my boots to escape customs. They were very nice to me but it's a strange mentality out there.'

Considering Jimmy's so sampled by rappers, what are his thoughts on Tupac and co?

'It's very negative, that gangsta element, full of self-hatred. Slavery has implanted too much anger and hatred in the US.' Jimmy walks out on to his balcony and looks across the desert. Twilight's gleaming and in the distance the Strip begins to glow. 'I don't know if we can ever truly put it behind us.'

Mean machine: Greyhound

chapter 4

Tucson: The Shadow Land

Restlessness… it's like an itching in my psyche. Must be a trait, maybe a gene even, inherited from ancestors whose mongrel bloodlines somehow made it from a variety of locations to the bottom of the world – *New Zealand* – to mate and mingle but never stopped wanting to escape, to keep moving. Occasionally I manage to relax, decide to settle, then the itch begins again so I open my nostrils, catch the scent of the breeze, listen carefully, hear the road calling my name, and… *hasta la vista, baby*. Sometimes the itch invokes a struggle, common sense suggesting 'stay put', but before long it's unbearable and tonight, well, I'm raw to move: Las Vegas, a city best seen in the rear-view mirror. Here gaudy opulence rubs against some of the most shitty locales imaginable. Jimmy Castor, dropping me back at my motel, was struck dumb at the sight of teeny hookers and their crack dealers. Jimmy, never having set eyes on the Vegas ghetto before, admonished me for staying in Fremont. 'I've seen too many ghettos in this life,' he muttered, then vanished into the night.

At the bus station Greyhound staff do their best to win 'most surly Nevada employee' award. I take a hard plastic seat, wait for my bus and watch downtrodden America pass, air sticky, temperatures rising. I start thinking of songs mentioning Greyhound – Robert Johnson, Steve Young and ZZ Top all deserve honourable mentions – many musicians have criss-crossed the US riding the dog but has any ever expressed just how miserable a Greyhound station is? Here you have a public building designed to be as un-user-friendly as possible: we're in a desert city and there is No Air Conditioning, just the tang of diesel fumes and sweat. Unbelievable.

Two security guards approach a mashed-looking white woman who, it turns out, was refused entry on an earlier bus so rang the police and claimed the driver assaulted her. One guard starts calling her a liar. She protests innocence. He raises his voice. She begins to shriek and amid the humidity misery saturates the night air. The situation takes on a Jerry Springer-style ambience with passengers shouting their opinions, few appearing to support the underdog. 'Yo sho' jus' shut yo' mouf,' snarls a shaven-headed black man, accent molasses thick, at the dishevelled woman, 'yo' talk too mush.' She pleads desperately until, finally, security march her away whimpering. Everyone's avoiding eye contact, bad vibes weighing heavy on the station, I'd best focus on a book: along with Twain's *Roughing It* I've brought Jack Kerouac's *On the Road* as US travel guide. Last read *On the Road* decades ago but as I start perusing the text my immediate surroundings fade: *'This was really the way that my whole road experience began,'* wrote Kerouac (page 9), *'and the things that were to come are too fantastic not to tell.'*

The Phoenix bus arrives late; no excuses or apologies offered. Those queuing to board mutter curses, the post-9/11 humiliation of security searching hand luggage and jackets fuelling a collective bad mood. 'If I'd a done well at the tables I'd be flyin' my ass back,' says a skinny white boy with vivid tattoos crawling around the back of his neck. Take a seat next to a Tom Joad – wiry middle-aged white guy dressed in the uniform of baseball cap, jeans, cotton shirt, worried eyes – and get a strong impression he has no desire to exchange even the most perfunctory of introductions. Maybe he's heading home and needs to explain just how much money he managed to lose. Or, considering his unblinking, stoic gaze, perhaps what weighs on his mind is heavier than lost wages. And then we're off, sweeping through downtown and into the Vegas suburbs, driver reciting rules and telling when and where the stops will be. On to Highway 93, neon phantasmagoria left behind, ancient American night enveloping the surrounding desert, small towns appear a blur of street lamps and road signs, glimpses of jackrabbits, stray dogs, desert-rat humans, the road still suggesting all kinds of magic and possibility. Tom Joad locks his fingers and stares into oblivion: *what psychic weight does this traveller carry?*

At night stops a loose camaraderie takes shape among those who get off the bus to smoke, eat junk food, stretch, swap tales of fortunes almost won and long journeys home: 'twenty-eight hours to Fort Worth,' says a youth in a cowboy hat, still fresh enough to chuckle at the thought of it. A black man who's travelling with his two small boys quietly announces, when prompted, that they're riding all the way to Monroe, Louisiana. Someone whistles, utters, 'Jesus, that's a couple o' days riding,' and he nods and draws on his cigarette. I want to ask what's pushed him into taking such a grinding journey but hold my tongue; no need to pry. The bus honks and all clamber on board again. Tom Joad sits in silence, staring into eternity. Contort myself trying to find a secret position that allows sleep while riding.

By the time we get to Phoenix I'm red-eyed, cramped, aching with cold: it's been a long night and as we unload desert chill permeates the air. This station looks a major improvement on the Vegas office; not exactly comfortable but the architect managed to consider humans making use of this space. I wash my face, buy watery coffee and slink out front to watch the motorway roar into life as rush hour takes hold. Fire up my first cigarette of the day. After a rough night's travel, tobacco-coffee-morning-sun, well, these are simple pleasures that never fade. Standing in the queue for the El Paso bus are the Stetson-wearing youth, thumbs tucked in belt, hat at an angle, still rising to the road's challenge, and Mr Monroe, Louisiana. One child's curled up asleep on a suitcase while he rocks the other gently in his arms, calm and strong: no need to lose grace or dignity on the road. A couple of tough-looking Latino guys I'd earlier noted hanging around the station appear handcuffed by Border Patrol agents. Reading Kerouac, I relish the passage where he meets Terry, the petite Mexican woman who inspired his most tender prose, in a Greyhound waiting room. That's what I need, a little road romance!

Today I mean to make it to Tucson – a few more hours on a bus south – and have no business in Phoenix. There are regular Greyhounds to Tucson but I skip the first few, not yet having recovered from the night's ride. Wonder whether there's anything worth experiencing in Phoenix? All I can recall about the city is it being home to Canyon Records, the great Native American label. Appropriate as Phoenix was built on the ruins of an ancient Native American settlement, starting life as a Wild West town, and today acts as the epicentre of a vast transhumance currently under way in the USA, citizens fleeing the north and east to sunbelt cities of the South-west. Named to signify resurrection, Phoenix continues to maintain a strong pull on those wanting to begin afresh. One wonders why; Phoenix is the hottest city outside the Middle East and produces a breed of extreme right-wing Republicans. Edward Abbey, author of *Desert Solitaire* and *The Monkey Wrench Gang*, adopted Arizona as home while dismissing Phoenix as 'the blob that is eating Arizona'. My *Rough Guide* struggles to find anything to say about Phoenix, neither Kerouac nor Twain mentioned it, and today you need a car to find your way around.

Back on the bus, heading south, Phoenix's suburbs appear to spread for ever, acres of lookalike houses, beige and grey and grey and beige, encroaching upon desert sands. Power pylons stretch across a horizon dotted with golf courses, exclusive gated communities, neat pebble gardens, gas stations, drive-through fast-food outlets. Crows. A freight train. Desert heatwaves. Cars. Trucks. Cars. The dog rolls in mid-afternoon silence, no voices raised, plenty of time to reflect on music and America: in Tucson I aim to catch up with maverick rocker Howe Gelb.

Is Arizona a musical state? It's home to the aforementioned Canyon Records, the longest-established Native music label, and their leading artist, Navajo flutist R. Carlos Nakai, whose ethereal recordings have won him a large New Age market. In the fifties Marty Robbins was a huge country-pop star, scoring with Old West narratives while cutting some of the most hardcore, right-wing jingoism in American music ('Ain't I Right'; 'My Native

Land'). Duane Eddy and his producer Lee Hazelwood opened things up with reverb-laden guitar instrumentals in the late fifties, Hazelwood moving to LA, where he produced all of Nancy Sinatra's hits and pioneered a Gothic country-pop sound. Dyke & The Blazers cut 'Funky Broadway' in Phoenix's small black neighbourhood. Five acid-fried dirtbags calling themselves Alice Cooper crawled from Phoenix to LA to Detroit and cut a half-dozen of the early seventies best hard-rock hits. Linda Ronstadt left Tucson for LA where she established herself as seventies soft rock's premier sex symbol. The Meat Puppets melded hardcore punk with an odd, scorched hillbilly aesthetic to impressive effect. And that is, ummm, pretty much all the Arizona hall-of-famers I can name. One could suggest a loose link between Howe Gelb and most of them, he's just a little weirder. And everyone listed enjoyed some degree of commercial success; little chance of Gelb replicating this.

Giant Sand – essentially a vehicle for Gelb and whoever he's got playing with him – have existed since 1980. The name fits the music as Gelb's songs often appear sun-damaged, meandering in a style suited to wide open, desolate landscapes. Discovering Giant

'I like it here': Howe Gelb, Tucson, AZ, 2006

Sand in the early nineties, their spiralling mess of sound, dusty and rough and full of strange, oblique angles, I heard American rock 'n' roll with a lazy, home-made flavour I thought had long since passed. Gelb's a solitary figure, something of a goof, who releases up to five albums in a year – this makes keeping up with him impossible. And unnecessary: Gelb's music varies from the lovely country rock drift of *Chore of Enchantment* to oddball doodling only a Howe obsessive ever need hear.

At Tucson's Greyhound station I head out in search of a late lunch and quickly find myself beaten back to the station by extreme heat. Be warned: food served at and around Greyhound stations is aimed at undiscerning stomachs. Hail a taxi and the driver, a wiry old Walter Huston lookalike, scans the address, hesitates and barks, 'Young fella, you aware this is in the Mex-ey-can part of town?' I wasn't but, all things considered, it makes sense. Tucson's a much more attractive city than Phoenix, lots of adobe and early-twentieth-century buildings, desert colours of brown and cream and white lending a calm flavour, even the freeway's sidings painted tan colours. Mention to the driver my distaste for Phoenix and he starts shouting, 'Goddamn Phoenix, turning the whole state into one big subdivision,' then begins cursing politicians, businessmen, East Coast pensioners and Mexicans. I start chuckling, not 'cos his rant is funny, more because of how he appears to share Edward Abbey's loathing of pretty much everyone, then he glares, ensuring my silence.

The taxi threads its way into a neighbourhood where the streets are dusty, sidewalk dissolving into gravel, houses painted bright colours, people walking, hanging out in front yards, tan skin, black hair, Anglo-America definitely some distance away. Walter's muttering, a slow hum of racial epithets, his taxi finally stopping in front of a large blue stucco home with cacti growing in the front yard, and there's the man himself, Howe Gelb, tearing the interior out of a van. Walter's shaking his head – 'crazy white trash living among Mex-ey-cans!' – then glares at me with disdain as I drop the exact fare. I mean, fuck giving this bigot a two-dollar tip. Not that I'm welcomed by Howe: he appears unsettled by my arrival even though I phoned from Vegas to confirm. I try some small talk and Howe wearily explains the van was purchased at a police auction, having surely been used by coyotes to smuggle people across the border, and right now he and his buddy Doug – a gregarious man with a broad, red face – are removing seats so the vehicle can be made to accommodate band gear for Giant Sand's forthcoming US dates. Touring constantly, Howe?

'No way. We never get in the van and do coast-to-coast tours any more. I prefer to just go out and do a bunch of gigs then come back home.'

Howe returns to mute van demolition while I stand in the yard feeling unwelcome. Not for long as Howe's wife, Sofie, soon appears accompanied by two tots. Sofie's a vision of Scandinavian blonde beauty and a good deal more welcoming than Howe, explaining that the neighbouring pink house's owner works for a paint factory and continually paints his house/fence/letter box/tree different colours. Turns out that the Gelb home is a historic building, thus the city council are helping finance refurbishments. 'When we got this place,' says Sofie, 'we were among the only white people in the neighbourhood. We had to live in this part of Tucson simply because it was the only area we could afford. Now a few of our friends and other Anglos have decided this is a good place to live. But at school our son is the only white kid in a class full of Mexican kids. You should see the school photo – his little blond head among all those dark-haired kids!'

As the light fades Howe's rushing to get as much done as possible. Considering the dry heat he and Doug are working in I guess a few brews may be appreciated; I take instructions from Sofie on where the nearest store is and go purchase a six-pack of pale ale. Everyone decamps inside and Sofie, noting how I'm ogling the house's interior, says, sure, look around. With its thick mud walls and high wood beams and worn floorboards and white walls and Native American wall hangings and musical instruments and toys the Gelb residence is the perfect house for a desert rocker. We split the beers in a large, sun-baked back yard and I start bitching about Phoenix, but Doug springs to its defence – 'it's got a dozen skateparks!' – allowing us to bond over seventies skateboard icons and how great it feels to roll across tarmac on a board. Howe says nothing so I wonder whether he ever skated and he shakes his head mournfully. 'I got on a board once when I was about fourteen and damn near broke my arm. Balance has never been my strong point.'

Howe's tall if a little stooped, handsome if somewhat dazed, hair and goatee tinged with grey, cautious with words and gestures, in person as in his music seeming to stand outside of conventional rhythm, reflective and intent on creating his own space. He and Doug muse on how both were born in Pennsylvania, coming to Tucson as children with parents looking for new possibilities in the West. Howe's roots are in Wilkes Barre ('coal mining') while Doug's are in Union City ('a Polish and Ukrainian ghetto'). '*Deer Hunter* territory,' adds Doug, and Howe nods assent. We talk Old West history, Billy the Kid having spent some of his short, violent life criss-crossing Arizona, while Tombstone is down the road. Tombstone's loved by Hollywood for the OK Corral gun fight but the town should be noted as home to a significant struggle in South-west labour history: in 1884, after the mine owners tried to force a wage cut, the union called a major miners' strike. The US government supplied the owners with federal troops, who set about disbanding the union and forcing the men back down the mines. This turned out to be one of the defining events of the West – broken unions, the threat of institutional violence, low wages and poor conditions – yet Hollywood never recreated it on film. Howe appears unaware of the strike but mentions that many of the old mining towns are now home to artistic communities. Sofie appears with plates of salad and as the heat drops the evening is tinged with bliss: good food, good ale, good people, kids tearing around the yard, a natural ambience filtering through the evening. Tucson, what a glorious place to live!

'It's not always this nice,' says Howe. 'We're now getting mosquitoes carrying the West Nile virus. Worst-case symptoms see the brain swelling up of people who get infected.'

Do Giant Sand receive much recognition in their home state?

'Phoenix is a miserable city to get around in, not a good place for us, and Tucson's even worse. We're locals here so everybody takes us for granted.'

Howe's lived in LA and New York: doesn't Tucson feel a little confining?

'I like it here. There's an airport, good coffee, a nice studio, you can get pretty much whatever you want. It's enough to pester you and yet it's enough to facilitate.' Howe pauses than adds, 'After 9/11 people were twitchy here like everywhere else, looking up at the sky a lot, but the funny thing is there's no tall buildings in Tucson to fly a plane into.' He shrugs. 'We try and spend four or five months a year in Denmark so it's not like we're stuck here. Denmark offers so many things you just don't get here. A very different society. When Sofie was pregnant with our second child we were struggling, just no money, no health insurance, so we went to Denmark, where everything is provided by the state.'

Giant Sand cut their teeth on the early-eighties US hardcore scene as American rock rallied for a final burst of feral creative energy. Their contemporaries were The Gun Club, Black Flag, Bad Brains, Los Lobos, X, Rank & File, Hüsker Dü, the Meat Puppets and The Minutemen – *scorched-earth rock 'n' roll* – yet where most of those bands imploded, Giant Sand keep shuffling along.

'Tucson was even more sheltered than Phoenix during that scene's heyday,' says Gelb. 'The Meat Puppets went on to become part of the LA scene while I was still trying to find my way, my own voice, so we were never that aware of what was going on then. X were my favourite of those bands. We used to support them when they came through Tucson and Billy Zoom's guitar-playing was an influence on me. But we did our music on a very independent scale and a lot of those bands were with SST, the big alternative label of the time, and doing the same thing as the majors with tough contracts and low royalty rates. I never fell for that. I've always leased my albums to labels for periods of three/five/seven years. That might have hurt us at the time but in the long run it's benefited the band.'

Gelb mentions how his music exists in 'the shadow land', which is a fine description of a sound that's unhurried, full of drift and dust, shaped by debris from American and Mexican culture, the notes of a border dweller. While there's little sonic comparison, I wonder whether he sees Giant Sand as descendants of Americana pioneers The Byrds and Creedence Clearwater Revival, The Band and Neil Young?

'Yeah,' he says without much enthusiasm, 'I liked to listen to them when I was a kid.'

I've met Howe once before in London and he appeared a much chattier character then, conversation spiralling into the amusingly absurd. Today he's blank, resistant. *Great.* I've come all the way from Vegas on a damn Greyhound, avoiding the shorter, simpler journey to LA so as to fit with his tour schedule, and he can barely be bothered to talk. OK, keep trying: Gelb's music is unconventional and a long way from popular – briefly signed to V2, Giant Sand were dropped, the label refusing to release the *Chore of Enchantment* album, declaring it 'uncommercial' – yet over the years he's found such gifted vocalists as Victoria Williams, Lucinda Williams, Neko Case and Lisa Germano all willing to sing on his projects. Even alt.rock siren Polly Harvey likes to hang with him. Admittedly, he's handsome, but why do these women play Nancy to his Lee when so few ever hear the results?

'Ah, we're friends.'

Speaking of friends, his former rhythm section of John Convertino and Joe Burns have become Calexico, developing Gelb's template for desert rock into a bigger, slicker production.

'John and Joey got so busy with Calexico we couldn't make our schedules fit any more,' says Howe. 'There's occasions where we get the chance to work together but now I have an American rhythm section for US dates and a Danish one for touring Europe.'

Rainer Ptacek, the Czech slide guitar player Gelb formed Giant Sand with and his best friend, died of brain cancer in 1997. Since then Gelb's continued to champion Ptacek, hosting concerts in his memory and employing recordings of his transcendent slide playing on new albums.

'He was the main guy,' says Gelb wistfully. 'I wish Rainer was here.'

He then excuses himself to go and put the kids to bed. I ask Sofie what she makes of this city on the USA's frayed frontier.

'I like it and I don't like it,' she says. 'What Denmark doesn't have it has. And vice versa.'

I'd willingly sit in the backyard all night and chat with Sofie but as Howe hasn't reappeared I take this as a silent 'time to leave' signal. Sofie calls a taxi and we say our goodbyes, her fretting about how to develop their dusty front yard while the Giant Sand man lurks somewhere in the house.

Howe insisted I stay at Hotel Congress in downtown Tucson, a hotel that's kept – or, more correctly, reverted to – its original 1930s trappings. My room has no TV, only a big box radio, and the phone and furniture are all period. Howe had suggested the Congress was 'full of history' and this history turns out to focus on one John Dillinger, a bank-robbing, Depression-era celebrity who caused quite a commotion here on 22 January 1934, when he and his gang stayed at the Congress and were subsequently captured by authorities. Looking at the Dillinger information on the Congress walls I'm surprised by how brief his career was (May 1933–July 1934), especially as his legend remains enshrined in US folklore: John Sayles's latest short story collection is *Dillinger in Hollywood*, William Burroughs dedicated *Tornado Alley* to him, Joseph Beuys re-enacted his death as performance art enshrined on screen by tough guys Lawrence Tierney and Warren Oates (and soft guys Mark Harmon and Johnny Depp), even *The Simpsons* once referenced John D. Aged twelve and just beginning my infatuation with America, I read a book on Dillinger; his daring lifestyle appealed so strongly I announced to my mum that when I grew up I too wanted to be a bank robber. To which she mournfully replied that if this was going to be the case she would have to get used to visiting me in prison. Talk about crushing a kid's dreams... and here I am, staying under the same roof as a man who came to represent wild, tearaway America, gun in one hand, babe in the other, pockets stuffed with loot, one step ahead

Cowboys & Indians, 1910

of the law, born to die violently. On reflection, there's little to admire about Dillinger beyond his bravado; his brief, brutal life suggesting the cult of Tupac will also endure.

I head to the Congress bar where a framed poster of Howe declares *'He walks the earth like Caine in Kung Fu'*, which somehow seems kind of apt, his persona fitting a similarly cowboy Zen archetype. Stepping into the warm night, I wander quiet streets peppered with cafés, bars and shops selling crystals. Kerouac and Cassady came through Tucson on their way back to San Francisco after visiting William Burroughs in Louisiana, stopping only to cadge $5 gas money off author Alan Harrington, who lived here and bemoaned the isolation to his friends. I've never read Harrington (who died in 1997) but it appears he remained in Tucson, seduced by the city's peaceful culture clash. When Kerouac encounters him he's *'brooding in the yard'* just as Howe had been. Kerouac ate well, as I did, then hit the road again, briefly noting a city in transition, one situated on *'beautiful mesquite riverbed country'* and surrounded by the Catalina mountains. I head into a bar, order beer, sit beneath overactive air conditioning. Downtown midweek and little is going on; wonder what Dillinger and his gang got up to in 1934? People around the bar discuss the Minutemen, a vigilante organisation who have set up in the desert outside Tucson to patrol for illegal immigrants: the Mexican border is 60 miles away.

The Texan and Californian borders were long the most porous region for 'los illegals' to cross into the USA but Operation Gatekeeper, Bill Clinton's $3 billion militarisation of the border, has led to the deadly Sonora desert being the turf migrants struggle through. It takes at least three days to cross the Sonora into Arizona and death by dehydration has claimed hundreds. The Yuma 14 remain the single most tragic statistic: in May 2001 fourteen undocumented workers crossing together perished in 110-degree heat. 'The Devil's Highway', they call this brutal endurance quest, and for those who make it, well, Tucson's their first US city. Incredible to think that so many people – up to half a million Mexicans annually and, with people-smuggling proving ever more profitable to criminal gangs, Chinese and East European migrants are now beginning to be funnelled through the Sonora – are willing to risk everything to reach a land where most will be valued as little more than menial labour. Incredible but unsurprising: to be poor in Mexico and Central America involves absolute poverty, entrenched discrimination, an environment brutalised by gangs, police, military. And then to arrive here and be greeted by a shotgun-waving Minuteman…

One of Edward Abbey's final essays, 'Immigration and Other Liberal Taboos', raged against Latinos and Haitians being allowed into the USA – Abbey was the founding philosopher of radical ecologist movement Earth First: their mantra desired sharing the earth with fewer humans, not more. Californian professor Victor Davis Hanson's *Mexifornia*, an angry diatribe on how Mexican immigrants are destroying (environment, society, crime) his beloved state, has also inflamed debate. Abbey and Hanson are different types, the former a self-proclaimed anarchist, the latter a military historian, yet both fear these seemingly feral non-Anglo immigrants without trying to understand where they come from. Neither Hanson nor Abbey suggested that to slow immigration the USA should focus on helping Mexico, Haiti and Central America develop into more equitable nations; the USA having been founded by people fleeing European war/discrimination/poverty. Then again, my migratory nature surely makes me empathise with the poor, brown masses from the South to a greater degree than many settled US citizens would. Didn't think to ask Howe what he made of Tucson as a flashpoint for the hot topic of immigration but recall Walter, my taxi driver; is he out in the desert with a shotgun hoping some poor peon will make his day?

I rise late, breakfast heavily at the Congress café, head full of old American outlaws, then return to the Greyhound station. Border heat, headache heat: pity the poor migrant trekking through this temperature. As we roll I content myself by imagining the Indians, Conquistadors and cowboys who ventured across this fierce terrain without maps, vehicles or suncream. Back in the Phoenix bus station there's an hour before an express bus to LA departs. I return to Twain, following his journey from Nevada to San Francisco. He describes those who rushed towards California's gold rush (many losing everything) as *'victims upon the altar of the golden calf'*, yet notes this pioneer population *'gave to California a name for getting up astounding enterprises and rushing them through with a magnificent dash and daring and a recklessness of cost or consequences'*. As the majority of illegal immigrants head for California this spirit surely still exists.

At 3 p.m. I take a seat on the LA Express. As the bus begins to reverse there's a knock on its exterior and the driver brakes. The bus's door opens with a hiss: enter the Border Patrol. Four agents, dressed in olive-green uniforms, start shouting for everyone to produce *'los documentos'* and all around folk start tearing out papers/driving licences/passports and waving them about. This should be interesting: *has anyone here fled Mexico, crossed the desert to Tucson, got to Phoenix, then as they aimed for LA found themselves busted at the last hurdle?* All seems to be in order until an agent leans over and says, 'Excuse me, sir, are you a US citizen?' No, I reply, I'm a New Zealand citizen. 'Can I see your passport?' 'Sorry, but I left it with friends in San Francisco as I fly out of that city. I do have my New Zealand driver's licence government-issue photo ID.' The cop glances at the licence and says in that heavy, monosyllabic tone men with guns like to use on those without, 'Get *off* the bus.'

My backpack's torn from the hold, emptied, searched and, once it's apparent I'm not smuggling plutonium or a kilo of coke, repacked. I'm then backed up against a wall. *Sheee-it, I've truly fucked up this time.* All four Border Patrol cops surround me, arms folded, mouths tight, pistols bulging: two are Mexican-American, one is white and one black. The team leader fires questions: *Why don't I have my passport on me? What am I doing in Arizona? Where am I going in LA? What's the purpose of my visit to the USA?* He's polite but tough, a handsome man who knows he looks good in uniform, hair buffed up, trying to find holes in my story. My passport's in Frisco 'cos I can't imagine taking it to Burning Man and on a tour of America's cheapest motels. I suggest he calls Howe Gelb to verify my journalist status. He dismisses this suggestion and marches off with my driver's licence. All around the station people are eyeing me, wondering what crime the scruffy white boy has committed. Meanwhile, my stomach is flipping. To make things even more unpleasant my naturally paranoiac mind starts imagining being locked up with the two hard-looking Latino men I witnessed being cuffed yesterday. An American jail... there are, surely, worse places to end up in. But not many. I've heard about how the prisons are run by gangs – Aryan Nation, the Mexican Mafia, Black Muslims – stabbings and rapes commonplace. Fear curdles inside me. Should I pray? Negative: not a believer. Run? Negative: that would lead to unthinkable consequences. Shout that my civil rights are being violated? Negative: in Bush–Cheney America civil rights have been peeled back. Feeling very unsettled, mind playing tricks, thinking of Dillinger held at bay in Tucson all those years back an— 'You sold your passport in Vegas, didn'tcha? Gambled it away? Admit *it*.' Oh, mama, the white cop's turned into Charles Bronson and wants to bust a confession out of me before his superior returns. How to tell this moustache-wearing, spittle-dripping redneck to back the fuck off? Best to say nothing, grind teeth and nip tongue. 'Did you know you're breaking federal law just by being a foreign national without your passport on you?' 'That right, Officer? Well, I apologise.' He continues, stating that they can jail my ass. This being a serious offence. Terrorists everywhere. Nod along – *like I resemble an al-Qaeda operative!* – imagining just how unpleasant a Phoenix cell must be, holding on to that old galaxy hitchhiker maxim: *Don't panic!* Nod and bob ('Yes, suh!' 'Yes, suh!'), imagining servility being what the cop mentality demands. The head officer returns, passes me my licence, says, 'You're OK. You can get on the next LA bus,' and off they head in search of Osama Bin Laden or John Dillinger or whatever other major criminals travel by Greyhound. I've got four hours to kill before the next LA bus. And it's a regional so going to take twice as long as the express. As the hours drift by I watch my Border Patrol guys busting a scared-looking Latino couple. No doubt about it, in the struggle to keep Mexicans out of the USA these guys earn their wages.

I take a seat by a black male and it turns out he's from Jamaica but living in LA and waiting for the same bus. We swap notes on our favourite reggae musicians and when I mention a taste for Lee 'Scratch' Perry's seventies productions he answers, 'We don' like him. He a *tief*,' which explains why Scratch now resides in Switzerland. I mention my experience with Border Patrol and his complexion takes on an almost Caucasian hue, not having any ID on him and maybe not being the most legal of Angelenos. So we both sit there, sweating that a new team of BP officers will arrive to repeat the disruption, while chuckling at the entertainment value my earlier arrest surely provided for those riding to LA – *a blue-eyed devil being the only person busted!* Sweet. By the time we leave Phoenix it's a night ride down Highway 10, stopping often to shovel passengers on/off, the usual flotsam gathering to spark cigarettes. One guy calls Arizona's capital 'a hell of a town. I didn't have nothing but trouble there', then asks whether he can get into the UK with criminal convictions. How serious, I reply, was your crime – murder? 'Nope,' he says, 'ain't killed anyone. Yet.'

It's 2 a.m. when we arrive in the LA Greyhound station. I resist going looking for a motel, certain cheap thrills would find me quickly. The bruised and beaten – a man holding a rambling conversation with himself, a woman covered in dirty bandages – stumble past likes moths to a lamp. The station's rammed but obviously designed to be extremely unaccommodating: steel mesh or hard plastic chairs frustrate any attempt at sleep and the atmosphere is stuffy, no fresh air. All around people are snoring, shuffling, moaning, sniffing, munching on food from a vile-smelling café and, occasionally, shovelling quarters into tiny B & W TVs attached to chair arms. A black woman keeps proclaiming 'I'm from god*damn* Dallas, *Texas!*' to anyone who happens to pass her while an obese youth seated alongside makes long, creepy calls on his phone, at one point muttering 'She said I had a nice face for someone so big,' and I wonder: *did she ever get to say anything else?* Beggars constantly do the rounds, the station's security seemingly oblivious to them, and a black guy with no teeth, seeing me trying to read Kerouac, says, 'A reader, huh? I got a book you will love,' and pulls out a biography of Albert Speer obviously lifted from a local library. He's only asking two dollars but I've no desire to read about old Nazis so shrink in my seat. Given I'm the only person in the entire station reading he keeps returning, at one point saying: 'Yo' gonna finish that book soon. This here a new one!' *'LA is the loneliest and most brutal of American cities,'* wrote Kerouac. He describes being surrounded by wild jazz characters while I'm dodging the ruined. Wrap myself into backpack. Feign sleep. Hope those demanding alms will – *please!* – stop.

Hours later I finally venture outside to find dawn's soft pink light illuminating a mess of warehouses and factories and streets and power lines. Everything looks forbidding, worn out, diseased, poisonous; even with this softest of light the atmosphere is one of ruination. Across the road I notice the golden arches of a McDonald's. Normally try to avoid eating such but, right now, it's hard to imagine a more welcome sight. The McD's is spotless and staffed by polite Asians and Latinos. Feast on hotcakes with butter and syrup and steaming coffee. By normal standards it's mediocre but after yesterday's diet of Greyhound café food and fear it tastes like, well, nectar of the gods. Fortified, I take basic

Bright lights, big city: Linda Lyndell in Los Angeles, CA, 1969

directions from a Chinese employee who hasn't yet mastered English but knows how the public transport system works. Back on 7th Avenue everything appears coated in lead, a bleaker shade of grey. Creatures drift out of alleys, shuffling along the sidewalk, humans reduced to pack-rat status, faces drained and boiled, many desperate for a drink, a hit, a fix, cornflakes dusted with PCP and doused in Night Train. No one makes eye contact, no one appears to see me as I step among and over them, collapsed on the sidewalk or loitering in shopfronts, men and women, black and white, young and prematurely aged, in rags, cast-offs, the ghost of clothing, feet bare or wrapped in plastic bags, scabby and terribly weary. A 60 Metro bus pulls up. I pay the unsmiling female driver $1.25 and ask to be warned when we hit 7th Avenue Station. 7th Avenue crosses Broadway, the crossroads between poverty and wealth in downtown LA. The city starts to pulse with people and traffic, a few more red lights and then the driver shouts, 'Seventh Avenue Station.' Another $1.25 and I'm riding the red line to Hollywood.

CALIFORNIA SOUL

Hollywood, East LA, Watts, Orange County, Joshua Tree

And so the people started to sing
And that's how the surf gave birth untold
To California soul, California soul.

Marlena Shaw

Latinos are without a doubt the most profound challenge to the American melting pot myth, in that they don't adhere to just English, or to the one-drop definition of racial Otherness, and they are themselves part of an American migration with a rich history in this Hemisphere. It is often asked why Latinos don't simply conform to established forms of assimilation to American life. One answer might be that Latinos are already deeply American, they derive from a North/South divide that is yielding a new geography, and they are thoroughly engaged in the project of further defining what Americanness means.

Roman de la Campa

LA's main drag: Central Avenue

chapter 5

Hollywood:
Everything Sings Except for a Buzzard

I check into a Hollywood Motel 6. Shower. Nap. To be clean and secure feels *so* good. The Latina at reception offers a basic Hollywood street map and I wander the few blocks to LA's most iconic structure, the Capitol Records 'Stack O' Records' building near Hollywood and Vine. Welton Becket's masterful 1956 design playfully anticipated LA becoming the planet's most powerful music industry city and it's the perfect place to begin a Hollywood ramble. A wall outside Stack O' Records features a mural of jazz legends – Nat 'King' Cole (whose huge sales financed the Stack), Billie Holiday, Miles Davis, Charlie Parker – artists I tend to associate with New York yet all recorded in the Stack's legendary studios. Strange but true: LA was a late developer as a music powerhouse, West Coast jazz and soundtracks being industry staples until surf music, especially The Beach Boys (who signed to Capitol in 1962), signalled an LA gold rush that – by the mid-sixties – had established the city as a hitmaker equal to London, Memphis, New York, Chicago and Detroit, one which would overtake all these metropolises in the seventies and reach its zenith in the late eighties, mid-nineties when the likes of Guns N' Roses and Snoop Doggy Dogg shifted zillions of CDs. Rock City/ Rap City, LA became popular music's Mecca with local heroes The Red Hot Chili Peppers currently the world's most popular rock band. But the Chilis' origins date right back to the early-eighties hardcore punk scene and I'm struggling to name any twenty-first-century LA stars. Even LA uber-producer Rick Rubin now focuses his energies on resurrecting the likes of Neil Diamond and ZZ Top. Perhaps the industry has reverted to its origins: a huge billboard not far from the Capitol Building advertises *High School Musical*, this Disney product doing bigger business than any recent feature film or pop/rock act.

The tourist in me glimpses the Hollywood sign, ogles celebrity palm prints outside the Kodak Theater and notes how the intersection of Hollywood Boulevard and Cahuenga is now renamed Raymond Chandler Square; Chandler, another displaced South Londoner, set Marlowe's fictional offices here and the exasperated PI wouldn't feel out of place today among the dusty palm trees and Scientology centre. Close to Chandler Square the Hollywood Walk of Fame finishes; this really should be renamed the Hollywood Walk of Shame, there being stars for name-calling red baiters Elia Kazan and Ronald Reagan yet none for those they persecuted. At Frederick's of Hollywood I peer through the windows, hoping Jessica Alba might have decided to drop in and check out the latest lingerie, then ride a bus along Sunset Boulevard – the other passengers are Russian babushkas – dismounting at the section of the Boulevard known as Sunset Strip.

From the mid-sixties to early nineties Sunset Strip was the epicentre of a burgeoning West Coast rock scene. It is to here people flock believing near-instant movie and music fame exists while hacks get gushy about Hollywood Babylon, certain excess-all-areas is constantly served up to the fortunate few. Admittedly, The Beach Boys, The Byrds, The Mamas & The Papas, Love, The Doors, Buffalo Springfield et al. all engaged in the Icarus-like pursuit of fame and self-destruction either on the Strip or in nearby Laurel Canyon, squandering both talent and considerable fortunes. But, for the most part, Hollywood feels very southern Californian, laid back in a congested, sunny way. Passing rock club the Viper Room I reflect on River Phoenix, twenty-three years young, man-child in the promised land, drawing his last breath on this sidewalk. Neighbouring club the Whisky-a-Go-Go is LA's most legendary venue – *imagine witnessing the 1966 Whisky concerts where The Doors supported Them, Jim and Van Morrison trading verses on an extended encore of 'Gloria!'* – psychedelia, country rock, singer-songwriter, punk, new wave and hair-metal hopefuls all debuted here in a tidal wave of media and industry excitement only to, inevitably, fade once the initial excitement and creativity were drained. Today the Whisky, Viper and the Roxy Theatre are all exclusive venues, hosting industry showcases and charging 'pay-to-play' rates for those not yet established. No youthful Axl and Slash preen outside, the Hollywood rock scene having seemingly dissipated among a mess of heroin and hairspray some time before the new millennium.

Crowning the Strip is Hustler's megastore, a silver-skinned sex supermarket serving up all kinds of penetrations. LA porn is a multibillion-dollar industry now, almost as mainstream as rock 'n' roll. Maybe more so. *Think about it*: today finding a porn store is much easier than finding a record shop. Some twenty years ago, in the hills above Sunset Boulevard, donkey-dicked porn star John Holmes participated in mass murder (retaliation for a drug rip-off), cocaine having chewed through porn as it did the movie and music industries, before dying of Aids. Hustler sell boxed sets of Holmes's movies, DVDs that should come with a sticker warning of porn's human cost.

At a vast Amoeba Records emporium I purchase a vinyl copy of *The Border*, a soundtrack helmed by Ry Cooder to Tony Richardson's feeble 1982 movie about illegal aliens and Texan border patrol agents. Cooder has long been king of LA's retro rock scene and I'll never fault his ability as a slide guitarist (as a teenage session guitarist he played on many fine sixties LA pop/rock recordings), but his solo albums are stuffy: recently he's begun a series of albums that look at LA's Mexican and working-class history. These sound right up my street; unfortunately, the first of these, *Chavez Ravine*, came on like West End musical *Five Guys Named Moe*, theatrical nostalgia for a bygone age. With *The Border* Cooder got everything right, taking a back seat and letting the likes of Freddy Fender, Sam the Sham and John Hiatt loose. Cooder's roots music leanings have long stood out as something of an oddity in an LA music scene dominated by glossy rock fashions, but the city once was a country music hothouse. Indeed,

Capitol recorded pioneering rockabilly singer Wanda Jackson and Merle Haggard, an ex-con (he witnessed Johnny Cash's performance in nearby San Quentin) who developed into the most expressive songwriter in country music history. In the 1930s Los Angeles' booming factories, shipyards and oilfields attracted many fleeing Oklahoma dustbowls and Southern poverty – Woody Guthrie first made a name for himself here – while the sixties found Arizona's Lee Hazelwood, Alabama's Steve Young and Georgia's Gram Parsons independently shaping a Gothic LA country rock sound. All three succeeded in their own way and helped mark Hollywood as a Cosmic Cowboy hangout, one the Eagles would emasculate as they turned country rock into the blandest of radio staples across the 1970s. Warren Zevon, Randy Newman and Jackson Browne each penned a handful of memorable songs here in the early seventies – if never matching the critical brouhaha surrounding them – while Joni Mitchell, Laurel Canyon's smug sovereign, ultimately inspired a boom in female singer-songwriters. Less mercantile but more suited to my ears was the city's early-eighties roots scene. Fired up by punk's eclectic do-it-yerself nature, The Blasters, X, Green On Red, Los Lobos, Victoria Williams, Lucinda Williams, Dwight Yoakam, Rank And File and The Jayhawks imprinted country, rock 'n' roll and Tex-Mex with a defiant, scuzzy identity. My personal favourites were The Gun Club, four Hollywood misfits led by doomed Mexican-American rocker Jeffrey Lee Pierce, whose scorched country/blues punk resulted in 1981's *Fire of Love*, the best American rock 'n' roll record of that decade.

Los Lobos, Lucinda, Victoria, Dwight, Chuck Prophet (guitarist of Green On Red) and Alejandro Escovedo (guitarist of Rank And File) remain active, but as metal and gangsta rap began to dominate most fled the city of angels. LA's a city of transients, people wash up here – *hungry for a deal, looking for a dream* – some stay, many flee, exhausted by tainted paradise. I consider all this in a Cambodian doughnut shop, awaiting my appointment with a singer who arrived in LA looking for work.

Drinking coffee in America is a challenge. There's the watery slop they serve in diners – last night's one served 'freedom fries', which should have alerted me to how bad everything else would be – and the overpriced, bland, supersized lattes of Starbucks and co. Experience suggests immigrants make the best coffee: strong, tasty, inexpensive. Greek, Lebanese and Italian delis do great paper-cup takeouts. And Cambodian doughnut shops are similarly reliable. This one, occupying the ugly symmetry of what was once surely a hamburger or fried-chicken vendor, is no different: entering, I chew on the aroma – percolating coffee and fresh doughnuts – the American urban diet par excellence, $1 a cup and you can choose between French Roast and decaf. Then there's some two dozen different doughnuts on display. As I slip into a seat an old black guy who's mulling over doughnuts at the counter shouts, 'Don't sit there. That's *my* seat!' I duck out, grab an empty pew, and as he shuffles into his seat a raggedy-looking white guy starts laughing in wild uneven patterns and asking the old dude whether he has a special reservation on that seat and the whole vibe is instantly very bad. The white guy keeps at it, teasing the black guy, who squirms in his seat, ignoring the riff of 'your seat, man? Own it do ya, man? Box seat, man?' while the proprietor looks edgy until the white guy finishes whatever 12 per cent solution he was mixing with his coffee and wanders off laughing in a strange hyena style. The black guy turns and says to me, 'That boy wasn't right in the head.' Well, this is Hollywood. The owner squeezes out a worried smile, hoping all is normal now, which inspires me to mention I backpacked in Cambodia. He asks what year and I say February 2001 and he considers this then adds how he's never returned since he fled almost thirty years ago. Doesn't he, I ask, miss Cambodia? He shakes his head and says, 'Why would I go back? My children were born here. They are Americans. Cambodians killed my mother and father and brothers. Only graves are there for me now.' Which is a great way to end unnecessary conversation. I thank him for the coffee and doughnuts, strong unfussy coffee and light doughnuts dusted with cinnamon and sugar, and return to thinking about Mable John.

Sister to Little Willie John, student of Billie Holiday, associate to Berry Gordy Jr, pioneering Motown artist, Stax artist at the height of Southern soul's achievements, deputy to Ray Charles and, more recently, a preacher and campaigner for the homeless, Mable John is formidable. That she has been based in Los Angeles since 1969 yet has no connection to the Sunset Strip rock scene suits me; tales of groupie abuse and drug gluttons take on a queasy sense of ritual in rock writing, as if readers have little interest in the music, hungry only for vulgarity. The media's continued fascination with the antics of Mötley Crüe and Guns N' Roses, bands who personify Hollywood at its most soulless and stupid, suggests tainted Western psyches. Even Brian Wilson is more celebrated today for his drug-fuelled crack-up than his best music – pulsing early-sixties hymns like 'I Get Around' are overlooked while studio doodles like the *Smile* album attract exegesis. Such thoughts occupy my mind as I say goodbye to the doughnut vendor and begin to walk across the City of Angels. Public transport in LA, I've realised, is abysmal. There's a skeletal metro line and an infrequent, slow bus service – back in the fifties General Motors managed to convince those who ran the city that public transport was 'socialistic' and thus un-American. So LA crawls, traffic locked in congested patterns, air thick with exhaust fumes, seemingly diseased palm trees wilting, sun heavy with glare, ashen sky. Latinos attempt to sell oranges at intersections and men of all races hold up signs suggesting they will work for food. I can sense that once LA did seem like a West Coast paradise, but when? Fifty, sixty or seventy years past? As I walk I sense a harshness, a brutality, inhabiting the city's spirit. Eventually, sweaty and eyes stinging from the smog, I reach the spacious, comfortable home of Mable John.

Ushered inside by an aide, I'm given a glass of water. Mable enters the room speaking in a strident, testifying voice. In her mid-seventies she looks fierce, a woman not to mess with. I compliment her on her distinctive bone structure and she replies that her mother was Indian. She then shows me a wall-sized black and white photographic print featuring her young and very beautiful self next to Motown founder Berry Gordy Jr and Billie Holiday, who, by then, had only a few months left to live. *'Wow!'* Corny thing to say but, really, what else is there?

'That was taken in Detroit in 1959. Berry had secured me a booking supporting Billie at the Flame Show Bar in Detroit. She was shy. I don't know if Berry knew her before that. I did not. She'd had such a tough life and the lessons Billie taught me she had not learned until too late. One of them was to know when you have given enough, when you've gone far enough. And then have guts to say, "I quit. I'm finished."'

Born in 1930 in Bastrop, Louisiana, Mable and her family moved to Arkansas and then on to Detroit.

'In Louisiana my father did what they call "log rolling". They cut the tree and it would fall into what they call a "log pond" and he would then roll it with his feet until it got to the mill. He left that and came to Cullingdale, Arkansas, where he was working with his hands at the mill that was making paper from the trees he had rolled with his feet! After that, when that work started to get slower, he heard that in Detroit he could get a job and he could

'Know when you have given enough': Mable John fronting Billie & Berry, Los Angeles, CA, 2006

make more money. Detroit was wonderful then.' She pauses after saying this, dwelling on how her home town is now the USA's poorest, most ruined city. 'Father came with some friends and got work at making nuts and bolts for the auto industry. He then went to work for the Dodge Chrysler factory on the production line. So the same nuts and bolts he had made were those he was putting into the automobiles as they came on down the assembly line. That's quite a history, isn't it? He then became road manager for my brother, Little Willie John. That's the history of my dad. My mother just stayed at home and taught us songs and cooked. My mother and father both sang and played guitar and everybody had to sing. My father said everything in the world sings except for a buzzard and we weren't allowed to be no buzzard.'

The oldest of ten children, Mable watched her teenage brother Little Willie John become a huge R & B star in the mid-fifties, cutting definitive versions of 'Fever' and 'Need Your Love So Bad'. Willie was the original wild child – 'he never grew up,' admits Mable, 'his life was music and ladies' – drinking, gambling, brawling, pulling guns and knives, even cheating Sam Cooke out of $5,000 (claiming he needed it for his mama's funeral – she was alive and well), qualities that are reflected in his abrasive, rule-breaking vocals. In an era of smooth harmony singers Willie ripped and roared, curling notes then biting them off, desperately inhabiting a song. As the hits tailed off in the early sixties he lived a feral existence, arrested for attacking a man with a broken bottle in a Miami club in August 1964, jumping bail and, two months later, stabbing a man to death in a Seattle speakeasy. He died in jail, officially of heart failure, although speculation suggests a severe beating, in 1968. His Detroit funeral found Reverend C. L. Franklin delivering the sermon and his daughter Aretha singing. In attendance were a galaxy of soul stars including James Brown and Sam & Dave.

'Our family always sang together. We had a group, a gospel quintet, then Willie broke rank and began singing blues. Johnny Otis said the greatest talent show he ever saw in his life was in Detroit featuring Jackie Wilson, Hank Ballard and Little Willie

John. There was none better than my brother. He knew how to stop your heart. He could stop you in his tracks. He was the originator of that soul sound. During the time he was alive no one had that sound. He could sing *anything*.'

Mable followed in her brother's footsteps, tentatively perhaps as she was already in her mid-twenties. Disowned by her church when she began singing blues, Mable found that a friendship with Berry Gordy Jr led to her becoming the first female singer signed to Motown. She released several singles on his Tamla label between 1959 and 1962, none of them hitting the charts, her vocal style closer to Dinah Washington than the ebullient pop of Motown's initial female stars, Mary Wells and The Marvelettes.

'I was friends with the whole Gordy family and I met his mother when I was a teenager. I was at school and she gave me a job in the holidays working for her insurance company. I met Berry years later when he went into writing. I had no idea that he was her son at the time. At the start he was wanting to be more of a songwriter so he didn't have that original vision. I remember we were in New York for an awards ceremony where Jackie Wilson and Berry were getting an award for a song and at the table I said, 'Since you can't find a place for me why don't you start your own record company and I'll stay with you for ever.' He looked at me and said, 'Don't ever say you'll stay with them for ever. What if I can't provide for you?' I don't know what's in anybody's heart but I know that I planted a particular seed in his heart. And I was the first female singer signed to any company Berry had. Sometimes I think we expected things of Berry that he had no idea he was supposed to provide. He was looking at the entire picture and we were just wanting him to do this and that for each of us. Unless you were a business person you can't imagine what Berry Gordy went through trying to establish Motown. Most people wouldn't have even dared to start it. Number one, we were all embarking into a field we didn't know. We were African-American people trying to get into a world that had not accepted us, a different world to today. Berry had to fight all of that. He had to get distributors to take the records. He had to struggle all the way.

I loved being on Motown. We were a big family. The Supremes and Temptations sang backing vocals! But my sound didn't suit the label so Berry dissolved my contract in 1962. We've remained friends ever since, he's a generous supporter of our scholarship foundation and Effort to End Homelessness and Hunger in America. Incidentally, he don't owe me a dime.'

Mable shifted to Chicago, recording for small independent labels of little consequence. In 1966 she was invited to Memphis to record for Stax, the Southern soul label shaping up as Motown's main competitor. Working with songwriters David Porter and Isaac Hayes and backed by Booker T & The MGs, John's first session produced 'Your Good Thing (Is About To End)', a Southern soul classic. 'Good Thing' gave her a No. 6 R & B hit and found her cool, clear voice fitting perfectly the Memphis sound.

'Memphis, I'd live there if I could!' she says. 'Stax was great, the people, the musicians. It's there I really found my voice. My first time there David and Isaac came to my motel, the Lorraine,

Soul men: Isaac Hayes & David Porter 1968, Memphis, TN, 1968

and they had a piano brought to the room and they didn't have any music ready for me so I told them about my life and they started playing music and "Your Good Thing" came about.'

Her voice is a powerful instrument, one that brooks no fools and bears no relation to her famous brother. Among the other tunes she cut at Stax was 'Don't Hit Me No More' – written by Texan soul singer Joe Tex and published under his wife's name – the pain in her voice almost prophetic: not only was John unhappily married and soon to lose her brother but three of her four sons would predecease her. Her face doesn't suggest a woman of constant sorrow, instead conveying intelligence, a sense of command. These qualities – and her remarkable voice – are surely what made Ray Charles insist she head The Raelettes, the female backing vocalists who constituted an important part of his sound. In 1969, with her Stax releases no longer charting, she took up Charles's offer and moved to LA. This proved fortuitous: Stax would collapse within six years while Gordy moved Motown to LA, hiring Mable as adviser for *Lady Sings the Blues*, his Billie Holiday biopic.

'Ray's studio is just down the road,' says Mable. Yes, I passed it on the way here: RPM International, a large stucco cube built for Charles in 1964 – 'people told me to build it in Beverly Hills,' Charles once noted of the studio, 'why not a working-class black neighborhood? Why not put some money back into the community? Besides, the location was great; close to downtown, close to Hollywood and a straight shot to the airport' – and home to much great music. Charles was both musical visionary and ruthless taskmaster but Mable demurs.

'I met Ray through my brother and he followed my career. When my time with Stax was closing I got a call from Ray. I sang with him from 1969 to 1977 then asked him to allow me to come home because I had a call to go study at the ministry. We remained in constant contact right until his death. I publish seventy-seven songs with him and we would e-mail one another every evening as Ray had voice-activated e-mail. I stayed with him when he was ill and prayed with him. Ray was a wonderful friend, a wonderful man to work with and for. I learnt many lessons through him. He taught me how to make money and how to save money. He was one of the smartest men that ever lived. Genius. That word is the true word for him.'

Mable founded the Joy in Jesus Evangelistic Ministry in the 1980s and has since fed and clothed hundreds of thousands of LA's poorest people. It must seem hopeless, I suggest, trying to deal with homelessness and hunger in California?

'Not when you look at it from an individual viewpoint. I thought twelve years ago that by now there would be no more hungry people in California because of the amount of the people we were feeding. But that was premature thinking. The Bible says the poor will always be with you so I have to deal with people one person at a time. It's a huge experience and undertaking because we reach out to the public to help underprivileged people. It's all based on the Bible – giving people food, clothing, toiletries, shelter and spiritual uplift. We teach them how to balance a chequebook, a budget, to prepare for famine in the time of plenty. It's a lifetime challenge.'

Mable John has risen to many challenges: what does she make of America today?

'It's more equal than when I was growing up. But it could be *more* equal. To get rid of the strife and hunger. If everybody made themselves into a committee of one and thought what they could do for others rather than just for themselves then we'd sort out the problems in this nation.'

chapter 6

East LA: Pure Mexican Fury

It's a classic LA day: sun shining, breeze blowing, blue sky breaking through the smog, radio blaring. Feel I'm inhabiting a Tom Petty song. Luis Rodriguez, poet laureate of East LA, manoeuvres into heavy traffic and starts spinning the dial, trying to find KBUE, the city's powerhouse Mexican station, when out of the static surfs a high, nasal voice rapping over doo-wop loops. Then the chant kicks in:

> Sawn off shotgun
> Hand on the pump
> Blasting on a 40
> Puffing on a blunt

Beautiful: on our way into East LA and here's the barrio's thug anthem. Luis looks over, wondering what's so entertaining. 'Cypress Hill, man. This is the East LA we consume at a distance. Gangsta rap.' Luis cocks an ear, listens, shrugs. 'That shit is ancient. Almost as old as Los Lobos. You know Los Lobos?' Course I know Los Lobos. *'La-la-la-la-la-la bamba!'* Jesus, I sing badly. Luis grins, mentions Los Lobos were his homeboys way back when. Then adds, 'All kinds of sounds coming out of East LA right now way tougher than that old gangsta shit.' 'Lead me on,' I say, 'take me to the promised land.'

Luis Rodriguez is an East LA veteran; back in the 1960s he lived a thug life of gangs, crime, addiction and prison time. Somehow, Luis avoided becoming just another statistic and he's now among the USA's most acclaimed Latino authors. His memoir, *Always Running: La Vida Loca, Gang Days in LA*, written for his wayward teenage son Ramiro in 1993, didn't sway the youth from gangs – he's currently serving a twenty-eight-year sentence for drive-bys – but it became a bestseller and saw Luis invited on *Oprah*. Poetry, short stories, a novel and a supremely funky spoken-word CD have all followed, Rodriguez's eloquent writing rooted in the Mexican immigrant experience as they attempt to build North American lives.

Cruising downtown, Luis points out huge cinemas from Hollywood's dawn, movie temples that hosted 1920s Academy Award presentations when the city was young and LA's possibilities appeared endless. Today these stucco-and-plaster wombs of the entertainment industry are transformed into multi-use precincts of Latin American culture – churches, markets, wholesale jewellers, vendors offering burritos, fried chicken, noodles – where golden-skinned entrepreneurs smile and laugh and bark out offers. And the music? The music pumps out: high, keen voices, swinging accordions, wayward brass, Spanish as the loving tongue. *Funky Broadway?* Uh-huh. Downtown is, if it can accurately be said of this sprawling metropolis, the heart of LA. And it now pumps a Latin pulse. What's going on? 'Simple,' says Luis, 'it's La Reconquista.'

La Reconquista – The Reconquest – refers to the lands of California, Arizona, New Mexico and Texas (all forcibly annexed by the USA from Mexico after the latter's defeat in the 1846–48 war) being peacefully recolonised by Latinos. This involves both the native Chicano community's growing confidence – LA recently voted in its first Mexican mayor – and the Mexican and Central American immigrants who keep arriving: the City of Angels has become the planet's second biggest Mexican city with the city's populace between 45 and 55 per cent Latino. Not that LA's entertainment or media industries would suggest this. But on Broadway evidence is everywhere. Leaving behind the old stucco-and-brick buildings, we arrive at Bunker Hill and the Civic Center. LA here is testament to how those in power envision the city: a financial district consisting of mirror-glass towers, vacuous art museums, condos and Frank Gehry's eye-burning titanium obscenity, the Disney Concert Hall. Talk about a billion dollars' worth of Mickey Mouse architecture. Although the sun is shining – no, *glaring* – off Disney Hall, there is a vibe hostile to anyone who lacks electronic-key access to the private loft space of many of these under-utilised skyscrapers, which have now been turned into exudes.

Bunker Hill is now LA's financial district and a monument to intolerance and corruption. Post-WW2, as Anglos fled to the suburbs, Bunker Hill's large Victorian houses became home to a fluid black and Latino community. This unsettled both the LAPD and the local power elite – from The Beach Boys to *Baywatch*, LA presents a white face – leading to Bunker Hill's housing being razed, its community dispersed; by 1970 any hint of its past existence was removed, developers destroying even the Angels' Flight funicular railroad. Luis points out the railway (rebuilt in the 1990s as a nod to old downtown), now rarely in service: ersatz recreation of history, a perfect LA genre. The neighbourhood cleared, LA's financial district was shifted to Bunker Hill at immense public cost; American and Japanese banks, fortresses of capitalist aggression, all battlements and reflective glass,

'I was born in Juarez': Luis Rodriguez in East LA

emphasise how those who run LA loathe much of the city. Today, the northern area of downtown is a corporate non-place, a clinical wilderness encouraging no one to linger.

'Broadway's changed a lot,' says Luis. 'I lived down here when I first ran away from home as a teenager in the late 1960s. Back then downtown was poor housing so you had all types living here. Now it's mostly Pachuca [urban Mexican] neighbourhoods. These days there are lots of homeless people. Thirty years ago I was homeless and hooked on heroin but being homeless now, it's far worse. I'd spend my days reading in the downtown library or mugging people and stealing clothes from shops. Nasty shit. I'd go to Clifton's Café where for five cents they'd give you bread, soup and juice and there were lots of all-night movie theatres that charged seventy-five cents entry and would throw you out in the morning. Those old movie palaces were beautiful buildings but, man, they were full of winos and junkies and perverts.

'Now, look at what these grand old cinemas are: the Rialto's a, uh, market. The Cameo looks like it's a jewellers. And the State is... oh... *shit!* It's been turned into an evangelical church. The evangelists are going into Latin America like locusts, converting lots of poor and indigenous people to fundamentalist Christianity. They're succeeding in the US among poor Latino communities too. People feel such despair, living in poor neighbourhoods with high crime while working minimum-wage jobs, they end up embracing whatever promises the fast track to heaven. My brothers and sisters have all fallen for it. Those fucking evangelists, man, they're a cancer on our community!'

Luis swings left on 4th Street, drives east for a few blocks into the warehouse district, turns right. 'Skid Row,' he says.

Now, I've travelled far and wide, passed through Calcutta slums and West Bank refugee camps, but nothing's prepared me for this bright Californian inferno. Unfolding in front of us are dozens, no hundreds, of people, mostly black, sharing an atmosphere of extreme human suffering. Some rest on the sidewalk, others huddle over shopping trolleys, most seem to stagger, run, shuffle, the street vivid with madness. Skid Row functions as an open-air asylum, a place where the crazies can be contained. Check those features – meth-ravaged, puffy, blunted – here roams feral America.

'LA has hardly any beds for the homeless,' says Luis, 'yet people keep coming here because they figure the city's not too cold so they can survive sleeping on the streets. Of course, the streets eat you alive. There's quite a lot of Salvadoreans on Skid Row, men who have escaped the awful situation down there only to find they can't adapt to the US.'

Skid Row spreads across several blocks and large numbers of homeless gather outside missions and shelters, waiting for food and clothing, medicine and bathrooms. We drive past the New LA Mission and the Union Rescue Mission, which shelters over a thousand souls a night, then pass LAPD's Central Division fortress on 6th Street. 'The LAPD see themselves as serving the suburbs and the wealthy,' says Luis. 'If you're poor or Latino or black then watch out, they've already marked you as a potential criminal. And if you're homeless they just love to harass you. You've got eight thousand, maybe ten thousand, people living here. There ain't nowhere near the number of beds available in the shelters. You don't have to be Einstein to work out how unpleasant that makes life for everyone in this region.'

Skid Row – the name comes from a Seattle street where logs were once skidded down before the Great Depression turned it into vagrant turf – is the kind of visible social ulcer most Americans simply blank out. Not Luis. He stares ahead, reflecting on how close he came to taking up permanent residence here, then asks what Europeans make of the US government's ability to burn billions on bombs while refusing to find the spare change to help out the 'largest stable transient society in the US'. Not that it's simply a federal problem; local government efforts make life even more unpleasant for these unfortunates: public toilets have been removed (LA has fewer public toilets than any other US city), benches designed barrel-shaped to discourage sitting and obstruct sleeping, sprinklers come on and soak sleepers in open areas while police and private security forces practise 'containment' (official term) of the homeless within these few blocks. The walls may be invisible but the homeless are, to a degree, caged.

'Seen enough of the Nickel?' asks Luis, employing the name given by those who have lived here as Skid Row centres on 5th Street. Enough for this lifetime, sure. Luis turns the car right, points out Hotel Rosalyn, a welfare hotel he once frequented, and the El Paso bar where he gave early poetry readings. 'I used to hang out at the old Greyhound station and mug people getting off the bus,' he says. 'Anyone who was green and didn't know LA's streets was prey. I've done a lot of bad things in my life. I'm trying to make up for it now.' I recall my night in the new Greyhound station – a mile or so east of the Nickel – and feel relieved my ass stayed put on those hard seats. Luis starts driving north on Broadway and as we pass the Civic Center I muse on how close the financial district and the Nickel are. 'The yuppies would love to get rid of Broadway,' says Luis, 'push the Mexicans and the homeless out. It makes them uncomfortable that they've pumped all this money into developing their part of downtown but they can't control somewhere literally just down the road from them. But that's the story of LA, a city where people are often unwillingly pushed together.'

Luis's LA story begins in Mexico.

'I was born in Juarez. That's one unforgiving city, perched right on the Mexican–Texan border. My family arrived in LA when I was a child. Immediately we found ourselves negotiating fierce racial barriers. LA was then and is now a very segregated city. We first lived in South Central and I remember my older brother getting beaten up by black kids all the time. I went to school in East LA and there was a lot of racism. I hated white people – *goddam gabachos!* – it was a superficial mentality but growing up in the 'hood whites were cops, judges, politicians. Later I realised poverty was a big part of what united us with blacks, poor whites, Indians. In the US people talk about race all the time but won't talk about class. All the politicians in Congress are millionaires and they're supposed to represent us?'

Reading Rodriguez, you encounter a USA few contemporary

writers touch upon, a literature of hard, filthy work and struggle. Words come chiselled from experience, words that, as he drives, echo around my head.

I dreamt I had a son.
His name was Ramiro.
He was a beautiful boy.
He loved his father.
He laughed and played and smiled.
I dreamt such a great boy.
I woke up.
And the nightmare of the reality told me.
I should be there.

Driving along Cesar Chavez, Luis points out a massive concrete haemorrhoid, squat and threatening, directly to our left. 'LA County Jail. That's the second largest prison in the world. LA County has 165,000 prisoners, the largest prison populace of any city in the world. And of those the largest group is Chicano.' The County Jail represents the nucleus of what's called prisonomics: in the USA many prisons have been privatised with each prisoner representing up to $25,000 in income for the surrounding community. With industrial and textile jobs being exported to Central America and South-east Asia, prisons, casinos and huge animal confinement units (for raising and processing pigs and poultry) have become major employers of working-class America.

'What you see in today's US is an authoritarian, racist, zero-sum political economy that has generated the most unequal distribution of wealth in the industrialised world,' says Luis. 'This has given rise to what I call a 'prison nation' concept. It's easier to lock people up than educate them. Criminality in this country is a class issue. You see this played out across the nation as economic differences escalate: there are more and more gated communities while working-class neighbourhoods become dumping grounds for underfunded schools, poor housing and youths whose options have been cut off. So they stand on street corners flashing hand signs, inviting the bullets, killing people who are their mirror image.'

All of which recalls a Rodriguez poem.

The outlaw life, idealized. Symbolized,
Even kids who've never truly lived are 'killas';
It's in the rhymes, in the bass, in the rhythms
From inside bouncing cars or yawning windowpanes.
Tattoos on faces – they're saying, you can't change this;
You can't change me.
Permanent pathology.
But that's only the body.
Inside, somewhere, there's a different song.
Who will listen to that song?
Who will know these cries because they've languished here, too.
The truth is we're all broken.

We drive across LA River and, my oh my, what a sad waterway, now nothing more than a concrete viaduct familiar from too many movie car chases, slick with graffiti and a tiny watery trickle hinting at this city's desert thirst. I think of doomed LA titan Lowell George singing 'Find Me A River' and wonder whether that tune wasn't inspired by the dirty, depleted banks of the LA River. We drive past junkyards and industrial lots and then Luis announces we're entering East LA. There are bungalows, small, compact homes with tidy front lawns and palm trees. Compared to the black neighbourhood where I stayed in Vegas everything looks quite, well, cosy.

'East LA has the highest population density in LA with a forty-six per cent poverty rate, twice that of the LA average,' Luis says. 'We live in the media capital of the world but if you live in East LA you're going to find it difficult to buy a book or see a movie.'

We drive under El Arco, a huge steel gateway symbolising East LA's official border. 'Whittier Boulevard,' says Luis, 'this used to be the heart of East LA. Growing up here Whittier was the main drag of the barrio. Today, to me, it's lost most of its flavour, but Whittier used to be the "cruise" capital of the country for low-riders [customised cars popular in Mexican-American communities]. In 1976, during a low-rider cruise, police arrested close to six hundred people and beat the participants. Since then large numbers of police have been deployed here to contain any real culture and expression.'

Indeed, these streets of East LA bear all the wounds of strip-mall culture: beauty salons, junk-food vendors, car and electrical repair stores, launderettes, groceries, chain and liquor stores. We pull up outside a boarded-up building. 'The Silver Dollar Café,' says Luis, recalling how, on 29 August 1970, the Chicano Moratorium against the Vietnam War had been under way in nearby Laguna Park. Proceedings were peaceful until the police dispersed the crowd with tear gas, forcing many on to Whittier Boulevard where a riot broke out. Covering events was Ruben Salazar, an award winning *LA Times* journalist who had recently become news director of KMEX-TV (a Mexican-American station). Salazar's coverage of LAPD violence against the Chicano community had led to him being warned three times to 'tone down his coverage'. At 7.40 that evening Salazar went into the Silver Dollar and ordered a beer. While he was looking at his notes a sheriff's deputy aimed a tear gas rifle through the door and fired, blowing half of Salazar's head off. The subsequent inquest found the deputy innocent of any criminal intent. Salazar became a martyr to the Chicano concept of Aztlan (a radical Mexican-American identity rooted in La Reconquista). This inspired Hunter S. Thompson to write a paranoid, perceptive feature, 'Strange Rumblings in Aztlan', for *Rolling Stone*. Luis, meanwhile, got slung in jail.

'People were angry because twenty-two per cent of the US casualties in Vietnam were Chicanos yet back then we only made up five per cent of the population. There were lots of slogans being shouted, bottles being thrown, and then the police waded in with tear gas and batons. I was arrested, beaten and placed on Murderers' Row in the Hall of Justice Prison in downtown next to

Charles Manson's cell. Every morning the deputies would make us stand with our faces to the wall while they marched Manson past to go to court. He'd be screaming racial abuse and going on about the coming apocalypse and we couldn't respond 'cos he was looked after, the celebrity prisoner. We were released after about ten days and by then my life had changed 'cos I met activists in jail and I, a little cholo ["low life"] gang leader, became politicised.

'Two years later, aged eighteen, I was arrested for fighting police and looking at a six-year sentence. Community leaders wrote letters on my behalf so I got a shorter sentence. I felt in debt to those people when I came out. And I wanted to own my life. In prison someone tells you when to get up, when to take a shit, and if you're with a gang inside you can never leave when you're out. Back then Cesar Chavez was organising the farm workers and there was a lot of Black Panther-inspired grassroots activism in our 'hood. I went to night school, worked in steel mills, found my way through. I wasn't the smartest or toughest but I survived while many didn't so I feel a commitment to do something.'

Luis pulls over outside a Korean grocery store. I buy candy and while service is fine I notice a different kind of tension. Nothing unpleasant, just the sense that running a grocery is not a relaxed thing to do and any strangers who enter, especially white strangers, are observed with a certain caution. 'Probably figured you were undercover,' says Luis. 'Koreans are the new minority here. They come to East LA to run stores just as they do in South Central. I don't know how they get on with the Chicanos. I hope it's OK. LA's the most volatile city in the US. The most minor incident can set tempers flaring. Especially when race is involved.'

We start to walk the 'hood and Luis points out Boyle Plaza, one of LA's legendary music locations. Known locally as Mariachi Plaza, Boyle is where musicians gather to get work at weddings and fiestas, people literally driving up, negotiating a price and driving off with a mariachi band. On the corner of the square is the Boyle Hotel where mariachis from Mexico have headed for decades knowing they will find other musicians there. But today the hotel appears closed. Work on the metro-rail has put the Plaza off limits to all but construction crew. I'd expected to see mariachis hanging out, dressed in all their finery, maybe singing to kill the time, waiting for work, but there's no one in sight. I love Mexican music, both traditional and contemporary, and start listing every East LA artist: punks Los Illegals, R & B monsters Cannibal & The Headhunters, funkateers Eastside Connection, teenage rocker Ritchie Valens—

'Ritchie Valens was from Pacoima,' interrupts Luis, 'that's out by San Fernando Valley, where I now live. Couldn't fit all of us in East LA.'

Doh! Luis adds, 'You know a lot about LA music. I'm just fixing your geography.' We discuss the failure of sixties idealism

Sharp-dressed men: Mariachi Real de San Diego, LA, 2009

and how the FBI's COINTELPRO programme infiltrated, disrupted and helped destroy the Black Panthers, the American Indian Movement, Students for a Democratic Society and East LA's the Brown Berets. Not that the likes of Panthers founder Huey Newton and co.' were innocents. 'Many of the radicals, they self-destructed,' admits Luis. Drug abuse, criminality hyped as 'revolutionary activity', violent machismo and paranoia, all were rife. 'Things are fucked up right now,' says Luis, 'but a lot of Chicanos are making connections with Native groups, doing sun dances, peyote ceremonies, and sweat lodges, realising that they too are natives, not this "immigrant" tag that gets slapped on us.'

Luis pauses then adds, 'You know what I'm most proud of right now? It's how the Latino students here have been shaking up California's education with Inner City Struggle. They've forced the Los Angeles School Board to agree to build a new high school in East LA – the first in eighty years. Two of the local high schools, Roosevelt and Garfield, were built in the 1920s for one thousand students. Today each school has more than five thousand students enrolled. ICS has also looked at why most East LA students fail to graduate and go to college. It's devised a campaign demanding every student be placed on a college prep track. That's the kind of militancy needed today. This state was once the nation's leader in education spending. It now ranks forty-fifth in the US. What does that tell you about the people who run California?'

'More than enough, sure, but let's talk on a smaller scale: your son's serving life for attempted murder – as his father are you willing to accept blame for his sins?'

'Having grown up in East LA then living with me in a poor, gang-infested part of Chicago... well, the odds were on that he might fall in with the gangs. I tried, man, I really tried. But you know how hard-headed young males are. What's done is done. I'm proud of how he's serving his time. Avoiding joining prison gangs. Working as a teacher's assistant. Hoping he'll get his sentence halved so he can get out and be a good father to his children.'

'What is the appeal of *la vida loca* – the crazy life?'

'It's hard to explain once you've left it behind but when you're living it you don't consider there's any alternative. *La vida loca*'s a killer but look at how it's shaped by American culture: this very materialistic, very fast-paced society that emphasises solving problems with guns and money. What goes on here with the gangs is the same as what happened in Colombine: they were kids from a gated community and they saw murder and violent death as the only answer.'

Luis broods – *lost homeboys, son locked down, weary conscience* – time for me to hush a little. I apologise for asking so many questions but Luis says the questions are fine, keep them coming. In the late afternoon sun all feels peaceful, almost suburban, not a gangbanger shouting 'lick a shot' in sight. 'Mexicans in LA pretty much invented gangbanging,' says Luis. 'The tattoos, hand signals, baggy trousers, shaven heads... all that shit is straight from the cholos. The black gangs copied it and now you even have Armenian and Cambodian gangs doing it too.' Passing Homeboy Industries Luis says, 'It's run by Father Greg Boyle. I don't always trust priests but he's a good guy. He's gone where the Church doesn't go. He helps with education, tattoo removal, job training, graffiti removal.' Luis pauses then adds, 'Actually, two workers were recently murdered doing graffiti removal so they've stopped that.'

We enter El Mercado, a three-storey market selling all things Mexican. Racks of snakeskin boots and broad-brimmed hats, the fashion choice of the Mexican campesino, hang alongside B & W photos of Pedro Infante, Mexico's most iconic movie star, and posters of Santo, the legendary masked wrestler. A mariachi duo serenade shoppers. Nothing here suggests the LA of Hollywood or Bunker Hill. We pass a store selling nothing but huge *piñatas* in the shape of The Incredibles, Spider-Man, SpongeBob, Piglet, Batman. They're a metre high, gaudy and opulent, stuffed full of candy, the ultimate birthday gift for the Chicano child. I check a stall selling CDs, cassettes and DVDs. Luis asks what's hot. 'Reggaeton and Lupillo are big,' says the assistant. Reggaeton's a Puerto Rican hybrid of Jamaican dance hall, US rap and salsa flavours. And Lupillo is Lupillo Rivera, the King of Mexican LA music.

Lupillo's rise to fame is the stuff of immigrant dreams; hard work and good luck leading to a musical dynasty reaping fame and wealth. This Mexican-American dream begins with Lupillo's father, Pedro, arriving in LA from Sinaloa, a rugged, north-western Mexico state infamous for producing large quantities of opium and marijuana and the brutal mafias that deal them. In 1960s LA Pedro worked as a jobbing nightclub musician, eventually setting up the Cintas Acuario label to handle Californian-based Sinaloan singers unable to find outlets for their music in the USA: the Latin branches of the major record companies and the big Mexican labels sneering at these hicks performing *norteño* (the Mexican equivalent of country music). Pedro established his label by selling cassettes in bars and markets, scoring a local hit with a *corrido* – a traditional Mexican narrative ballad format (during the vast social upheaval of the Mexican Revolution they acted as musical news reports) – about the capture of Panama's General Noriega. In the late 1980s a young Sinaloan *corrido* singer-songwriter approached Pedro looking for a deal. The singer's nasal voice and fierce presence suggested little commercial potential yet Pedro recognised a fresh talent – the youth's *corridos* about Sinaloan drug soldiers (thus '*narcocorridos*') contained intense, detailed narratives – and agreed to handle distribution. The singer was Rosalino 'Chalino' Sanchez and rapidly, very rapidly, his raw songs and short, violent life established him as *narcocorrido*'s ruling icon.

The legend of Chalino goes like this: raised in Sinaloa, at age fifteen he shot dead a man who had raped his sister. Fleeing to LA, he worked harvests, dealt drugs and assisted his older brother Armando in smuggling people. In 1984 Armando was murdered in a Tijuana motel: Chalino wrote his first *corrido* to commemorate Armando. He then spent time in a Tijuana prison where his talent for writing *corridos* proved profitable; in a land where literacy is never a given, *corridos* still retain an important social function. Chalino soon began recording *corridos* that celebrated local drug

Pure Mexican fury: Chalino, Los Angeles, 1992

lords and the trade's fallen soldiers. His nasal voice, campesino clothes and brutal *corridos* were the antithesis of Mexican entertainment-industry standards yet migrants across LA and the South-west recognised a man who shared their experiences. Returning to LA, he worked in a car wash, singing as he scrubbed, selling his tapes at swap meets and car washes. Photos show him dressed in slacks, cotton shirt, cowboy boots, Stetson, large belt buckle, pistol tucked in trousers, whippet thin, gunsight eyes, pure Mexican fury.

Cintas Acuario promoted Chalino and he rapidly became a street phenomenon, from unknown to commanding $20,000 a performance – a street legend. Chalino's songs were dense, descriptive affairs, appearing as direct communiqués from the recently dead or imprisoned. Such subject matter meant he attracted intense reactions: in January 1992, a man leapt onstage and shot Chalino in the thigh. The singer pulled his pistol, returning fire, while gangsters in the audience joined in, blasting at one another, staff and patrons flinging themselves through windows to escape. Somehow Chalino survived the carnage. Yet only five months later, following a concert in Sinaloa, he was abducted by a group of men bearing police ID. The following day Chalino was found dead in a ditch. The who and why of the thirty-one-year-old's execution remain matters of conjecture; as with Tupac Shakur, whose career followed a similar trajectory four years later, Chalino lived the songs he sang. Murdered, he kicked off the *narcocorrido* boom.

'Luis, did you know Chalino?'

'No. I was living in Chicago when he came through LA. Even if I had been here our paths probably wouldn't have crossed. I'm Chicano, grew up listening to R & B – War, Charles Wright, The Dells – while he played for the Mexican immigrants who wanted *norteño*.'

Chalino's fearless manner helped make Mexican folk music hip to Mexican-American youths and the Riveras' saw Chalino's sales rocket as *narcocorrido* became part of LA's soundtrack. Realising the market was hungry, Pedro promoted his son Lupillo, then in his late teens, as the heir to Chalino. Lupillo mixed an urban LA element into his sound. His sister Jenni did a similar thing, documenting life as a female hustler. The Riveras sang about dealing kilos and getting shot and living fast and dying young and their releases sold and sold and sold. I pick up a Lupillo cassette called *Despreciado* ('scorned/despised'). Here Lupillo stands smug and shaven-headed, thin moustache and *Scarface* suit, in front of a Lexus.

'Let's hear it,' says Luis, and the sound of a wonky Mexican brass band blares out of the speakers.

'Banda,' I say, and Luis nods, adding, 'Party music for the campesinos.' Lupillo makes his entry burping and hollering and the horns fart and honk and lock down the groove and the atmosphere is wild Mexican machismo, real cinematic spectacle, a raucous march towards the cemetery. Luis smiles, surely recognising his former bad-boy self in the tune. The orchestra, some sixteen horns, blow a weird Mexican funk descended from Austrian military marching bands and village brass bands, music reinvented by the poor as party music. Lupillo bites a vowel and curses and the horns go crazy and the whole thing reeks of good-times-for-bad-boys music. No wonder LA's Latino youth love this cat.

'You checked out any banda-rap?' asks Luis.

'Only in your car. Who should I listen to?'

Luis barks in Spanish and the assistant starts pulling CDs out: Akwid, Azteka, Jae-P, Mexician. All sport hip-hop's uniform of shaved heads and baggy trousers. The assistant slips Jae-P's CD on and a gorgeous accordion melody builds and swells before a voice enters rapping in Spanish. 'It's the kids who grew up on Chalino and Cypress Hill making their own records,' says Luis. The tune rises to a chant of *'Latinos unidos'*, the music bursting across the market, a Spanglish hip-hop melange. The next track employs banda horns, sampling and looping them beneath strident rappers. Purchase *Despreciado*, Chalino, Jae-P, *El Movimento de Hip Hop Vol. 2* and a CD of Pedro Infante. Back in the car Luis points out Hollenbeck Division Police Station. 'They have an infamous basement where they'd beat people. Not me but a friend of mine lost his hearing down there.'

'How are relations with the LAPD today?'

'On one hand it's not changed; on the other it has. After LA burned in the '92 riots some have been trying to reform but others refuse to. It used to be all whites, now lots of black and browns are cops but some are terrible people. When I was coming up we'd shoot at cop cars. Shot the police helicopter down once. I figured I didn't have to go to Vietnam as I already was in a war zone. Today the police presence is more effective when dealing with gangs so the gangs are less obvious, more underground. The eighties and nineties were when it peaked but if things get worse economically then the gangs will rise again.'

We drive under the 4th Street Bridge and Luis starts to talk about the White Fence, the oldest established gang in the USA. This remains their turf.

'Mexicans bought land here in the 1920s when it was considered worthless by the Anglos who owned most of LA. They sold land for a dollar a plot so a lot of Mexicans headed up from Arizona and Texas. When I was a kid this area was still dirt poor but people have done it up. The Pachucho gangs of the 1930s and '40s originated around here, initially as protection against racist gangs inflamed by the Hearst newspapers. Remember the Zoot Suit Riots? That was US soldiers who were encouraged to attack Pachuchos. Those gangs became the cholos, speaking their own street language, Kalo.'

'In Spain Kalo is the name given to the Romany dialect some *gitanos* still speak. Is there a connection?'

'I'm not sure but I guess that when the Spanish were colonising Mexico they sent lots of Gypsies down as slaves and others followed later to escape war and persecution so their language became a kind of underground dialect. I think it's appropriate we speak Kalo as, for most Anglos, Mexicans are the Gypsies of LA. We're treated like dirt, yet our music, food, exuberance, it gives the city soul.'

Luis points out apartments he once rented, a church he got married in, explains how to read the neighbourhood through its urban codes (tags, graffiti, colours, hand gestures, headbands, cap angles). Hoyo Mara Vin, East LA's second biggest gang, are based in this region, says Luis, but today the streets remain quiet and only tiny pockets of graffiti are visible. We head up Juarez Hill, the car snaking around narrow streets, Luis still the East LA homeboy who knows exactly where he's rolling. 'This is a real barrio,' he says as he parks, 'hardcore gang area. The roads are narrow so it's difficult for the cops to come up here and also for other gangs doing drive-bys 'cos it's hard to get out of quickly.'

'Well, Luis,' I say, looking over my shoulder, 'I certainly hope you don't have any old vendettas floating round this barrio.'

Luis laughs. A good deep laugh, that of a man who's come through slaughter and now smokes the peace pipe. We exit the car and stand in the sunshine, looking across LA. Banda-rap blares from a nearby bungalow, the rapper's slurring Spanglish over a tangle of beats and horns. In the distance downtown's skyscrapers shimmer, ringed by smog, offering up an iconic Anglo LA of wealth and opportunity, close yet so far away to those who dwell here. Luis looks across his kingdom.

'I love LA,' he says, 'but I'm continually expecting explosions, big and small.'

Dreamscape: Watts Towers, South Central Los Angeles

chapter 7

Watts: Not in Raceriotland…

South Central LA bleeds warehouses, strip clubs (*'To our customers: lock your cars and take your keys'*), wreckers' yards (*'We Buy Junk Cars'*), fast-food joints, gas stations, tyre merchants, railway lines, omnipresent striped taco stands, shabby factories, faceless office blocks. Flat, dusty, tense, inimical – the LA of *Point Blank* and *Reservoir Dogs* – hermetic environs, designed to isolate, keep paranoia levels high, conduct near-invisible business. Grid roads, telephone cables, traffic lights, city gristle. Those resident here are constantly reminded just how fugacious their existence can be.

Out of East LA we'd cruised down Alameda, Luis noting where working-class white, black and brown communities once existed, divided by race and railway tracks. Back in the day South Central's workforce filled local mills and factories. 'LA had the second largest industrial base in the US after Chicago,' says Luis, 'huge steel mills like you wouldn't believe! I worked in them in the seventies, doing pipe fitting, carpentry, lots of stuff. The racial tension from the streets carried into the factories but, for the most part, people got on. Now, well, almost all of the heavy industry has gone. The owners shifted the work to Mexico or China.' The 1965 Watts Uprising encouraged white flight – 'cops told the whites blacks were coming for them so people were standing on their front lawns with shotguns and rifles' – followed by an exodus of black residents who could afford to shift: South Central's now becoming a barrio for new arrivals from Mexico and Central America. This being evident at our intersection: moving among traffic a girl (maybe twelve) begs, one man sells oranges, another soft toys. We drive on and at the next intersection there're coconuts and flowers for sale. 'Imagine leaving your home town,' I say, 'crossing the desert, going through all those extremes to enter the US and finding that the better life you dreamed of involves standing at these lights all day.' Luis mentions how the US–Mexico free trade agreement as brokered by Clinton screwed Mexican farmers, dumping cheap maize on Mexico, forcing a wave of landless farmers north. He adds, 'LA's a tough place to survive in and getting tougher. The way the system is now it's much more difficult than when my family arrived. That's one of the reasons gangs thrive, they offer security, a sense of belonging, to a lot of displaced people.'

Luis turns into Slauson Avenue and recalls the Slausons, a black gang of the 1950s and '60s. We pass a McDonald's with Spanish signs, past bungalows with barbed-wire fences and pit bulls behind them, past concrete walls with broken glass embedded, past droopy palm trees and youths with shaven heads and baseball shirts. A police helicopter floats overhead. We turn left and Luis says, 'Central Avenue.' Well, I say, all right. Yet 'all right' isn't the correct expression. For Central Avenue, which connects downtown with Watts, looks anything but all right: a Jack-in-the-Box trash-food emporium, Nails outlets, 99c shops, empty lots, Louisiana Fried Chicken, a caged Chinese food vendor, Central Liquor Bank, Kick-Boxing, Missionary Baptist Church. Central Avenue resembles East LA in its strip-mall shoddiness, if poorer, more threadbare; yet Central Avenue once provided LA's musical heartbeat, comparable to Harlem, packed with clubs and juke joints pumping jazz and blues. Jelly Roll Morton, self-styled 'inventor of jazz', played and recorded here in 1918 while Jack Johnson ran Club Alabam here in 1932. Kerouac turned up in 1947, breathlessly enthusing about 'the wild, humming night... chickenshacks barely big enough to house a jukebox, and the jukebox blowing nothing but blues, bop, and jump.'

The presence of famous white LA citizens mixing with the locals at clubs on Central Avenue infuriated Chief Parker, then the LAPD's ruling bully. Through citing 'interracial vice', Parker viciously succeeded in snuffing out much of LA's jazz/blues scene by the mid-1950s. Parker's LAPD viewed blacks and Chicanos as a criminal class so policed South Central with a brutality that, when twinned with the discriminatory hiring policies employed by LA's construction, aerospace and entertainment industries, lit a racial powder keg: on 11 August 1965, Watts exploded into a week of violence and arson leaving 34 dead, 1,100 injured, 4,000 arrested, 600 buildings damaged or destroyed. Several miles north, LA's psychedelic era took shape around Hollywood, yet beyond Frank Zappa's riot-referencing 'Trouble Every Day' on *Freak Out* little attention was paid; to pop's pampered elite Watts was as distant as Morocco, if not quite so romantic.

The riots led Thomas Pynchon to travel, almost a year later, into South Central and write the rambling, if illuminating, 'A Journey into the Mind of Watts' for the *New York Times* magazine (12 June 1966). Pynchon's fiction is unfathomably dense and hubristic yet his essay's unfussy, stumbling only when he romanticises ghetto dwellers à la so much rock/rap journalism: '*Everything seems so out in the open, all of it is real, no plastic faces, not transistors, no hidden Muzak, or Disneyfied landscaping, or smiling little chicks to show you around. Not in Raceriotland... These kids are so tough you can pull slivers of it [glass] out of them and never get a whimper.*' Perhaps Pynchon's legendary social reticence is due to him being fearful someone will ask him how the tough kids in Raceriotland are. But when he steps back and reflects on how Watts is both connected and removed from mainstream America he's eloquent, perceptive: '*Though the panoramic sense of black impoverishment is hard to miss from atop the Harbor Freeway, which so many whites must drive at least twice every working day. Somehow it occurs to very few of them to leave at the Imperial Highway exit for a change, go east instead of west only a few blocks, and take a look at Watts. A quick look. The simplest kind of beginning. But Watts is country which lies, psychologically, uncounted miles further than most whites seem at present willing to travel.*'

Well, I'm off the highway and travelling into the heart of Watts – admittedly with ex-resident Luis Rodriguez as guide – and the surrounding urban landscape mixes those LA totems of scruffy palm trees with off-kilter suburban ruination: Chief Parker, his successor Daryl Gates and the '92 riots have all left a lasting imprint. In the late afternoon heat a sense of subjection hangs across the 'hood. Little of LA's fabulous wealth and fantasy trickle down to Watts: the community has the lowest household income in all of Los Angeles County at $17,987, with 49.7 per cent of families and 49.1 per cent of individuals below the federal poverty line. Sociologist Carl Taylor has coined the phrase 'Third City' to describe places like Watts, places abandoned by mainstream America, places heavy industry has left so bequeathing high unemployment and low expectation, declining public services and spiralling crime rates, the drug trade now an economic mainstay, crack cocaine and automatic weapons terrorising the community. 'A lot of this area burned during the '92 riots,' says Luis, 'and there's been little reinvestment.' 'Were you here,' I ask, 'during the riots?' 'No, I was living in Chicago. My brother worked for a phone company and was down here when the city went off. He had to hide in his work for three or four days. Couldn't go home. Fires everywhere. Gangs rampaging.'

Turn off Central Avenue and roll along 109th Street, passing Luis's former residence, bungalows with neat gardens looking homely, past public housing (something scarce in LA; investment in it was destroyed along with the city's trolley buses as 'socialistic' during the 1950s anti-communist crusades), past kids playing and dogs barking and cops cruising, past a vacant lot – 'burnt out in '65 and still empty' – until we pull up in front of Watts Towers. The Watts Towers are an odd construction, folk art of sorts, built by Simon Rodia between 1921 and 1954, he labouring alone, paying to build this baby Gaudi edifice from his wages as a window cleaner, using scrap pottery, glass, rocks, seashells, all kinds of colourful refuse, alongside cement and iron, to create a taste of urban magic. The Watts Towers are enclosed behind a fence now, recognised as a genuine LA artefact, but Luis recalls a childhood where the Towers were a playground.

'We used to climb this thing. It's amazing it hasn't fallen apart. Rodia was a little guy, only five foot tall, but a real visionary. I always found it inspiring that he built the Towers for no practical purpose, just out of creative spirit.'

In front of the Towers black marble plaques honour Watts's finest. I recognise critic Stanley Crouch, athlete Florence Griffith Joyner and a whole host of musicians: Aaron 'T-Bone' Walker, Charlie Mingus, Johnny Otis, Eric Dolphy, Esther Phillips, Etta James and the man who truly put his 'hood on the musical map: Charles Wright, leader of The Watts 103rd Street Rhythm Band. I mention my love for Charles Wright's music and Luis nods assent.

'Back in the day any low-rider with style would blast Charles Wright. That was hardcore LA street music.'

Charles Wright is more than just a local hero; his musical legacy links delta blues with soul, doo-wop to hip-hop. Underlying Wright's finest music is the essence of *funk*: African-American groove, pride, sensuality, earthiness, an aesthetic seemingly derived from the Ki-Kongo word 'lu-fuki', suggesting both bad body odour and artistic achievement, an expression employed by black musicians in New Orleans since the nineteenth century.

Some songs never die: Charles Wright, Orange County, CA, 2006

Funk, in the music of Wright and James Brown, establishes a raw sonic beauty. Seeing Wright's name in Watts stone made me want to meet him and Luis, of course, knew where to find Charles.

Aged sixty-five, Wright now lives in a spacious house in Orange County. Upon arrival I find him leading a band rehearsal. Initially, things are a little uneasy, the bear-like keyboardist – huge grey afro, ham-hock arms and sour eyes – less than enthusiastic about my presence, suggesting 'maybe he a Bush supporter', which makes me laugh: I've been called many names but no one's ever before said I bent over for Republicans! On bass is Melvin Dunlap, original Watts 103rd Street member and the guy Bill Withers champions on his awesome *Live at Carnegie Hall*'s penultimate track as 'Melvin's quiet but he likes to shake 'em on down'. Dunlap's a slim, friendly man who, when I enquire whether he's a native Angeleno, admits he was born on the East Coast, arriving in LA with the O'Jays, whose early recordings he played on. 'Lipstick Traces?' I venture and Melvin's mouth falls open – *little white boy knows his shit!* – and Charles chuckles. Why, even the bear on keys stops growling at me. Across the afternoon Wright directs the band and, during breaks, answers my questions. He speaks with unshakeable conviction, his rasping voice and granite features speaking of hardscrabble, determination, a refusal to flinch. 'Most of the neighbours are Korean,' he says when I ask about this 'burb, 'they ain't too friendly but they don't cause no problems either.' His house is a long way from the sharecropper's shack he was born into or the small Watts bungalow he and his fifteen-member family shifted into in 1950, Wright's hard-won musical success having ensured him a degree of comfort.

'I was born nine miles outside of Clarksdale, Mississippi, on a cotton patch. My father was a sharecropper. I spent my first ten years in that shack. They call it sharecropping, I call it slavery. The way we were living down there at that time... My dad insisted I pick one hundred pounds of cotton a day. I couldn't do it. I'd get ninety-two, ninety-four, ninety-eight pounds. But I couldn't get one hundred. Each time I didn't get to one hundred he whupped me. Reason I say it was slavery is each time at the end of the year a sharecropper would have to settle with the guy who owned the land and my father always ended up in the hole. No matter how hard he pushed us, how hard we worked, how hard he tried not to buy materials from the man, he always ended up owing the man money. Each year at a certain time of year he'd come in the house with a look on his face and my mother would say, 'He gotcha again, didn't he?'

'When I was ten we moved into Clarksdale but the guy we used to do the sharecropping for was trying to force us back, he had connections with the police, so we shipped out. LA was like day and night. I'd been in Clarksdale but I'd never really been in a city. Los Angeles was huge. I had to catch on quick but you can't believe what a change LA was to Mississippi. My family settled in South Central Los Angeles. It was all kinds of ethnic groups living together. Whites, Japanese, Mexicans and blacks, we all got on. Integrated schools. And my parents could buy a lot of food for their money. Today it's not a good city to live in and your money buys nothing. Ronald Reagan got elected governor in 1966 and he ruined the state. Then he got elected president and he ruined the country.'

Wright's importance to LA's black music scene is undeniable: his slangy, drawling sing-rap delivery, loose, spiralling guitar playing, hip street philosophy and raw, under-rehearsed sound gave black LA its groove back after Central Avenue's cessation. He opened doors for the likes of Barry White (his drummer in the sixties) and War, the superb South Central funk-Latin-blues ensemble.

'The first day I went to high school I heard singing. It was raw, four guys singing and looking into one another's eyes, and I thought, 'Man, I gotta be a part of that!' And then this neighbourhood guy Jesse Belvin started having hits and I loved his records so I found his number in the phone book and rang him, told him 'I sing just like you' and he cussed me out, said, 'You gotta find your own style,' but he introduced me to his record label and that's how things got rolling. Everyone would come around Jesse's house – Ray Charles, Johnny "Guitar" Watson, all the vocal groups in LA, The Jacks, The Turks... his house was open. And we always made music. He would sit at the piano and we would all harmonise. It was a great way to enter the music business.

'I was in a doo-wop group [The Shields] that had a massive hit called "You Cheated" in 1958. I decided to learn guitar as the people that backed us never sounded right. And I'm left-handed so I had a real problem learning guitar. But I kept at it. Once we had the hit all the girls came around and the guys lost focus and that was that. Then I got involved with The Galahads and we had a regional hit ["Lonely Guy"]. We tried to stick it out and practised all the time and looked forward to making better records but we got in trouble with Alan Freed. We got caught up in his payola thing – appeared on his show and he expected a kickback. Dick Clark started playing our record on his TV show and the kids loved it but Freed hadn't paid us so we filed against him at the union. He had Dick Clark drop our record and that was it.

'I got involved [as producer] with a group called Cardinal Caesar and The Romans and had a huge hit, "Oldies But Goodies Remind Me of You". We got screwed out of our royalties by Del-Fi [the label], so I quit that job and tried to set myself up as an independent producer. I went to this recording studio next to the Hollywood Palladium where guys would hang around, producers looking for work, and the lady who owned it, she would always tell me, "Never give your publishing away. It belongs to you, not the record company," and that stuck with me. I own seventy-five per cent of my publishing. That's why I live like this. "Express Yourself" has been licensed for movies or TV seventeen times.'

Comedian Bill Cosby, then trying to carve out a career as a singer, hired Wright to lead his band. Cosby's singing career never took off but he got the Wright Sound a deal with Warner Brothers and renamed them The Watts 103rd Street Rhythm Band.

'Everybody wanted me to play on their records and so I did that from '65 through about '67. Played on a lot of hit records – Bettye Swann, Leon Hayward, Dyke & The Blazers. I was in the studio all day and with the band all night. It was a great trip.

Watts 103rd Street Rhythm Band: Charles Wright seated centre, 1970

Warner's signed us on Cosby's advice. They were looking to get into the R & B scene and they began to see us as the way to that market.'

Whether preaching soulfully on 'Comment (If All Men Are Truly Brothers)' or drawling 'bout 'Good Things' over a spacey, minimalist groove, Wright's music is constantly full of surprises: rhythms tug, guitars go to interesting places, talking-drum music, African music made in America.

'I created my own rhythms and stuff. I tried to be different but effective. I admired James Brown and Otis Redding, would do a lot of their stuff in the clubs. James Brown usually played only two or three changes in a song. I brought in more chords, more arrangement. Sometimes we would find a rhythm and work up a song from that. "Express Yourself" came out of me improvising over the end of "Do Your Thing" in Texas and the kids goin' crazy for it.'

The Watts 103rd Street Rhythm Band left Wright in 1972 to back Bill Withers (then scoring with 'Ain't No Sunshine' and

'Grandma's Hands'). Withers' early seventies recordings are extremely eloquent, his songs matching the earthiness of blues with a craft equivalent to any in the American canon, but Wright resents losing the Watts Band. 'Withers was a guy hanging round us who wanted me to produce him but as he was pretty annoying I was taking my time to do it. So he took my band.' Wright continued, making the most radical music of his career on 1973's superb double album *Doing What Comes Naturally*. From the title and sun-bleached panoramic cover through four sides of vinyl (as yet unavailable on CD or download), Wright and band deliver one of the great LA albums. Sexy yet weary, reflective but full of wild party spirit, *Doing What Comes Naturally* is matched arguably only by War's *All Day Music* as an early seventies West Coast soul-funk masterpiece. Here Wright moves from doo-wop to organ-drenched blues groove to soul ballads to 'Nonsense', a seventeen-minute slice of rip-it-up raw funk 'n' jazz that surely influenced Fela Kuti and slays Miles Davis's seventies fusion efforts.

'You heard that album?' says Wright with genuine surprise. 'Man, I cut that for ABC-Dunhill and they did nothing with it, no promotion, no push. Guy in charge was a black man but he was so insincere, treated me with contempt. I've pretty much forgotten that stuff. But I hear what you sayin' 'bout Miles – he used to come to my gigs and say, "How you do that?" 'cos he couldn't figure how I put my chords together.' Wright pauses, adds, 'I felt like a baby when I went to see Miles play 'cos he could be so good.'

Wright smiles. A rare smile. He's aggrieved about many things, not least the way his music gets ignored.

'They rarely play us on LA radio. Black radio don't play us now and oldies stations don't play us like they do the other groups. See, Watts is still getting blamed for the '65 riots and so we take that blame by not getting played.'

What are Wright's recollections of the riots?

'I don't know, being the first people on the block to start a riot, people don't like that. At that time I was studying at Malibu College so was living over that way. Could see the smoke coming up. I had lived in that situation and I had got out 'cos I couldn't take no more. If another policeman had stopped me and felt my balls I would have really lost it. So I got out. I could have participated but I didn't. I don't think people really wanted to riot but enough is enough – it was an emotional outburst. We'd been backed up as far as we could go. Our humanity had had enough. 'Cos the LA police and sheriff's department, their job was to keep us in our place and they loved to do that. I always heard they recruited from Southern whites and those people had a mean attitude. So it was a hot night and it happened. And what happened in LA and what happened in Detroit, they were gonna happen. Ninety-two? That was what I call a fair riot. 'Cos we knew those guys beat Rodney King to a pulp. That was a non-racial riot, lots of Latinos and blacks involved.' Wright pauses, thinks about what he's said, adds, 'Personally, I would love to see people sit down and talk rather than go to war with one another.'

Throughout the late 1960s/early '70s there were attempts to revitalise South Central: the success of Wright and War uplifted the community, giving Watts such focus Memphis's Stax Records organised 1972's WattStax, a black Woodstock of sorts, which myopically failed to book any local talent (Wright remains aggrieved at this), proto-rappers The Watts Prophets laid down militant verse, the Black Panthers set up an LA base here and, most recently, the urban dance form of krumping has attracted much media coverage. Yet South Central's legacy is, finally, more poisonous than artistic: the Black Panthers' early-seventies implosion splintered youths towards aspiring South Central street gangs, the Crips and the Bloods. Both gangs eschewed Panther politics while retaining Panther hostility, paranoia and organisation structures; the gang culture they created unleashed a virulent cultural virus that has swept the USA, infected Mexico, Central America and beyond: gang drones being evident on the streets of both London and Auckland.

Rappers NWA's 1989 album *Straight Outta Compton* (Compton borders Watts) harnessed Watts Prophets-style militant rhymes via a gangsta rap vision: on 'Fuck tha Police' decades of harassment and humiliation crystallised. Hear it and understand why LA exploded in '65/'92. NWA's protagonists were a tiny crack dealer, a chubby architecture student and a lisping roller-disco DJ: this misfit trio gave their community a voice and reinvented both how urban music sounded and what it could say. NWA heavily sampled The Watts 103rd Street Rhythm Band. One track on *Straight Outta Compton* is called 'Express Yourself' and features Ice Cube busting rhymes over Wright's groove.

'Ice Cube? Yeah, he's still afraid of me. I didn't threaten him. I just called him up and said, 'That's my song' and he gave it up graciously. He never should've stolen it. People always perpetuatin' fraud. That made me some money so I'm not complainin'.'

NWA's late leader Eazy-E was Eric Wright: is it true you're his uncle?

'Nah. I been asked by enough people that it ain't even botherin' me no more. O. V. Wright, the soul singer, he was related to my father.'

I love O. V. Wright's music!

'Man, you must be kiddin'. O. V. passed while you were in short pants.'

Rap producers sample Wright regularly: what's his take on how his music empowered hip-hop?

'Y'know, some songs never die and will always live because nobody's come along to do any better. The kids today say they're doing something new but they're just building on what we've already done. Hip-hop is funk recycled. See, funk was such a beautiful thing but the business couldn't control it so they invented disco. Scott Hamilton, a very fine bassist, told me in '81 that from then on they wouldn't play any black music on the radio that didn't have keyboards and drum machines on it. I didn't believe him but he was telling the truth. The record industry is all about youth, people who are naive and can be exploited. I've been shut out of the music business. Like a lot of other people. With this music that we bought to this country, the treasure we contributed, we should have been able to build our own media empires. But that's been disallowed. I'm still a second-class citizen.'

You feel that?

'Damn straight I do! Thank God that I don't have to live in the ghetto but my people, as a body, a lot of us are in worse shape than when the original riots started. Go five blocks from Union Station, to Main Street, and you'll see how a lot of people live. Their homes are boxes. Look at the mess in New Orleans. See, they don't need black people to pick cotton no more so a lot of us ain't got no place in America. It don't have to be this way. Don't make sense to me that we can't open our hearts and even things out. World should be a better place but here we are, just like in the sixties, back in a war again and divided among ourselves again.'

Today little artistry can be said to speak for South Central. Instead, tales of the city are left to ultra-violent films (*Menace II Society*) and video games (*Grand Theft Auto*). And Walter Mosley's novels – here Watts is a historic backdrop for slight (if super-righteous) parables. Closer to Wright's vision is Charles Burnett's rarely seen seventies films (*Killer of Sheep*, *My Brother's Wedding*) which celebrate black working-class LA's everyday humanity. Maybe it's the banda-rappers' and narcocorridos' turn to tell city tales. Not that I'm surprised at the falling off of Dre, Cube and Snoop, fame tending to do bad things to talent; LA being the burial ground for many who once promised much. None more so than Sly Stone, who shifted from San Francisco to LA in 1969 as a rising funk-rock star of seemingly infinite possibilities. Sly's long LA sojourn found him more interested in ingesting industrial quantities of cocaine and PCP than making music, his talent burnt up a freebase pipe.

'Sly destroyed himself but not the funk,' says Wright defensively when I mention the musical Icarus. 'Sly is misguided because of drugs – he thought he was too smart – but he made some beautiful music. I know and admire Sly but this business is not something to play with.'

As the afternoon progresses the band work through many Wright classics and when they strike up a groove Charles relaxes, loses himself in music full of soul and warmth. At one point he leaves to answer the door and the band continue to sing 'if all men are truly brothers' in unison. Charles returns up the stairs singing with the band, voices hanging in perfect harmony. *Magic!* Alongside LA atmospherics there's lots of Mississippi in Wright's music, mud and grits and barefoot walks to school and a spine aching from picking cotton; I hear it in the way the music builds and shuffles, a slow jam in no hurry to move, in the way the band stretch out – *take their time, do it right* – and the music's sense of dignity and lived experience. On 'Express Yourself' instruments snap and pop, raw funk, Wright bending forward, starting to shake, stomping his foot, shouting 'in the jungle, babe!' over and over. I imagine a young Luis cruising East LA in his low-rider, listening to an eight-track of Charles and The Watts 103rd Street Rhythm Band and thinking of all the ideas he wanted to – *yes!* – express. Wright builds the opening of ''Til You Get Enough', pulling a flurry of blue steel notes from his guitar, and I shake my head in awe at the Mississippi–Watts master located in Orange County's suburbs. *Magic!* Charles stops the band, instructs that they're not locking with the piano. 'Leave it like Chuck Berry,' the bear suggests. 'Chuck Berry don't care no more,' says Wright. 'I do.'

Keep on truckin': Mexican woman and children in motion

chapter 8

Joshua Tree: Mojave Desert Shivers

At LAX I hire a Hyundai Accent: the cheapest vehicle going. Not that driving even the simplest rental to Texas is cheap – if the car isn't being returned to LA the price gets spiked. To handle this I'm sharing driving and costs; I'd studied Craig's List for anyone looking to head south and came across a traveller wanting to get to Austin for a music festival. Lee and I meet outside the arrivals portal at LAX; he's easy to recognise, a moustache-wearing, big-bellied, black-haired giant. He lacks bags and front teeth but has a welcoming smile and an Irish-American way with words ('*whadafock*'). Lee's a chain-smoking bartender from Philadelphia and this is his first time in the West. He possesses little idea of how to get to Austin. I spell out my desired route. 'Sounds OK, buddy. I got just over a week to do everything. Alrighty?'

The traffic's heavy as we head on to Highway 10, driving through a concrete wilderness where flyovers eat up the sky, crawling along for an hour, flipping dials trying to find a *narcocorrido* or soul station. Quit the station search and slip a Stones CD into the player, 'Gimme Shelter' echoes around the Hyundai as the traffic starts to move, Charlie Watts kicks things along, Keith scrapes out a descending guitar pattern and Jagger wails '*rape... murdah... it's just a kiss away*', a perfect LA anthem. The light softens and the foothills of LA turn cumin hues as we cruise past the Monolo Indian Casino and the exit for Palm Springs, turning on to Highway 62, now beyond LA city limits. Darkness falls and soon we're entering the Mojave Desert and Joshua Tree city limits (tattoo parlours, gas stations, burrito joints, bars and a Wal-Mart). Pull over for a drink but as we're still in California Lee's told he can't smoke inside. He swallows his beer whole and heads back outside while I take my time and elicit instructions on how to get to Pioneertown.

Pioneertown is several miles of winding side road outside Joshua Tree and, as the name hints, existed once as a set for TV westerns. Howe Gelb mentioned living here in the eighties and Brixton DJ Pete Z told me that when he visited some twenty years past various refugees from Charlie Manson's Family were still creepy-crawling around. Pioneertown's also home to a bar with a reputation for featuring live music. We park and search for accommodation but it quickly becomes apparent that Pioneertown has been given a gentrified gloss: only venture capitalists could afford to spend time here. We pay $10 each to enter Pappy & Harriet's Pioneertown Palace, a big bar area with lots of outside areas which suits Lee's craving for nicotine, and soak up a few more brews while local rock bands blast electricity into the desert night. The bar's beautiful, spacious and built out of assorted recovered timber – Howe mentioned helping Pappy build it and getting Pappy to sing for Giant Sand before the old cowboy took up residence in Boot Hill – I ask whether Harriet's around as Howe suggested I should pass on his regards but it

Endless sleep: Joshua Tree Inn, CA, 2006

appears she sold up some time back. Those populating the bar have the polished look of Californian drugstore cowboys, dressed western but with soft hands and smooth features. I ask whether Lee's got a girl back East and he quotes the Henry Fonda movie *My Darling Clementine* where Wyatt Earp says to the bartender, 'Mac, you ever been in love?' and Mac replies, 'No, I've been a bartender all my life.'

The band playing are loud and creaky – *rock music, how did it become so dull?* – the music's lethargy inflaming Lee's hunger. We slip curves back down to Joshua Tree, feasting at a late-night burrito shack, then take a room at a shoddy-looking motel run by an East Asian whose face we never see, he handing forms and keys through a small hatch, just the sing-song phrasing of his voice giving away ethnicity. There's no hot water and the air conditioning works fitfully but – '*whadafock*' – it's somewhere to sleep. Lee can't smoke while asleep so snores, a rattling gurgle of a snore, lungs surely making up for every minute they're not chugging tobacco. I flip through two books found in LA: Henry Miller's *The Air-conditioned Nightmare* and Mark Twain's *Life on the Mississippi*.

Rise at 8 a.m. to ferocious Mojave Desert temperatures and head back to the same joint as last night for breakfast. Sunday morning and the restaurant is filled with those on their way to church, all pressed jeans and starched shirts, a crowd very different from Pioneertown's. Five dollars 35 cents gets coffee, eggs, beans, peppers and rice. Lee then insists on visiting Wal-Mart – appears he went on a bender in LA and lost most everything but what he was wearing – I protest Wal-Mart's many crimes against the American worker. Lee shrugs, says, 'But ain't it *cheap!*' stubs out his cigarette and grabs a trolley. Stand outside in protest – '*We Sell For Less. Always!*' reads a giant sign – but the heat drives me indoors. Looking at the cheap merchandise, I recall George W. Bush calling for 'another American century' – the writing's on the Wal-Mart wall (well, shelf): *Made in China*.

Searching among Wal-Mart CDs I find Bobby 'Blue' Bland's

Two Steps from the Blues for $10 so make a guilty purchase. Twenty minutes later Lee has toiletries and a change of clothes and we're on the road. But not for long: almost immediately the Joshua Tree Inn appears. This is where Gram Parsons, country-rock pioneer and trust-fund cowboy, took his last breath on 19 September 1973. It's early but I'm surprised there's no one at reception. Find a concrete plaque with 'Gram Safe at Home' scrawled on it and, aware that room 8 was the scene of Parsons's fatal misadventures with morphine and groupies (who stuffed ice cubes up Gram's ass to revive the tyro), consider knocking to see whether the current inhabitants will let me have a look. But that would be rude, especially if they had celebrated Gram in a hedonistic manner last night. I wander back to reception and a cleaner enters, thinking we want a room. Explain my interest and she fetches a walrus-moustache-wearing man who's amiable enough. No, the motel isn't owned by rabid Parsons fans (as one story had it) and not that many actually drop in. Only room 8's mirror survives from '74. Yes, it is occupied. No, you can't have a peek. Fair enough, looks a cosy place to sleep a night. Or, in Gram's case, eternity. Parsons's messy life continued in death with his road manager kidnapping his coffin from LAX airport, returning to Joshua Tree and attempting to cremate Gram. As he was a drunken sot this didn't successfully transpire but as a metaphor for the costs of LA excess Parsons's ignoble exit matches Sly Stone's spectral presence.

Back on the road and we're impressed by the landscape: barren desert populated by tall cacti and the Joshua trees – huge, Triffid-like yucca trees named by Mormon pioneers sure the rising branches were symbolic of the prophet Joshua. 'Didn't U2 record an album called *Joshua Tree*?' asks Lee. U2... *those awful purveyors of stadium cheese*... we've got a long way to drive together so it's not in my interests to get into a musical rumble, but U2... 'Maybe they did.' Answered as diplomatically as possible. Lee sucks on his cigarette then says, 'That Bono, he's a fockin' bozo,' and all is well in the world.

We pass through 29 Palms, a small settlement with the ever-present Burger King, McDonald's, KFC and an Oasis Community Church alongside a selection of murals depicting historic events. Barely a soul visible in the heat, landscape baked blond and impassive. A convoy of tanks and US army vehicles trundle past, the Mojave being, I guess, appropriately harsh training ground for those off to Iraq. Local legend tells of soldiers who became separated from their platoons while on training exercises here, vanishing into the desert. The sky's a stark, unrepentant blue, empty of anything other than the occasional condor... yes, this would be an awful place to be stranded. Ahead seemingly endless lines of telegraph poles drift into the horizon. Wind hums and drones through the power lines, singing its strange South-western song, twanging like a barbecued theramin. *Sing, wind, sing.*

As we drive alongside railway lines I note a unique form of desert graffiti (spelt out with loose stones) running for miles on the banked rail sidings, spelling out names, anti-war slogans, Hendrix, rave rallying crys... who comes out here to do such laborious work for so few witnesses? At Vidal Junction there's a solitary gas station/minimart decorated with posters declaring Ronald Reagan A Great American. Imagine living here, imprisoned by the desert and an insane right-winger... *brain boiling, mind melting...* scary America. Head straight up the 92 – known as the loneliest road in America – shivering in the sunshine, passing from Mojave into the Colorado Desert, winding the window down so letting air blow furnace hot into the car, whipping Bobby Bland's voice into strange atmospherics. On to the 40, a blue highway that runs over where Route 66 once rolled towards LA, and soon we're crossing the Colorado river and into Arizona. A canary-yellow building boasts '10,000 *Videos: The Original Truck Driver's Store*' and a middle-aged man sits by an on-ramp in front of his pick-up with a sign saying '*Stranded. Gas and food appreciated.*'

We pass the 93, which leads directly north-west to Las Vegas. 'You don't mind if we skip Vegas?' I ask. Lee shrugs, 'Whadafock,' then thinks about it and adds, 'Better I stay away from dose tables, anyway.' A fierce mountain range rises across the horizon and I think of Geronimo and other ancient warriors who once made this terrain their kingdom. Stop to use the restrooms in a siding and a sign warns 'NO PETS IN THIS AREA: Poisonous Snakes & Insects Inhabit This Area', which gets my trainers back on most ricky-tick. Heat like a whip. The road rolls and curves, rises and dips, apricot sands, juniper bushes, little outposts in the desert left by those nineteenth-century colonisers: Hell's Canyon, Horsethief Basin, Montezuma Castle, Dead Horse Ranch, Little Squaw Creek, Bloody Basin Road, Wet Beaver Wilderness... such sweet cowboy poetics!

I feed Blind Willie Johnson into the CD player and big blue notes resonate as we climb, winding among trucks, dodging high-powered pick-ups that charge up mountains, cutting air conditioning (to avoid overheating), rolling down windows and letting hot Arizona air whip around our skulls. I suggest a detour, Lee spins the wheel and we're heading down the 89, winding our way through retirement communities and prefab houses, into the mountains, coming across Sedona among canyons of rich red sandstone. A burnt sienna being the closest colour comparison possible, yet that doesn't suggest how resonant this land is, so absorbent of light, dappled with blond and grey shades... *no wonder Sedona's been turned into a New Age Lourdes!*

Flipping through the *Rough Guide to the USA* I discover Max Ernst lived here, Sedona's landscape suiting a surrealist, while Zane Grey set pulp westerns in the surrounding terrain. Today Sedona is a New Age tourist pit packed with strip malls selling crystals and Native jewellery and sub-Georgia O'Keefe canvases alongside hustlers offering 'healings' and 'tarot readings'. Odd that what appears to be an outpost of LA exists in rural Arizona; Page Bryant, a psychic who 'channelled' Sedona as *'the heart chakra of the planet'*, having turned what once must have been a tiny mountain post into an oasis of tack. We settle for sampling Sedona coffee and decline offers of enlightenment.

On through Oak Creek Canyon, deep gorges, wild canyons, giant mesas and buttes reinforcing why this is called Red Rock Country, Lee spinning the wheel as the road zigs and zags, and then the rocks take on a pale hue, casting fractured shadow patterns across us, the road offering even tighter twists and turns – *here we go loop de loop!* – and we're both laughing, caffeine madness, as the Hyundai surges forward, instant death only inches away from every high-speed turn. *Think about it*: we're feeling the American road and all the possibilities – freedom and adventure – suggested, rising and rising until we're on the mountain top, surrounded by pines (flayed and illusory beneath the late afternoon sun). Suddenly the road is smooth and straight and downhill almost all the way to Flagstaff.

All I know of Flagstaff is its mention in the song 'Route 66' – singers always love to snap out those six syllables 'Flag-staff Ar-*I*-zon-*a*' – and hitting it at rush hour wastes an hour among heavy traffic. Then we're on the 180 towards the Grand Canyon. Eighty miles to go and the light's beginning to slip – funny, I thought this region would be sun-kissed until the wee hours – so Lee keeps his foot heavy on the accelerator, curving across a flat, windswept land, no cops, thankfully, no cops, and we arrive on the outskirts of Grand Canyon National Park, pay $20 entrance, drive down to the Canyon, park, jump out, hurry to ledge edge and observe this vast stone panorama return to the shadow world. 'The Grand Canyon,' says Lee as he flicks a butt, 'whadafock so special 'bout this hole?' He laughs, adds, 'It's all right, buddy, I'm impressed, don't worry.' Darkness quickly settles, reducing visibility to naught beyond the hint of a fire on the Canyon's northern perimeter.

The only accommodation available is beyond our budget: what to do? We're here for the Canyon so might as well spend all night beside it. Drive back in, park and lean the Hyundai's seats back. Just before dawn a host of private and commercial vehicles arrive to catch the sunrise. I exit our car but the freezing morning air – *so cold it hurts* – forces me to take up something between hopping and jogging along the Canyon's edge. Hop-jump-jog and watch as the Canyon embraces the dawn. Mist drifts up from vast depths, a primal sense of new day rising, lack of comfort and warmth made up for by the strangeness and sheer wonder of it all – *what mighty depths! What a vista!* – the first rays of the new dawning sun peeling shadow away and kissing colour into rocks. Imagine what it must have been like when the only humans who knew this place were the Havasupai tribe... *what kind of world did they inhabit, living in this grandest of canyons? What kind of dreams did they dream? What kind of gods did they worship?* I note that almost everyone else observing the Canyon is elderly – obviously, the USA's million-plus pensioners who live in their RVs (recreational vehicles offering most of the comforts of a home) consider this mighty gash quite a meeting place. I relate all this to the still-dozing Lee, whose only response is 'Coffee. Let's go get some coffee.'

Reservation industry: Navajo weaving and sheep rearing

RESERVATION BLUES

Grand Canyon, Flagstaff, Navajo Nation, Monument Valley, Grants, Santa Fe

It cannot be too often repeated in this country now, that, where there is no vision, the people perish.

James Baldwin

The Navajo Reservation a lonely place?
It is Not!
The skies are sunny,
Clear Blue,
Or grey with rain.
Each day is gay –
In Nature's way.
It is not a lonesome place at all.
A Navajo house shabby and small?
It is Not!
Inside there's love,
Good laughter,
And Big Talk.
But best –
It's home
With an open door
And room for all
A Castle could have no more.

By a fifth-year group in a Special Navajo
Program in 1940 called 'It is Not!'

Hoop dreams, Navajo Nation, AZ, 2006

chapter 9

Navajo Nation: It is Done in Beauty

Having done our tourist duty – the Canyon is very grand indeed – we return to Flagstaff, where I've arranged to meet Navajo singer Radmilla Cody at Flagstaff's Greyhound station. When we pull up a slim, golden-skinned young woman is waiting. 'Miss Cody?' She smiles, shakes hands, suggests we go for lunch. Radmilla takes us into a stylish café and is recognised by several people. 'Are you famous, Rad?' 'People tend to know of me, sure, but I wouldn't say they were particularly interested in my music. Flagstaff's a conservative town and I have three strikes against me. Firstly, I'm a felon. Secondly I'm a woman. Third strike, I'm Native and black.'

Brief résumé: born of a teenage Navajo mother and an African-American father, Radmilla Cody was raised on the Navajo Nation Reservation by her grandmother, Dorothy Cody, initially speaking only Dine (as the Navajo call themselves – Navajo is a Pueblo Indian term bestowed on these people when they settled the South-west half a millennium ago – and their language). Across two albums recorded for Canyon Records she's marked herself out as a distinctive Native voice. Radmilla's 2001 Canyon debut *Seeds of Life* found her interpreting tribal chant songs. The simplicity of the music is its key, just voice and hand drum. There's no attempt to dress up or synthesise the material; instead she simply sing-chants songs steeped in Dine tradition. At the time of recording *Seeds of Life* Cody was still glowing from winning Miss Navajo Nation 1998. Then, as she bluntly says, 'I had a run-in with the law,' so spent almost two years incarcerated. Released, she returned to recording, issuing 2005's *Spirit of a Woman*. Again, she sings in Dine (pronounced 'Din-*eh*', it means 'the people') and employs traditional rhythms. This time there's also acoustic guitar and English lyrics employed, shifting her closer to Buffy Sainte Marie-style Native folk singer.

Radmilla describes a childhood spent herding sheep on foot and horseback, carding and spinning wool, searching late into the night with Grandmother for lost sheep and lambs. Sounds idyllic. Not so, says Radmilla. 'Things weren't easy. My mom was eighteen when I was born and was away living her life while my dad wasn't 'round at all. Being mixed race I attracted a lot of racial abuse. Kids were always teasing me about it; black kids doing war whoops and saying all Indians were drunk. Indian kids calling me "nigger". I never took sides when people were rude; I stood up for Navajos and for African-Americans. I'm not bitter about this. It hurt, yes, but I've put all these incidents behind me. My grandmother has been a great teacher. She raised me planting corn, shearing sheep, gathering water from the well. Living this life you take on tasks and responsibilities which teach you life lessons urban existence can't.'

These lessons served Cody well: she entered the 1998 Miss Navajo Nation contest – the winner must exemplify the essence

Miss Navajo Nation: Radmilla Cody

and characters of the Navajo deities First Woman, White Shell Woman and Changing Woman – and won. Where most beauty contests involve wearing a swimsuit and uttering baubles about wanting to work with children, Miss Navajo Nation is judged on the entrants' excellence in traditional technologies: butchering sheep, filleting the mutton, wrapping achee, carding and spinning, making tortillas, contemporary public speaking, traditional public speaking, fluency in English and Navajo. And appearance, attitude, bearing and conduct. But no swimsuits. 'I learnt a lot from my year. When I won the title I knew how to weave and speak Dine and shear and butcher sheep but once I held the title and I was attending all these traditional ceremonies I began learning a lot more from our elders.' Radmilla's a natural beauty – skin glowing, eyes smiling – and recalling her reign she blushes with pride. Modelling and media attention and the Canyon recording deal followed the title yet Radmilla's boyfriend, who she met while a student in Phoenix, made life difficult: running a drug ring across the South-west, he savagely ensured clients, dealers and Radmilla did as ordered. When the law caught up with him they also arrested Radmilla: she pleaded guilty to wiring him money knowing it would be used for illegal activities and served a twenty-one-month sentence. As Miss Navajo Nation Radmilla had visited Rez schools to warn children against drug and alcohol abuse; her trial and incarceration provoked much condemnation from other Navajo.

'There was an element of hysteria in the local media. The *Gallup Independent* tried to associate me with murders and all other kind of things I had no knowledge of. Even recently I played a Rez concert someone tried to stop 'cos I'm supposedly this bad-ass ex-con. I apologise for the bad things I've done but it's time to stop judging me by past mistakes. Personally, what hurt the most was disappointing the children I'd been working with. Yet kids are forgiving and my mom and my grandmother really supported me and Canyon stood by me. That helped me get through the sentence.'

What provided the attraction to the gangster life?

'I was madly in love with this guy. Mad in the sense of sick: he employed violence to ensure I stayed with him. I had a pistol forced in my mouth. Got slapped upside my head with a pistol. Beaten black and blue. I didn't know how to escape. I've since learnt that battered women often form a psychological dependence upon their partner even though they are risking their lives by staying with him.'

Healing songs and chants are an important genre in Native American ceremonies; does Radmilla feel her music contributes to reconciliation?

'Definitely. Though I should emphasise that none of my songs are ceremonial. Some are used with ceremonies but my Uncle Herman, who writes many of my songs, leaves out the more important deities that are used with healing ceremonies. Every album has been approved by a medicine man before its release. I don't want to cross those boundaries. What you hear when I sing is a part of our traditional songs; it's the way we sing, the styles, the tempo, it's our tradition. What makes my style of singing is I have a little bit of soul. That comes from my dad's side of the family.'

Radmilla suggests we head out to the Navajo Nation, paying by placing her money face down 'out of respect for the dead'. Lee, unexcited about the reservation anti-alcohol stipulations, opts to stay in Flagstaff. Radmilla drives a four-wheel drive and as we exit Flagstaff I check her vehicle CDs – *Mariah Carey! J. Lo! Tupac!* – and chastise her for listening to such corporate chaff. 'Hey,' she jests, 'you're forgetting how black I am.' We drive out of Flagstaff's suburbs and into desert terrain, passing a sign welcoming us to the Navajo Nation, *'Where Ancient Voices Gather'*. Here we are, entering a land once described in a chant as 'A House Made of Dawn', a land with its own tribal police, its own time, its own language, two radio stations, a flag, a nation that extends across the borders of Arizona, Utah and New Mexico. And a land that has suffered some of the worst abuses in US history.

In 1864 Kit Carson's cavalry waged scorched-earth war to

destabilise the tribe then forced 8,000 Navajo to trek to Fort Sumner, where they were held as prisoners on barren New Mexico plains, 2,000 dying in captivity. Survivors were freed to the reservation in 1868 and today the 180,000 residents of the largest US reservation continue to face huge hurdles: 43 per cent unemployment and drug/alcohol abuse are the most prominent problems. Uranium dust from mines (both active and disused) leads to high cancer rates while mining operations tear up sacred lands and siphon off pristine waters for slurry. Government investment is scarce and Native politics are often corrupted by those willing to work for Washington, DC's despised Bureau of Indian Affairs. To make matters worse 'G', a form of crystal methamphetamine dumped on the Navajo Nation, has led to social havoc. Radmilla groans when I mention G. 'Meth is a huge problem here. Responsible for half the crimes committed on the Rez. I'm anti-drug now 'cos of what my experiences of living with a drug dealer taught me and meth is just the worst. While in prison there was a woman whose face kept twitching uncontrollably; I found out this was 'cos she damaged the nerves in her face smoking meth.'

How tough was jail, Rad?

'When you deal with something extreme like imprisonment you experience all walks of life, all kinds of personalities, so I learnt to differentiate between those who were outright shysters and those who were good. At first a lot of the other inmates thought I was going to act like an Indian princess and I had to prove to them that I was as normal as they were. One of my first tasks was raking and I mentioned that I'd grown up harvesting corn and they were amazed – they had an idea that I was going to act like I was superior.'

Meth's ravages are matched by the urban gang turf wars that now exist on the Rez: *la vida loca*'s infiltrated and drive-bys now occur in this rural wilderness.

'A lot of our young ones resort to gangs as they don't have a strong and stable home environment,' says Radmilla. 'The gangs become substitute families for them. The gang problem's gotten worse just as the drug problem's gotten worse. The two go hand in hand.'

That *la vida loca* and its culture of drive-by shooting, turf war and psychotic devotion to the gang has taken hold in the sparsely populated Navajo Nation appears paradoxical until you consider the Rez is home to much poverty and alienation, makeshift schools and stimulant abuse. This provides a hothouse for youths who feel both racially inferior and very angry. Stanley 'Tookie' Williams, founder of the LA Crips, described the birth of a South Central gangbanger as involving *'no boys' clubs, no cub scouts, no social organisations of any kind for kids in my neighbourhood, except what we eventually created – the Crips... and everything about being a Crip revolved around negativism.'* And for the Navajo youth who join the Dragons and the Cobras those sentiments surely ring true. This connection is strengthened by the 'reservation dogs', Natives returning home after contact with gangs while in cities (or prison), youths finding no purpose in anything but violence.

If Rez territory initially appears harsh, unforgiving, there is also much beauty; the raw, rolling terrain shimmers in the heat, red-purple sands and huge skies offering amazing vistas. Radmilla stops at Leupp school (*'Welcome Braves & Bravettes'*) to collect her nine-year-old sister and sis's best friend. 'The Rez school now teaches kids in Dine,' says Radmilla, 'which is a real achievement as it used to be a punishable offence to speak Dine. My mom recalls having her mouth washed out with soap for speaking Dine. I went to school at the tail-end of that era.' We sight a circular grouping and Radmilla pulls over. 'C'mon, let's go check the powwow.' A group of eight men sit around a large drum, each banging on it rhythmically with a stick while chanting. The sound is amplified, rhythms and voices taking on a powerful drone quality. Each dance is announced at the start and those participating in it perform while everyone else watches from outside the circle. Many of the dancers are dressed in traditional garb of moccasins, buckskin outfits, beads and feather headdresses. The dance involves a shuffling of the feet and chanting, very different from the Afro-influenced dancing that accompanies most popular music.

Boom-boom-boom goes the drum and the drummers' voices are pitched high and strange, a banshee wail of sorts. Not an easy sound to adjust to. I focus, listening hard, this raw sound, genuine trance music. The atmosphere is South-west elemental, a culture quite apart from what I know, yet intoxicating, the trance power of the voices and drumming echoing through the skull, sounding as natural as a heartbeat. There're parents with kids and youths hiding behind hoodies and veterans wearing medals, the slim and the fat, those in traditional garb and those in Levi's. No one pays any attention to me – the sole non-Navajo – but as Radmilla knows many here there's plenty of introductions and all are friendly. The closest comparison I can make is to observing an Orthodox or mosque service, the way all around understand the initiation, the ritual, yet remain relaxed about outsiders. The

Powwow, Navajo Nation, 1891

booming drum, chanting voices, dancers stomping... the sense of something ancient, still living among the sagebrush and cactus and dust. I'm bearing witness to a pre-American culture, one that has survived so much, older than the recorded time of this land.

Light begins to fade, and while the powwow will last all night Radmilla's intent on getting the kids home. We navigate gravel roads until way out in Rez wilderness then draw up by a simple homestead. Radmilla's grandmother, wandering the yard, looks up and offers a greeting in Dine. I wonder what Dorothy Cody, aged ninety-one, will make of me, she surely having had innumerable run-ins with my pale-skinned brethren over the past century. Radmilla makes introductions and Dorothy's as welcoming as someone who has never learnt to speak English can be. She keeps busy by building a fire and providing for the children, who rush around shooting hoops – basketball being a Native passion. Radmilla apologises for Dorothy not speaking any English, 'she used to say, "Teach me, Millie, teach me" when I was at school but, of course, I was just a kid and couldn't be bothered.'

A pick-up arrives with Radmilla's mother Margaret, teenage brother and Uncle Marcus. Margaret's strong features and merry eyes stand in contrast to Marcus – alcoholism, life's disappointments and a hit-and-run driver having conspired to break his body and spirit. He stumbles around, slurring, Margaret and Dorothy keeping a watchful eye on him. Native author N. Scott Momaday wrote of the slow death that embraced Navajo painter Quincy Tahoma, *'He died as a young man of alcoholism, so they say. I wonder if he did not actually die of a broken heart. It seemed to me that he had been severed for many years in his mind from the world in which his roots were planted. This is not a rare affliction among Indians, especially those who have the old ways fixed forever in their blood.'* The average life expectancy for a Native male in the US is forty-five, alcohol-related diseases culling thousands annually. I try to express sympathy but Radmilla is unmoved by Marcus's plight. 'When I was a child he and his brother used to call me all kinds of bad names in English as Grandma couldn't understand. They were cruel, abusive towards me as a child because they felt so bad about themselves. That hurt a lot and I guess I've never truly forgiven them for it.' Grandma obviously likes things simple: beyond a TV and electric stove, chairs, table, sink and beds there's little else occupying the house. Dinner is served – fry bread, potatoes, scrambled eggs and coffee – and stories flow across the table.

'When I got out of prison I came here and was sitting in the dark and my grandma entered and flipped on the light and said, "Yaahteee! Don't sit in the dark – we have electricity now!" She finally got electricity in 2003!'

'I've been here since I was eleven,' says Margaret. 'Before that we lived in a hogan [traditional Navajo adobe dwelling]. The stove's been here since day one. Mom likes to be out here. My dad too, he was real traditional, never drove, always rode horses. He'd grow big leaves of tobacco and use it in his ceremonies. But my mom became a Christian so she burnt all the tobacco. She divorced my dad forty years ago. He didn't like her becoming a Christian and he was a tall, charismatic guy so had quite a way with the ladies and she didn't like that either. We'd stay at the Rez school all year long. Dad would take us in the wagon, fifteen of us, and we'd not see them again until our holidays.'

Dorothy smiles and nods as Radmilla translates into Dine, a beautiful language full of high, expressive flights and strange, angular vowels, a language so difficult to master that Navajo code takers were used for the Pacific War, the Japanese being unable to break this ancient, secret language. I'm fascinated by Dorothy's hands. Such tough, gnarled hands. Hands that recall Bill Withers's song 'Grandma's Hands'. Dorothy's always earned her living shepherding and weaving Dine rugs. Radmilla tells me that they convinced Dorothy to sell her sheep – she being too old to chase them – but she still weaves. Her weather-beaten features suggest wisdom and compassion. No wonder Radmilla expresses such a fierce spirit, having been bought up by this woman.

'The traditional way of living means you never really lose the core part of Dine living,' says Margaret. 'The weaving, the songs, the prayers, the way my mother dresses, the jewellery – no matter how much she may consider herself a Christian she's never going to lose this core Navajo being.

'My grandfather would always come riding over the hill on his horse chanting,' adds Radmilla. 'He once sat me down and said, "Yaahteee, my child, get your education, value what your grandmother has taught you, and come back and work with our people." He never tried to teach me his ceremonial knowledge so I think he'd be surprised if he knew I was continuing his tradition.'

As the evening wears on other Rez dwellers drop in. Everyone's friendly and entertained by the idea of London. Questions are asked about Camilla and Charles while Margaret wonders whether the newspaper cartoon character Andy Capp is a typical Londoner. Considering Capp's always drunk and beating his wife he's an odd figure for Rez dwellers to find entertaining but the Codys think he's hilarious. Being farmers, everyone beds down early so I tuck up with Twain's *Roughing It*, trying to work out whether he passed through this region. Instead, he used Nevada as his highway yet what's noticeable is his virulent racism towards Native Americans, *'A silent, sneaking, treacherous looking race... descended from the selfsame gorilla, or kangaroo, or Norway rat, which ever animal-Adam the Darwinians trace them to.'* These views were prevalent in the nineteenth century yet it's odd that the man who wrote about black Americans with such empathy detested Natives. If I'm remembering correctly *Tom Sawyer*'s villain is Indian Joe – the archetypal demonic 'other' currently being played out by Osama Bin.

Beyond the rustle of wind the Rez is silent. Occasionally I hear Marcus gurgling in his sleep. Poor Marcus, loved but unable to withstand life's furies. Margaret recalled a younger Marcus reading widely while Radmilla mentioned that certain Navajo criticise her for dating non-Native men, yet with drugs, alcohol and depression devastating the Nation's males finding a suitable partner isn't easy. The Navajo are matriarchal in many ways and today their women continue to be icons of fortitude. I think of the Night Chant – a series of Navajo practices including dances, the construction of sand paintings and the use of prayer sticks that constitute a nine-day healing ceremony – and wonder whether they are used to help those wounded by whiskey and meth. I know only one Navajo ritual chant and in the darkness I whisper it, a prayer of sorts for Marcus:

Reared within the Mountains!
Lord of the Mountains!
Young Man!
Chieftain!
I have made your sacrifice.
I have prepared a smoke for you.
My feet thou restore for me.
My legs thou restore for me.
My body thou restore for me.
My voice thou restore for me.
Restore all for me in beauty.
Make beautiful all that is before me.
Make beautiful all that is behind me.
It is done in beauty.
It is done in beauty.
It is done in beauty.
It is done in beauty.

The family that weaves together: Radmilla's mother, grandmother and sister

chapter 10

Monument Valley:
A Few More Nowhere Towns

I awake to find Dorothy preparing coffee, fry bread and eggs. After a warm farewell, Radmilla and I and children are back on the Rez's bone-rattling roads. We drop the kids at school and talk turns to tribal issues. Indian casinos have proved huge money-spinners for certain tribes but, so far, I've not noticed any on the Navajo Nation. 'They're about to build one,' says Radmilla. 'I voted against it simply because I feel whatever issues we are currently dealing with will only worsen. Gambling can become an addiction and we already have too many addictions on the Rez.'

Lee's waiting on South Beaver Street. 'How was Flagstaff?' Lee shrugs, mutters, 'Hard night.' Goodbye to Radmilla, who looks relieved my bleary associate didn't accompany us to the Nation, and we're off, me driving, heading along the 89, avoiding the turn-off for the Canyon, taking the 180 east, re-entering the Navajo Nation's northern territories, passing stalls and shacks selling jewellery and buffalo jerky and decorated with signs saying *'Friendly Indians'* and *'Chief Yellowfeather's'*. The landscape's lunar, amazingly empty, mining turning up bulbous hills of pink earth and piles of slate, very little growing, everything dry and desolate. At the Kayenta Trading Post we buy fruit then sit outside to eat and people-watch. I'm taking notes when an old Navajo man approaches, says 'Yelli' and explains it means 'hello'. He enquires where we're from and at Lee's mention of Philly recalls being stationed in New Jersey during WW2, rolling up his sleeve to show a faded tattoo of a naked woman. 'You write about us?' he asks me. Yes, sir. 'Thank you,' he says, then adds, 'Too windy and too dry here.' And hot and dusty. The only comparison I can make is with Australia's outback, the same crimson earth and flyblown, brain-boiling climate.

Most of the locals drive pick-up trucks, some decorated with 'Support Our Troops' bumper stickers, others 'Alcoholics Anonymous' (an emblematic Native warrior as decoration), many plastered with US flag decals. A strange place to find patriots. Love the land, the ancestors, yes. But the US state? Radmilla sings a tribute song to Lori Piestewa, a young Hopi woman raised on the Navajo Nation who achieved a tragic double first: the first US female soldier to be killed in Iraq and the first Native woman to die in battle for the US army. US media canonised Piestewa as a patriot but reality tells of a solo mother living in a community suffering from 50 per cent-plus unemployment. Her parents now call on all Native soldiers to return home, decrying the US government's Iraq invasion. US army recruiters, aware how limited opportunities are on the Rez, siphon youths into the services, a wretched irony considering the military were once employed to brutalise and conquer North America's Native people. Currently more than a thousand Navajos are serving in the US military – more than one soldier for every 200 Navajo. Remove those ineligible to serve (under eighteen, over forty, physically/mentally unsuitable) and the statistic leaps – *one in every eighty men and women* – the highest representation of any American ethnicity in the military. Like Piestewa, many must feel the army offers better odds than the Rez.

Native kids trudge past, heading to a jumble of fibreglass houses and trailers surrounding this elemental trading post. The Navajo are reclaiming their language and culture but this doesn't guarantee food, shelter and wages. The US army offers these and more. Education. Adventure. Discipline. Training. Death. Crippling injuries. Violent psychosis. Well, they don't advertise the last three, but only a fool would deny that damaged Iraq vets will litter the USA in decades to come. And it's towns like Kayenta that produce today's soldiers. Places you've never heard of. Places Texan essayist Michael Ventura describes as *'a new American geography – a geography of places with fewer and fewer choices, fewer and fewer opportunities, where the young would rather risk death than endure the death-in-life of towns where most shops on Main Street have long since been boarded up. And so it goes. Every day there are a few more names from a few more nowhere towns – towns made "nowhere" not because they were incapable or insignificant, but because a "free market," run by the 1% who profit from the Bush tax cuts, decided Asia or Latin America could contribute more to their portfolio than Utica, Miss., or Apex, N.C., or Flint, Mich.'*

I mention this '*new American geography*' to Lee and he suggests that in small-town USA today the smart and the talented head off to college. But for the rest, well, if there's no work available then military recruiters gobble. 'Places like this,' he says, 'I don't see much here providing work. Maybe they will head to Flagstaff or Phoenix or Vegas. Or maybe they want to stay here, close to their families, the tribe. But welfare's hard to get an' it won't buy you a pick-up truck. See, the army's big business. They clean out places like this and where you went in LA, South Central. Ghettos produce tough youths familiar with guns, unafraid of fighting, quick reflexes, good grunt material.' We stare through the haze of heat and dust at the teenagers drifting past; their ancestors once were warriors and they too may live to fight.

On country roads again, passing tiny outposts of Rez dwellers, and I start to laugh. Lee asks what the joke is. The Temptations. '*The Temptations?*' Yeah, remember that tune 'Ball Of Confusion'? It builds to a head when Dennis Edwards screams '*and the only safe place is the Indian reservation*'. Laugh again. Lee chuckles some. Maybe coming from the Detroit ghetto the idea of an Indian reservation appealed: fresh air, open spaces, wild horses, running free...

Down the road, twenty miles or so on US-163, and we're at Tse Bii' Ndzisgaii: *Monument Valley.* I've seen this site in countless American movies, unsurpassed natural spectacle for John Wayne or Henry Fonda or Billy Jack or Clint Eastwood to strut their kick-ass stuff through, but cinematic familiarity doesn't prepare for the majesty of this land. *Look, look... red, red... the mystery of stone of time and tide and wind so creating a field of bright humming stone more Mars than America...* Lee pulls over and we stand and stare at the craggy vista in front. Lee's nodding, muttering something under his breath; it sounds like a prayer. Whassup, Lee?

'Oh, don't rightly know. Just, man, not often I wanna talk with God, but this...'

'All right, let's go check those rocks. Maybe you'll find a shaman who can put you on the hotline to God.'

Lee and I laugh and the world tilts a little and we chug into the landscape, eyes on the prize, turning right, driving through a shanty town of plywood shacks selling soft drinks, jewellery and Navajo food (mutton, fry bread). It's $5 a piece to enter the Valley. We pay and get on a dirt road that slopes steeply, stones and potholes designed to snap axles. While the Grand Canyon is observed from the ledge, we drive into Monument Valley, spraying up a mist of rich, tawny dust. The road twists, buckles and reveals a film crew. 'Welcome to Marlboro Country,' says Lee, and he's right, this is the landscape used to sell a zillion cigarettes. Better to recall John Wayne and Jeffrey Hunter criss-crossing Monument Valley in *The Searchers*. Do I qualify as a searcher? No Natalie Wood at the end of my journey. Immediately ahead, paired east and west, are the Mittens, huge rock vessels, abstracted ocean liners surfing a tapered base, a thumb splintering off from each Mitten's central bulk. A few vagrant clouds float above their 1,000-foot peak, enforcing the majestic bulk of these sandstone temples against a severe blue sky. I think of Willie Nelson singing 'Blue Skies'. Indeed, nothing but blue skies above.

'Fockin' awesome,' says Lee, and I, I'm lost for words. Lee continues, saying this is what he always wanted to come west for: see some LA palm trees and check those big rocks Henry Fonda rode beneath. The Three Sisters, three rakish pillars of stone, knobbly and severe, recall not the feminine but H. R. Giger's phallic lunarscapes. What are their Dine names? I wonder. There are places where the earth concentrates its strength and Monument Valley is one of them. What a place to camp, build a fire as the sun sets and giant shadows fall across the land, a sense of the ancient and the numinous sweeping across puny, fragile humans. Wake in the morning, cook coffee over the embers of your fire then mount your pony and ride and ride and ride. Well, that's my Arizona dream.

We pull over to check a Navajo youth selling jewellery. The work is good, prices fine. Lee starts marching towards what he imagines is a ruined pueblo in the near distance and the youth starts shouting at him to stop. 'That's my hogan! My house! You *can't* go in there!' Lee apologises: 'Just being a dumb tourist. Just wanted to look.' Well, says the youth, softening, if you only wanna look, you can. No problem. Lee smiles his Irish smile, nods, lights a cigarette, says, Hey, that's OK. The youth – big belly, buzz-cut hair, constant grin – laughs loudly at my attempts to speak Dine, teases that we're on the run, calling us Thelma and Louise. 'I'm Thelma,' says Lee, 'he's Louise,' and the youth says, 'Yeah, guessed dat,' and starts trying to sell us horse treks out to the stones, describing his horses, corralled behind his makeshift stand, with great affection. Your horses, I say, they look a little surly. And they do, especially one, a white horse dappled black, who snorts and stomps, hinting he could tear the stockade down. 'Wanna go?' asks the youth, easy smile tinged with challenge. 'Thanks but time is tight.' A German couple approach and enquire as to the price for horse treks – $25 for thirty minutes, says our chunky Navajo. That's expensive, they say. He smiles, shrugs, offers a my-way-or-the-highway gesture to the palefaces. They look at one another and decide, yes, the highway, and return to their vehicle. I ask about the film crew. Turns out they're here for a few days, shooting an advertisement. 'We've got plenty of film crews here,' he says. 'Whole lotta people wanna film in Monument Valley.' He then states that he and his family make all the jewellery on site – which I find hard to believe – adding, 'I got a car. We got two pick-ups. We're living good!' He laughs, pride bursting from his eyes and creasing his smooth brown face. 'Keep living good,' I say, and offer my hand. He laughs again, gentle but a little squirrelly, slowly offers his hand. We shake methodically and he looks me straight in the eye and says, 'You really want to buy a ring.'

We could drive to the outskirts of Tsé Bii' Ndzisgaii, get as close to the stones as vehicles are allowed but, no, Austin is a date we don't want to break: time to hit the road again. Lee sticks the car in reverse and we blow red dust all over the youth, he laughing and calling to his horses. Back at the Visitors' Centre I read the *Arizona Republic*. The news is local politics and business, farming and crime: *a homicidal robbery of a fast-food outlet (less than $300 in takings)... a pedestrian beaten to death by a meth addict so high he was unaware of his actions... wild, violent, brutal America... a culture experiencing sensory overload.* Then again, the *South London Press*, my local paper, dishes up a similar diet of gore which has never made me feel much more than a little unsettled.

On the 163, our once shining white vehicle now coated a thick, dusty red, we pass a sign informing us we're entering Utah, where 'headlights are compulsory'. Through the town of Mexican Hat – *landscape aglow with red* – through the Valley of the Gods and into Bluff, where gigantic cliffs of red offer a fortress of stone, rock that shimmers and absorbs heat. Big sky country? Yep, and big rock country too. Open roads, little traffic, little habitation, wild

HOMELAND SECURITY

"Fighting Terrorism Since 1492"

horses canter across vast expanses. Crossing the San Juan river, landscape spreading, Lee recalls growing up listening to Waylon Jennings and this being what he imagined Waylon's West to be. *It is done in beauty.* Note Lee's cigarette consumption has slowed right down, a little natural magic from the land, the people, oiling his soul, relaxing addiction. N. Scott Momaday observed the South-west was *'essentially a spiritual landscape'* and here, twilight falling, the land transformed into a tangerine dream – *bold and glowing!* – I shiver with positive tidings. Lee spins the radio dial and The Beach Boys' spooky pop mantra 'Good Vibrations' fills our car. Perfect. *Good vibrations.* No crystals or acid or anything else needed. Be present. Be mindful. Good vibrations.

The radio returns to the seventies flatliners now marketed as classic rock – Led Zeppelin, Pink Floyd, Kansas, Heart – so stretch the dial across the wavelength but this station appears to be the only one out here. To further destroy the beatitude Lee says, 'Check it: we're almost outta gas' – *uh-ohhhh!* – petrol dial hangs south. At that moment Jackson Browne's 'Running On Empty' begins and a red warning light starts flashing, as if the DJ were tuned into our situation and taunting us with soft rock. No use turning back – haven't seen a gas station since Kayenta – follow the 191 south towards Mexican Water, night coming down, feeling increasingly nervous: no traffic, no settlements, no farmhouses... running on empty in a big nowhere! Suddenly – *praise be to whatever gods roam this empty land!* – a gas station's up ahead.

We tear up, slam brakes, leap out and run inside waving $20 bills and shouting, 'Fill 'er up!' The women running the station, pale prairie girls wearing matching heavy glasses, look at us, sunburned, coated in red dust, wired on weird reserves of adrenalin and relief, a half-smoked cigarette stuck in the corner of Lee's mouth as he fills a Giant Coffee, and shake their heads mournfully. *More weirdos. Martha, check the .22 beneath the counter's cocked.* But we're harmless, just a little loud, a little excited, happy not to be spending the night stranded in this vast land. In a glass case Navajo jewels gather dust; I suggest to Lee our Monument Valley fat boy might claim to have made them in his hogan and he laughs, agrees. *Whooh!* I buy peanut butter cups – sugar rush guaranteed – and name the gas station Happy Gas and Lee complies by spilling coffee on the forecourt and shouting, 'I christen thee Happy Gas.'

Back on the 191, nothing but thick black night and the occasional onrush of a vehicle heading north with lights on full beam. Lee's starting to fade – *brows fluttering, foot drifting off the accelerator* – too long at the wheel. Over, I say, pull over, time for me to drive. Lee sinks in the passenger seat but no chance to sleep, uh-uh, for this is one primitive highway, nasty driving, trucks coming out of the darkness, lights swamping us in glare, while the surrounding land is devoid of light, even the moon's in hiding, a night swamp that demands concentration to get through. Then a battered Chevy's in front of us, waltzing down the median line. Lee gets uneasy, tells me to slow down, stay away, pull over. No, no, I say, Austin is too far away for us to pull off the highway every time some space cadet gets on the road. But Lee, who is, admittedly, a seriously careful driver, is freaking, shouting about drunken Indians causing traffic chaos and how we'll end up as just so much roadkill if we try and overtake him. All right, all right, I say, we'll let him lead, won't get too close. Sit on 40 mph while cars and trucks rip past, the Chevy driver – *and who's to say he's a Native son?* – wobbles along, seriously unglued, finally veering on to the road's shoulder, too fried to go any farther. Step on the gas again, no more crawling, simply wishing to escape this tar pit of a road. Within the hour we've crossed into New Mexico, got on to Interstate 40, hit Gallup – *another town name-checked by all who sing 'Route 66'* – but no stopping; gun the car towards Albuquerque.

All day I've figured we would make it to Santa Fe by midnight but the 40 is thick with heavy traffic, multi-ton Mac trucks bear down on us, screaming beasts of steel and diesel, and rolling among this roaring, big-wheel fury is way more intimidating than tailing a drunk driver. Not that Lee sees it like this, claiming the truckers don't want to deal with the insurance hassles squashing minnows involves. I keep my foot down, punching forward, overtaking some, overtaken by others, the 40 obviously not a highway famed for police as everyone's speeding, truckers surely fuelled on crank, and it's late, all wanting to get somewhere, desperate to squeeze each extra mile possible out of the road. I'm hunched forward, fists slippery with perspiration, pushing our grungy vehicle onwards... *onwards*... massive eighteen-wheel truck-trailers rumbling either side of us on this multi-lane highway, monsters of the American night, until – *fuck it!* – a particularly close call with a demented redneck determined to hog the road with his death star juggernaut and blaring horn suggests I'm re-enacting Dennis Weaver's car-truck duel in *Duel*. Slice towards the next turn-off, pulling over in a dark nowhere, heart pulsing, temples throbbing, feeling terrified, vulnerable... the road as death trip.

The town's called Thoreau but I doubt it connects with the author of *Walden*, nothing seeming to exist here beyond a post office and a locked-up gas station. We ask a passing pedestrian where a motel might be found and they say take the next town a few miles up on the freeway. Breathe deep and long, try and mutter the memory of a mantra, then it's back on the 40 and playing dodgems among these beasts of steel and rubber. I hug the far right lane, nervous sweats sticking T-shirt to seat and skin, eyes popping, arms aching, hungry and scared, New Mexico night moves chewing up my psyche. After several miles we see a sign indicating a town called Grants up ahead. Start to indicate and grab the exit, literally gasping with relief. I switched the radio off hours ago, tinny tunes only adding to my anxiety as we moved through this brackish night, and now, having escaped being crushed by the auto-Armageddon that is twenty-first-century America, I think of all those musical road warriors carving across America night after night: blues guitarist Hubert Sumlin complained he spent so long sitting in cars he developed haemorrhoids while The Ramones, stuck in a van year after year, learned to loathe each other. Still, Hubert helped build electric blues and all that came from it while The Ramones were the last

consistently great American rock 'n' roll band. I start to sing a
Ramones tune:

I give what I've got to give
I give what I need to live
I give what I've got to give
It's important if I wanna live
I wanna live
I wanna live my life

I'm unsure of what Dee Dee Ramone was getting at but want
to believe it stands as an American road mantra. Lee, sleepy and
unfazed by what we've just driven through, says, 'Buddy, don't
give up the day job.'

Entering Grants all relief is displaced by an atmosphere of despair;
heavy industry detritus, seedy motels, gas stations, bars, boarded-
up shops, used car lots... urban decay hangs in the midnight air.
We choose the Desert Motel and the owner, a quietly spoken man
with a tidy grey quiff and sad eyes, asks if we want one bed or two.
Both Lee and I laugh. 'I like this guy,' I say, 'but not that much.'
Grants is backstreet America, cheap motel territory, income
generated by hookers and trysts. Inside our room (thick brown
carpet, faded nylon curtains) there's a sign warning not to open
the door to strangers and how preparing drugs is strictly illegal.
Another sign announces *'Notice: Contents of Room Are Checked
Before and After Being Occupied. Anything Missing Is Reported to
the Police. Your Car License Is on Record'*. Yet beyond a plastic
lamp and a small TV there's nothing to even contemplate stealing.
The owner brings clean, threadbare towels and stays to chat. Like
Howe and Doug, he was born in Pennsylvania, landing in Grants
in the 1960s to work uranium mines. The mine closed twenty
years ago and with Route 66, which everyone rode ('even Bonnie
and Clyde'), usurped by the building of Interstate 40, Grants is
dying on its feet. Literally: uranium poisoning has given the town
a dramatic rate of cancer fatalities. 'Santa Fe, now that's a rich

town,' he says, 'but not here.' I ask him to recommend a bar and he simply shakes his head, looks at me with those sad grey eyes and says in his inimitably slow manner, 'Just be careful.'

Lee takes this as a signal to go to the local gas station for a beer run but once we arrive it turns out there's a midnight curfew on beer sales. The two men running the station are prickly–suspicious–agitated even as Lee purchases his fuel of Twinkies–coffee–cigarettes and I get the feeling that products beyond those made of oil and sugar are being sold here. Outside the station several local zombies gather, so thin they're barely recognisable as Americans, tattooed necks, body odour, furtive glances. Grants, man, what a place to live and die.

Back at the Desert Motel we decide to venture into a cinder block bar near by, both of us convinced that after all the miles and dust and Mac monsters we could use – *dammit, we deserve!* – alcohol. The bar looks to be jumping, music and laughter spraying across the street. Lots of Harleys are parked outside but Lee says he knows biker bars and they're generally OK. Fine, I say, let's get a beer. The interior's like a million other American bars, a pool table bathed in harsh neon light providing the centre of attention. The clientele are men with ponytails and swollen bellies and their women in too-tight Levi's, mostly white, a couple maybe Navajo, all drinking, smoking, playing pool, shouting unintelligible shit at one another and laughing haw-haw-haw. They check us as we head towards the bar – *fresh meat* – Lee who has spent a lifetime in such joints keeps his eyes lowered, shoulders hunched, while I'm still a tourist, busy looking until Lee taps me and says, 'No need to stare. Unless you want to start something.' I most certainly don't. The bartender resembles Mo from *The Simpsons*, permanent scowl, uneasily eyeing us, hissing when I complain about the beer choice being Miller or Budweiser. *How can Americans drink such awful beer?* Lee says shut up and drink, sucking on his Bud and ordering bourbon chasers. Fire up cigarettes, sink upon bar stools and watch the wild things at play. The jukebox plays metal – Judas Priest, Ozzy, Metallica – no one paying attention to what tune comes on, women occasionally shaking ass between pool shots, a wall of white noise to shout over. Then Pantera's 'Fuckin' Hostile' comes crunching through, music to break bones by.

Lee's weary, concentrating only on smoking and sipping Jack, oblivious to the bar's atmosphere. I nudge him, suggest maybe we should step out, gut instinct hinting a less than affectionate vibe is drifting our way. God knows what started it but a short, stocky man with long black hair and onyx eyes is talking louder than you need to in a flat monotone about the 'fucking pussies who come to *our* bar to check out *our* women'. Maybe my interest in observing surroundings made him think I was casing his woman. Or maybe he simply likes to fuck strangers up. I noticed him earlier, tears tattooed beneath an eye warning of wasted years inside. And beneath a cut-off denim jacket there's the kind of abs one builds in prison. Scary? Hell, he's terrifying. Lee's listening now, silent, barely moving, nodding to himself. Lee's big, missing a few teeth, surely knows how to look after himself, having spent too much of his adult life working behind bars or drinking in front of them. He lights a cigarette, says, 'We could, with the wrong word or gesture, have the entire bar on top of us. Understand?' Understood. 'Straight out the door,' he adds, 'no eye contact. And then we run to the motel.' I nod, keep sipping foul-tasting Bud, feel the sweat of fear start to drip from armpits, groin retracting. Lee looks at me, real casual, like he's about to ask about the football, his tone deadly serious. 'Let's go,' he says. 'No attention paid to the psycho.' OK, I whisper, *OK*. The exit's only seven metres, perhaps less, but feels like miles. As we walk he's shouting directly at us, starting forward. There's a spring in Lee's step, ready to run, but the psycho's woman gets between him and us, insisting he leave the fags alone, surely adding sagely, 'Remember, it could fuck up your probation.' Then we're outside and sprinting like Jesse Owens.

Back inside the motel room, both panting, short of breath and courage, fired by fear, freaking that maybe the bar's clientele are following us back here, a real-life horror movie. Lee starts cursing the American underclass and how instead of venting their anger at those who keep them poor, instead of organising and agitating, they turn on strangers. 'When I lived in Florida and worked bar I used to consider getting a bike and joining one of the motorbike clubs,' he says, 'but those people are too stupid, too nasty, to really want to hang with.' I can barely speak. Trauma. *The nightmare that is New Mexico.* Lee does what he always does in times of stress: lights a cigarette. 'Fockin' white trash,' he mutters. I reply, 'They weren't so much white trash as white toxic waste!' We laugh aloud, hysteria tingeing our merriment. I retreat to the bathroom and scrub teeth, take a shower, singing 'I Want to Live' loud as I can. Today counts as nasty travel. Hard roads. Hard people. Water scalds my skin, scouring sweat and fear, deep cleansing.

Re-enter the bedroom and Lee's already asleep, cigarette smouldering in the ashtray. Having survived the wild American road, the bleak American night, my adrenalin's jumping, sleep nowhere in sight. Crack open Henry Miller's *The Air-conditioned Nightmare* and note how Hank, exiled from France by WW2 so exploring his native land for the first time via jalopy, experiences a different USA to the one Kerouac would celebrate only a few years later. For Miller there is no spiritual engagement in crossing America, only decline and loss. A suitable guide, then, for those of us foolish enough to take to the road dreaming American dreams: '*Try to think of North Africa when you are in Algiers, Louisiana. Try to think of the dreams of the Spaniards when you are motoring over the old Spanish Trail. Walk around in the Old French Quarter of New Orleans and try to reconstruct the life that once this city knew. Less than a hundred years has elapsed since this jewel of America faded out. It seems more like a thousand. Everything that was of beauty, significance or promise has been destroyed or buried in an avalanche of false progress.*'

Rail tracks, New Mexico

chapter 11

Santa Fe: Desperate Spiritual Outlaws

We rise early, say goodbye to our gentle proprietor, a man who must wonder what twist of fate assigned him to a life sentence in this glowing tombstone, and hit the road. Route 66... never imagined it could seem so sad. Chuck Berry, The Rolling Stones and Van Morrison all sang its praises, suggested a path to glory, the supreme American highway. Before them John Steinbeck celebrated the great unwashed taking to Route 66 in *The Grapes of Wrath*: '*and they come into 66 from the tributary side roads, from the wagon tracks and the rutted country roads, 66 is the mother road, the road of flight.*' Now 66 is a ruin, a highway to hell, the desperate and the defeated clinging to the road's frayed pockets.

We head back on to Interstate 40 and signs loom out of the grey morning haze announcing Albuquerque's up around the bend. Lee notes a road sign detailing the distance to Tucumcari and I recall a trucking song, 'Willin'', where Lowell George sang '*I've been from Tucson to Tucumcari.*'

'You've been to Tucson and we are kind of heading to Tucumcari,' Lee announces, 'so that's our song.'

I quote the line where Lowell sings '*I had my head stoved in*' and Lee laughs, asks, 'Did you see that guy's eyes? Straight loco! A crystal meth freak if I've ever seen one.' Agreed, one scary cat. 'Yeah,' adds Lee, shaking his head in disbelief that we got to leave Grants intact, 'towns like that, they just breed psychotic mutants.'

What is it with meth? Having cut a swathe through the Southwest for more than a decade now, crystal appears to be gaining in popularity. If largely ignored in the UK – crack cocaine being the preferred high – I'm aware of meth's terrible legacy after biker gangs introduced crystal into early-nineties New Zealand, a surge in violent crime following. And here, in the raw-ruined Southwest, is where meth first found a congregation intent on following its creed of *no-sleep-no-pain-ultra-violence*. A familiar black and white poster hangs in public buildings and, occasionally, shops and bars, displaying a series of mugshots of a lantern-jawed blonde woman taken over a period of five years. In the first photo she's cold-eyed, tough, but handsome, attentive. By photo six she's a horror show: cheeks sunken, eyes glassy, teeth rotten, skin tarpaper, stinking of the grave. The model's a woman regularly busted for dealing/using meth; as she demonstrates, the shit chews through you faster than cancer, eats speedfreaks alive.

We drive on, through the vast open spaces where few appear to live, an ancient land so bereft of mineral wealth that the white man left it for Indians. We're obviously now in urban Indian country as every few kilometres there's another casino sign (Sky City Casino Hotel, Dancing Eagle Casino, Route 66 Casino) and big digital billboards flash messages – *Come Play Your Favourite Slots, High Stakes Poker, Cowboy Buffet, Liberal Blackjack* – designed to entice drivers off the road. Native gambling was legalised with the Gaming Act in 1988 and since then has proved a spectacular earner for casino operators and the Native tribes who agree to allow casinos on reservations: Indian casinos pulled in a combined revenue of $19.4 billion in 2004 with tribal members getting a share of casino profits. I'd heard Radmilla discussing the Navajo's possible casino at the powwow and a tall leathery man, black hair falling way down his back, mused 'after the land rush and the gold rush comes the gaming rush. It's all aimed at creating corruption and animosity among Native Americans. The Gaming Act is just another act of Congressional genocide.'

Road signs warn: *'Loose gravel, high winds, ten percent grade – every hazard known to man is here.'* Another sign: *'Do Not Pick Up Hitch Hikers – Illegal By State Law.'* Thing is, almost no one but the homeless and the wild hitch these days. Everyone's scared of everyone. But making hitching illegal; American freedoms just keep getting squeezed. We hit Albuquerque as morning sun kisses this grey city awake. Billboards advertising a Gathering of Tribal Nations pepper the highway. Wasn't Bo Diddley, inventor of rock's most primal groove, once a sheriff in Albuquerque? *Hey, Bo Diddley!* I heard good things about Albuquerque, New Mexico's largest city, when a local band called Hazeldine released *Where Bees Fly,* the best album to come out of the 'alt.country' movement, in 1998. Hazeldine, fronted by three women, played a raw, loose, very soulful country grunge. Championed by the likes of me, they were then signed by Universal; the resulting album found them cleaning up the sound and losing their spirit. As we drive through Albuquerque I wonder whether the ex-Hazeldine members are tucked in beds near by, dreaming of the days when they rocked capitals from London to Zagreb.

Boxed in by Mac trucks I get nervous and insist we take the 25 north. The Sangre de Cristo Mountains loom in front of us, the land around us raw, tough, lacking lyricism; even the scrub resembles Dick Cheney: nasty, brutish, dour. Lee, a seriously lapsed Catholic, starts reminiscing about the properties of Christ's blood but admits the Hispanics have it all over the Irish when it comes to getting a baroque groove on God. Traffic's dense and

Ceremony: Jemez pueblo, 1891

we're in no hurry so detour on to the 550 then take the 4, a back-country road, winding and bobbing through hills until at the bottom of a valley we come upon Jemez Pueblo, a small Native settlement. Lee brakes hard – a sign advertises tax-free cigarettes! – leaps out and bangs on the front door of a modest house. The door opens and there stands a bemused-looking Native woman, mid-forties, smiling eyes, wearing sweats. 'Looks like you could use a cigarette,' she says to Lee, and welcomes us into the tiny shop she's built in what might be, for most Americans, a poky bathroom. Skydancer is the brand she sells and they retail at $1.29 a pack. Being made on a reservation in New York State by Iriquois (Mohawks to most) and sold here by the Jemez tribe means they're tax free under some Byzantine US law. Lee asks whether Skydancers are a good smoke and she shakes her head and says sagely, 'Sorry, no idea. I don't smoke.' Lee buys a pack and steps outside for a taste.

I purchase good filter coffee and Ms Smiling Eyes explains Jemez Pueblo is an independent sovereign nation with a government and tribal court system. I try to recall a Dine expression learnt while with Radmilla and she chuckles and says, 'We speak Towa here. Jemez is the only place in the world that speaks Towa. It's an oral language because tribal lore maintains it cannot be written so outsiders can't learn it.' Well, a secret language only spoken in this pueblo! Lee returns, buys a carton and we say 'thank you, ma'am' and she smiles with her eyes, fabulous eyes full of merriment and good cheer. On we cruise, admiring rectangular mud buildings, their compact, cubist flavour and the valley's lush vegetation suggesting a place of strong spirit. Stopping for gas, I purchase the *Albuquerque Journal*. Headlines are 'Majority Supports Banning Cockfights' and 'Crystal Meth Lab Busted'. Louisiana and New Mexico are the only two states in the US that allow cockfighting – the 'sport' is hugely popular among Hispanics – and New Mexico is debating a ban. As for the meth lab, the science involved in creating the toxic high is highly combustible: build a lab within proximity of other citizens and you can be charged under terrorism edicts.

The road curves like a serpent as we sweep through the valley floor, surrounded by dense scrub and tangled trees, luxury houses on hilltops representing the new New Mexico. Pine trees, rock formations named Battleship Rock, the Sisters of the Precious Blood Convent, cemeteries, small gatherings of pueblos, those under construction employing a grid formation of timber and mud brick, children playing in the sun, Natives with hair so black it shimmers, red sandstone mesas, road rising, road falling and then, finally and suddenly, we're there, Bandelier National Monument, home to what remains of an ancient Native pueblo. There's a sign saying access closed until afternoon so Lee spins the wheel and we're back on the 4, drifting into Los Alamos, a spooky small town of sheds and very high security. This is where US plutonium's stockpiled; fittingly as Los Alamos National Laboratory was home to the Manhattan Project, whose director, Robert Oppenheimer, oversaw production of the bomb that flattened Hiroshima, misquoting the Bhagavad Gita verse as *'I am become death, destroyer of worlds'*. Lee suggests lunch and I ask what he fancies: contaminated chilli, radioactive ribs or H-bomb hamburgers? Ha ha, buddy, he says, spins the wheel and out of Los Alamos we roar.

Less than an hour later we're entering Santa Fe, the oldest capital city in the USA, and a stucco wonderland erupts in front of us. Every goddam building is dung brown and cube shaped. Initially, this appears a charm offensive, these stucco suburbs standing in contrast to the poverty of much of rural New Mexico, but central Santa Fe, glutted with art galleries selling Native jewellery and junk paintings, is stucco *in extremis*: even the fast-food joints hover in stucco shells. Lee and I rapidly agree: *we loathe Santa Fe*. Not that the city need worry, wealthy Americans flock here, splurging on silver, crystals, ashrams, imitation Georgia O'Keeffes, enchanted by whatever New Age wisdom seemingly wells from this plaster disaster. Indeed, it's hard to believe Santa Fe was once a Wild West town; today any real cowboy would be ticketed by the omnipresent cops and told to get out of town. Lee, I say, let's get the hell outta here. He nods,

High plains drifter: Kell
Robertson

mutters something about Atlantic City at least being honest in its
hustle, and we point the car at the 25 then slip off on to the 14
and find ourselves on the old Route 66, a long, straight and dry
road littered with strip clubs, fast-food joints and second-hand
auto dealers. And still the damn stucco façade remains. A mean
South-west wind blows long and hard and Lee laughs as a mess of
Styrofoam cups and newspaper pages, dust and leaves, skip across
the road, smothering the windscreen. 'Hubcaps flying… shingles
flying,' he says, 'a wild ride outta Santa Fe.'

We follow the 14 and then turn off on to the 45. In the country
now, hard, baked land, not much growing, not many people
wanting to live in the rolling plains outside Santa Fe. We drive
past the Lone Dude Stone Store and a bleak prison. 'What's out
here?' asks Lee. 'An old cowboy poet and country singer called
Kell Robertson,' I explain. 'I want to talk to him about the South-
west.' We take the Saltbush Road turn-off and then we're on a
gravel road and I think of Percy Sledge singing 'True Love Travels
a Gravel Road' for no good reason other than it is a great song
and this certainly is one loose gravel road. Down a driveway to a
small house, kit-set style. We encounter a long-haired man with
the red skin of those who never tan, paint up to his elbows. I ask
for Kell Robertson and he directs us along a garden path towards
a clearing where a large chicken coop stands. In the mud out front
there are several chooks. I bang on the coop's door and a man, no
feathers attached, comes out.

He's a small fellow, slightly hunched, wearing old boots and trousers too big for him and a cotton work shirt and a Stetson, grey ponytail falling across his shoulders. Kell's face, well, it's a face of the West: worn and well-boiled, mapped with lines and wrinkles, a prominent nose and mirthful eyes that meet my gaze, look right into me, eyes that have seen much and lived long. 'Howdy,' he says. 'Come on into the coop.' Inside is a cramped, if not disagreeable, residence: one small room hosts a bed, clothing, guitar, hotplate and assorted personal items while the small entrance area holds a bookshelf, desk, ghetto blaster, typewriter, a couple of chairs. Every item is coated in South-west dust. Introductions are made and Kell Robertson (seventy-five, poet, country singer, cowboy) gestures for us to sit. Lee opens a six-pack of pale ale and passes a bottle to Kell. Lee then lights a Skydancer and Kell, who's rolling loose tobacco wrapped in newspaper, asks for one. 'I'm so poor I can't afford to buy real cigarettes,' says Kell, 'so I 'preciate it when I get to smoke one.' Lee flips him the pack, says, 'Keep it,' an offering to a man whose poems, charcoal black and pulsing with wise blood, rank among the finest US verse of the last half century. Self-educated and never aligned to any poetry movement/school, Robertson's ignored by those who curate modern American poetry. 'What I've managed to read of yours,' I say by way of breaking ice, 'is as good as American poetry gets.' 'I 'preciate that, son,' says Kell, puffing on a Skydancer. The first Kell poem I came across was called 'Song'. Mention this to Kell and he recites it.

SONG
Up in the mountains, an afternoon
of good whiskey and country music
and John said we should just keep going
and ride right on down into Mexico.
You called us a couple of old fools
but chorded alright on the turnaround
even if you did forget the words.
I suppose it's a matter of genuine

Ride the hard land

folk art and wonder when the women
were asleep and we killed the whiskey
in the kitchen, staggering out into
the snow to piss hollering into the wind
warcries for dreams to be fought,
songs as impossible as the light
when the sun came up on all that snow.

We clap and Kell draws deep on his cigarette. 'Song' is, I suggest, one of his more optimistic poems, Robertson's writing often involving desperate poverty, casual violence, sour cowboy myths, bus station blues, homages to associates who ended up marrying ranchers or dying of exposure or getting their guts cut up in a barroom brawl, a hardscrabble life lived with much reflection but little remorse. Admittedly, he finds joy and camaraderie in this big-sky land and few can match him in expressing the tangible pleasures of a cigarette, that last shot of whiskey, the can of pork and beans warmed over a roadside fire, of song and those who sang. The voice of the hobo, the hired hand, the renegade, is present in his poetry. Lawrence Ferlinghetti described Kell as 'one fine cowboy poet, worth a dozen New York poetasters'. Yes, says Kell, he's punched cows but also run guns to Mexico, managed a hotel, worked a carnie ('I was Mephisto the Magician. We gave a good show'), sold insurance, washed dishes, been a soldier: why the 'cowboy poet' tag? 'Been an outlaw all my life,' he says, 'so call me an outlaw poet. Or the wild dog of poetry. Cowboy poets tend to write rhyming poems 'bout their horses. I sure as hell don't.'

And cowboys live on ranches, not in chicken coops.

'A friend of mine who lived here got tired of me calling him up at three a.m. saying I was homeless at the bus station so got me to live in this chicken shack he converted into a house. It's a mess but it's all right. All the women I been with are dead. So I sit up here and write poems and listen to cassettes and get by. I've been singing since I was a kid but never thought about doing anything with the songs. Would tape them on a boom box and send them to friends and for my seventieth some kids got them put on to CD so now I've got CDs to sell. On a recent tour we drove from here to Denver, to Kansas, to Indiana, to Akron, to Chicago, to Minneapolis, to Ohio – lived in the car for thirty days, playing coffee houses, selling books, CDs, fucking tough thirty days. Don't know how I made it to this age – I've done as much drugs and alcohol as anyone. Guess only the good die young.'

Kell chuckles, a dry survivor's laugh, talks of growing up on his grandparents' Kansas farm, how his stepfather, a rounder and gambler, disliked Kell's tendency to read books so 'threw a pistol on the floor and said "go for that or get out" so I got out at thirteen. Been on the road ever since.' A couple of marriages, five daughters, time in Mexico and Texas and Arizona and San Francisco, but here's where he wants his bones to rest and, sure, Santa Fe is a tourist town but 'it's the one place where you can go in at Tuesday at noon, meet all the old timers, get drunk – Mexicans, niggers, honkies – at the Cowgirl Hall of Fame on Guadalupe Street. The last time I played with Townes Van Zandt was there', says Kell, and it soon turns out that he was not only tight with the late TVZ but something of a Zelig figure, friendly with Janis Joplin, Sam Peckinpah, Lenny Bruce, Lightnin' Hopkins, Jack Kerouac, Charles Bukowski.

'Met Sam in Montana. I was punching cows. Got drunk with him for four days and at the end of that bender he said, 'I'm making a movie, Kell, come with me.' Went to these little towns in Mexico, drinking, getting stoned, banging whores. Took him six months to shoot. Took one and a half months to shoot the first scene. The actor who was playing the gang member who gets blinded during the initial bank hold-up quit before he had his big scene. Called Sam an asshole. Which was true. But he was, on his good days, a great guy. So we're in Mexico and Sam can't wait for another actor and he knows I can ride a horse so he says to me, 'Kell, you're about the same size as that asshole. Do it and I'll pay you five hundred dollars.' I said, 'Does that make me an actor?' He said, 'No, Kell, you're a poet. Don't become one of those Hollywood fruits.' So my scene's where I fall off the horse and I say, 'I can ride, Mr Bishop, I can ride. [pause] I can't ride. *Shoot me.*'

Kell's recital makes me think he could have joined Slim Pickens as a cowboy character actor. But Peckinpah was right: he has the soul of a poet and in such collections as *A Horse Called Desperation*, *The Leveling Wind*, *Bear Crossing*, *Honky-tonk Cantos* and *All the Bar Room Poetry Can't Mend This Heart of Mine, Dear* he's chiselled out verse infused with the dust and blood of the South-west. He's also a country singer and songwriter. Not that he ever chased a deal; instead music's an extension of the poetry. I ask to hear either of his two self-produced CDs: *Cool & Dark* and *When You Come Down from the Mountain*. He sifts through the mess, finds one, sticks it on his ghetto blaster. The songs are wry, lyrical, his voice equal parts croak and rodeo yelp. Reminds me of the old honky-tonk singers, I say, Hank and Lefty.

'I saw Hank Williams on June twenty-sixth 1952, in Corinth, Mississippi. He was on the bill with Ray Price, Red Foley, Kitty Wells and a girl they were calling "an up and coming country singer", Patsy Cline. Imagine that for one buck and a quarter! I took my mom along to see him. It was a big show, he came out drunk, knocked down the mic then started to sing "I'm So Lonesome I Could Cry". The whole auditorium went silent. And I thought, "Damn. Imagine if I could do that!" Hank, Milton and Shelley were my heroes and I decided back then life is not worth it if I can't write poetry and sing songs and drink whiskey. It's like some warped priesthood, a holy grail for me with a cup of cheap muscatel. See, I'm just part of one long song that has kept going through time. Any creative artist who is not just trying to be successful is. I'm singing the same song as Ugh and Org when they lived in a cave. Hank was an ignorant hillbilly with little education who read comic books. But he was a genius, he touched people in a way few ever can. That's the power of the blues. T. S. Eliot's best poems were blues songs. I used to do Prufrock with an electric blues band.'

A long sojourn in sixties San Francisco allows Kell to recall Frisco's glory days. 'North Beach was an interesting scene. Worked on *Rolling Stone* in the early days. Friends with Oscar Zeta Acosta. He was a good writer, better than Hunter S. Thompson. Thompson ripped him off for a considerable sum. I'd met Janis Joplin back in Port Arthur; she took guitar lessons from a friend of mine. We backed her one night in a coffee house. She needed someone who could play three-chord blues, not this twelve-bar shit. We were friends in San Francisco and she told me, "Kell, get in a rock band!" "No, I hate that electric rock shit. Gimme Ernest Tubb, Lefty Frizzell." I kick myself for not getting on that now – I made the wrong decision money-wise.'

I mention to Kell how we're heading to Texas and I'm hoping to meet Lydia Mendoza, queen of Tejano music. He recalls seeing her sing in the 1950s.

'I don't have any Lydia recordings,' says Kell, 'but I love Mexican music.' He pulls out his CD, throws another in and lush Spanish flows forth. 'That's Lola Beltran, she's a contemporary of Lydia's although long passed from this world. Listen to how she drops in on a note. Sings like Charlie Parker or Beethoven. Mexicans are not afraid to put emotion in a song. That's why Janis was so good. Miguel Osever Mejas said, "A good Mexican singer can get teardrops in their voice," and that's true of Lola and Lydia.'

The beers are finished and Lee, having spied a bottle of bourbon, asks whether he can have a nip. Kell agrees and soon the bottle's being passed, as Kell puts it, 'mano a mano'. I'm not averse to bourbon but want to be waking up in a Texas motel tomorrow, not a Santa Fe chicken coop, so when the bottle comes my way I fake a slug and pass it on, letting Lee and Kell get merry. Kell quotes Thomas Hornsby Ferril's verse then gives a great recitation of 'The Old Man Goes Home', a poem he wrote about returning to the site of his grandparents' farm only to find it now buried beneath shops and a car park. Kell reads well, dry and tough but tender on 'Under all this asphalt and concrete/plastic and steel, I learned to cut/a calf, learned to drive a team of horses/learned to work in this earth'. The poem's final line finds him meditating on what's replaced the farm and declaring 'all I can see is what we've lost'.

Applause. Kell grins, grabs the bourbon, sucks on it. 'What,' I ask, 'have we lost?'

'Innocence. The sense of wonder. Spirituality. We've lost an awful lot. The cheap beads they once gave the savages for land, well, it's the same thing now with technology: iPods and cell phones and laptops... it's the same old trickery, taking us away from our animal instincts, from who we are.'

Kell takes another hit of bourbon.

'America's getting worse. No healthcare 'less you got insurance. A poor man like me, I just gotta ride it out when I get ill. Bush managed to push this country back five hundred years. Look at New Orleans, goddam! Everyone's scared. He's committed impeachable offences so why isn't he on trial? In jail. Lied to the nation and they still want to believe him. We have the constitution and he and his cronies tore it up. I'm glad I'm an old guy. If I was young I'd have to do some revolutionary stuff.'

I ask whether Kell's ever read Randolph Bourne. He hasn't. OK: Bourne was a progressive writer best known for his essays, especially 'War is the Health of the State'. During the First World War American progressives split into pro- and anti-war factions. Bourne took issue with the concept of using the war as a tool with which to 'spread democracy', arguing America was using democracy as an ends to justify the war yet democracy itself was never examined. He also argued the USA should accommodate immigrant cultures into a *'cosmopolitan America'* instead of forcing immigrants to assimilate to Anglophile culture. Bourne wrote, *'One keeps healthy in wartime not by a series of religious and political consolations that something good is coming out of it all, but by a vigorous assertion of values in which war has no part.'* 'Damn straight that's true,' says Kell. Bourne also wrote: *'Now, while everything that is respectable in America seems to be putting its effort, with a sort of joyful perversity, into the technique of destruction, are there no desperate spiritual outlaws with a lust to create?'*

Kell chuckles, says 'hell yes' and asks me to write Bourne's name down. He's animated, enjoying the company, an audience, but now feeling the bourbon, beginning to repeat stories, unable to light cigarettes, propping himself up on his elbow. I suggest the highway's calling and Kell sours. 'Can't believe you're leaving,' he snarls. 'Wish you'd never come here.' We shout 'adios' to Kell and he sends curses after us.

WALTZ ACROSS TEXAS

Truth or Consequences, Austin, San Antonio, Gruene

Texas is *big*.

Joe Cummings

The thirties and forties showed more clearly than before the dilemma of working people in the United States. The system responded to workers' rebellions by finding new forms of control – internal control by their own organisations as well as outside control by law and force. But along with these new controls came new concessions. These concessions didn't solve basic problems; for many people they solved nothing. But they helped enough people to create an atmosphere of progress and improvement, to restore faith in the system.

Howard Zinn

Rock the house: hillbilly boogie, North Carolina, 1939

chapter 12

Truth or Consequences:
American Death Trip

Back on gravel roads and then we're riding the Turquoise Trail – an ancient, winding road that carves through the hills, dipping into ghostly mining towns, rolling across paths Civil War soldiers, Kit Carson's subjugated Navajo, Billy the Kid and countless others used – night so dark I'm steering by moonlight, a fat old full moon helping us escape. We hit Interstate 40, rejoining the 25 south and here we stop for Taco Bell, served by Rosa, surely not much older than nineteen but work wearing around her eyes. On the road again and Lee tips his seat back, descends into a bourbon stupor. I find a Mexican radio station for company and soon the sound of high voices, voices with teardrops in them, fills the car, singing of love and *narcocorrido* soldiers. The traffic thins and I push the Hyundai to ninety, hear the engine purr, digging the rush while Lee snores. The emptiness of the road makes driving a pleasure: last night's gladiatorial Mac dodgems are a thing of the past, tonight we rip forward, eyes on the prize, *onwards onwards onwards*. As the road empties a woman's voice elicits big, beautiful painful vowels – *is Lola Beltran sharing the ride?* – a chanteuse for those rushing towards Texas, all flowing, all beautiful.

The American highway once stood as a key to Kerouac's kicks, offering new frontiers and impossible freedoms; these days it's a heavy road that too many spend too much time on. These days, also, the consequences of burning petroleum products are beginning to haunt: climate change, those three syllables successive US administrations refuse to recognise, is upon us because of the flights we take, the cars we drive. In London I cycle. But to make this journey, well, that's not possible. For now the car remains king in the USA, the nation torn up and sluiced with lanes of tarmac so combustion engines can roll forth. Not that I'm about to sweat on it: foot down, stretched out, staring at destiny in the headlights' glare, this highway's mine, yes, this highway's mine. Only on late, late American nights do you taste life like this, the road wide open and empty and inviting you to engage, to flow, to roar down it in search of the last frontier. And so we do, car rolling smooth and fluid, no one in front of us, none coming from behind, a four-wheel blur.

I relax my grip on the wheel, listen to those loving Spanish tongues, let the night whistle around me, certain this is the territory Juan de Oñate, a Spaniard born in Mexico and desperate to make his fortune, entered in 1598 leading four hundred European men and an unknown number of Indians, women and children (and some seven thousand cattle), searching for the mystical Seven Golden Cities of Cibola. Crossing what was the proscribed border of Mexico around where the city of El Paso now sits, Oñate called the land New Mexico and proclaimed himself its governor, then began a long trek north through the most severe ninety miles of desert found between Mexico City and what is now known as Santa Fe. Oñate wrote that his group suffered for lack of water until an expedition dog appeared with muddy paws. The travellers followed the dog to water, where animals and people slaked their thirst. Known from then on as Los Charcos del Perillo – *the pools of the little dog* – it became a '*paraje*' (camping place) where caravans watered, preparing for the harsh trip ahead. After three days, Oñate reached the river near present-day San Marcial. Pueblo dwellers of the village Teipana showed compassion to these sunburnt strangers. Oñate promptly christened the village Socorro (*Help*). The kindness Native pueblo dwellers showed to the colonialists was soon to be regretted as Oñate began enslaving them. After a failed uprising of Natives at Acoma Pueblo, Oñate demanded the amputation of the right foot on all males aged twenty-five and over. Not that such cruelty could vanquish Native spirit: in 1675 a Spanish campaign across New Mexico to destroy ceremonial objects fired the only successful Native revolt in North American history, pushing thousands of colonists back south, over eight hundred dying as they fled across the deserts. Since then this desert's been called Jornada del Muerto – *Journey of the Dead Man* – and it was here that the scientists of Los Alamos chose to detonate the first atom bomb in 1945. *Think about it*: I'm cruising through borderlands, American death-trip turf, accompanied by Mexican voices and fresh early-hours air.

A town called Truth or Consequences looms in the distance. My eyes are leaking, the long-distance stare that comes with driving for too many hours, and figure any town with a name like that deserves our custom. *Truth or Consequences*: I imagine it being a code to live by for many of the individuals I've met so far on this journey. We swing off the 25 and the first sign says *White Sands Missile Range* and then there's a Super 8 Motel, glowing heavenly up front. I pull up, jump out, run in and the receptionist (name tag Star) says, 'My, haven't you been driving for a long time?'

'It shows, huh?'

'Eyes like a werewolf.'

As the werewolf's credit card details work their way through cyberspace Star mentions she shifted here from Atlantic City as she's allergic to damp. And how her husband has a bipolar disposition but putting him on lithium was a mistake. Staring for hours at an illuminated highway has strained eyes and levelled mind so I can barely take this in. *Lithium? Sounds good to me! Got any under the counter?* Payment through, I grab room key, return to car, kick Lee awake. He groans. 'Bro,' I say, 'a bed, rather than a car seat, is awaiting your bulk.'

Thought I'd sleep for ever but impulse has me up early. I drink the lobby's feeble coffee and Cheryl, this morning's receptionist, gets flirty, cooing about the wonders of Truth or Consequences. Turns out the town doesn't owe its name to biblical prophecy or a stoic explorer or even Los Alamos' Vedas-quoting scientists. The prosaic truth revolves around a popular 1950s radio show whose host offered a competition to find a town that would change its name to that of the show: New Mexico's Hot Springs won, hoping the name-change publicity would consequently lure tourists to this town of natural mineral baths. 'Y'all look like you could use a good soak,' says Cheryl with a wink. Agreed. But my senses are picking up on a barely audible hum in the background: *highway's calling.*

Lee's driving, claiming he slept well in car and motel. I'm definitely jaded, the rush towards Austin starting to wear. I stare into the distance where a long, rolling spine of mountains, soft pink-blonde-grey tones running through them, appears to hover. Eyes obviously still burnt from last night's expedition. Flip through the radio dial: country stations play flabby ballads while the classic rock stations appear to have The Cars' 'Just What I Needed' on auto-play. Lee's requested 'anything as long as it's in English' but the radio's blandness finds us agreeing on silence. Which is a national tragedy as the Texas–Mexico border just south of here once hosted border radio stations blasting country and blues, R & B and tejano, zydeco and jazz, across the USA. These stations were allowed by the Mexican government to far exceed the 50,000-watt maximum for US stations: XERA, launched by notorious quack and Nazi sympathizer 'Doc' Brinkley in 1935, had 500,000 watts and could be heard, on a good night, as far as Alaska, Australia and the Mediterranean basin. All border stations started with an X: '*hillbilly-Jesus-country-blues,*' sang ZZ Top on 'Heard it on the X'. Jim Morrison also saluted border radio on 'Texas Radio and the Big Beat' ('*Comes out of the Virginia swamps/Cool and slow with plenty of precision/With a back beat narrow and hard to master*').

Those wild sounds – unfathomable, *unimaginable*, in white-bread, picket-fence, Eisenhower/Nixon America – were the product of alligator hunters and crawfishermen, sharecroppers and railroad hobos, religious zealots and those whose tongues spoke Spanish and Creole and Native dialects, artisans who cooked up a great gumbo of regional flavours. Suburban brats like Gibbons and Morrison listened hard, paying attention to wired DJs like Wolfman Jack ('*I wancha to lay hands on ya radio, lay back wid me and squeeze my knobs. We gonna feel it tonite! Ooooooowwwwwwooooo!*'). The toughest music ever made burst forth on shows sponsored by snake-oil salesmen and preachers intent on separating poor Americans from their wages (sex, health and religion were the border blasters' currency).

Rules were few, X stations operating as sonic pirates, invading North America with the sounds of a genuine underground, all kinds of skullduggery being invoked across borders. Independent broadcasting was slain in 1996 with the wretched Telecommunications Act; the Clinton administration allowed corporations to purchase as many radio stations as they wished, public service eschewed for maximum profit: today a bland, corporate agenda owns America's airwaves. Clear Channel Communications (a Texas corporation that owns 1200 radio stations, forty TV stations and many thousands of billboards, and maintains close ties with Bush family business interests) has aggressively promoted a policy of running canned material on stations across the USA, its policy embracing extreme right-wing shock-jock Rush Limbaugh and a corporate music agenda: now you can drive across America and hear the same dozen songs over and over. Last night's station? We were picking up on a Mexican radio station with a good night-time signal. I gripe on this to Lee and he recalls hearing about a city in North Dakota that suffered a train derailment a few years back. 'The train was carrying ammonia so real poisonous and the police said "we've got to let the whole community know to stay inside" and went to the radio stations to announce this immediately. Found the doors all locked: they were owned by Clear Channel so broadcasting from a thousand miles away.'

We cross the New Mexico–Texas border. A big bronze star stands aloft. The smell of cattle fills the air. *Don't Mess with Texas*, states a road sign. Surrounding land stretches towards the horizon. Some fields grow crops, irrigated by the Rio Grande, home to assortments of trailer homes and prefabs. Much of the land is scrubby, dusty. Don't know if I expected Texas to look

Flatlanders: dirt
farming, Texas

somehow different but feel disappointed that everything's so, well, flat. To our right sits El Paso, a rough, dusty-looking city built across small hills. Then Patriot Freeway 54 – a labyrinth of flyovers – is upon us, a huge weave of eight-lane highway, Texan wide and patriot dense, a concrete wave, sluicing through the city. The highway's bordered by billboards – fastest auto repairs, best-value motels and litigious law firms ('*I Sue Drunk Drivers & Negligent 18 Wheelers*') – and fibreglass flags. A billboard for Romans 13.9, '*Love thy neighbour as thou loves one self*', sits next to an advertisement for Adult Mega-Store.

There's nothing here commanding us to stop but I'm tempted to turn off the highway and drive through raw, angry El Paso and cross into Mexico. Then again, maybe Ciudad Juarez, the Mexican city that's forever El Paso's distressed, unloved sister, is not the best place to begin a Latin odyssey: this city of femicide (370 women murdered and 400 reportedly 'missing' by February 2005) appears engulfed by a wave of psychotic misogyny, hosting competing packs of serial killers. Juarez is a city of factories, factories set up by US business interests to exploit Mexico's cheap, unprotected labour and thus attracting poor women from across Mexico. And the homicidal hurricane engulfing this city? All kinds of theories speculate on why so many women die brutally in Juarez, but with 97 per cent of Mexican murders going unsolved it appears there's little chance of this being (re)solved. How many of those murdered dreamed of crossing the borderline and enjoying 'the good life' supposedly available here?

We drive on through the flatlands – fields of dust, fields of crops – get stuck behind a convoy of trucks, lane dancing; freight trains rumble south, rumble north. Nothing appears to grow and no one lives here. Flashing lights and a sign stating all vehicles must exit. The highway becomes one lane. Inspection station. We're waved through by a Texas Ranger. A truck in front of us has '*I Support Our Troops and President George W. Bush. God Bless America*' stencilled on its rear door. Another has mudflaps of Old Glory and the statement '*These Colors Don't Run*'. Looks like we're also not going to run: gas tank's near empty again. I'm too tired to care, feelings of futility overcoming what should be excitement that we're on the main line to Austin. Lee grumbles and growls, angry that we didn't refill when stopped for McDonald's. I counter by blaming the junk food – it kills common sense – and we trundle on, scorched by hard Texas sun, expecting to hear a horrible clunk. Then, *hey*, a Phillips 66 station appears, situated off the highway, moored among desolate flatlands.

As we pull in a carload of young Japanese are cleaning their car, very fresh looking in contrast to our dishevelled appearance. The woman running the station sits surrounded by autographed B & W promo photos of entertainers (country, Mexican, rappers); tour buses heading to and from Austin obviously stop here. The station's coin phone swallows my quarters yet refuses to work. *Goddam, I hate the US phone system!* I start bashing the phone till Lee suggests I could end up spending tonight not in an Austin honky-tonk bar but behind the bars of a county jail. Sounds like a Tom T. Hall song and not one I wish to experience. We roll onwards, the landscape parched and unforgiving, the highway slicing through toadstool-shaped clay hills. Texas is the biggest state outside Alaska and, so far, visually the dullest. Wispy clouds float overhead. The sun sits high, a tangerine orb, as brutal and unforgiving as the Texan in the White House. Condors feed on roadkill and cops feed on cars, hiding in shady spots, and – *bam!* – they've got the Japanese who were at the gas station. Evening falls as we turn off the 10 and on to the 290, passing through Fredericksburg with its German beer garden and Lutheran church. *'Tell Your Problem'*, reads a church billboard. *'How Big Is Your God?'* reads another. And then – *finally! After twelve hours' solid driving with only occasional breaks. Finally!* – we're approaching the outskirts of Austin.

Slowly work our way towards central Austin until we find ourselves on Burnet Road, and we're trying to find number 5434. All appears to be used-car lots or small office blocks and then – *there it is!* Ginny's is a small A-frame building notable from the outside only for a large set of long steer horns prominent above the entrance. We park and run in, desperate to escape the Hyundai's sticky seats, the numbing Texan landscape. Ginny's is that now rare venue: an urban honky-tonk. Up until the 1980s pretty much every white, working-class American neighbourhood (in the South) had a honky-tonk: a bar with a hardwood floor for dancers. *Honky-tonk*, one of those uniquely American expressions, perfectly musical in its three rolling syllables with its dry 'o' and high 'y', a term that conjures up all kinds of wild, white-boy wizardry. Honky-tonks were once declared buckets of blood, skull orchards, by the cops and doctors who had to deal with the nightly carnage: Hank Williams employed Cannonball Nichols, a pro wrestler, as bassist, to ensure his safety. But as the children of the Southern rednecks – so called because their necks were sunburned and rubbed raw by the stiff cotton collars worn while working – took to rock and disco while Nashville reshaped country music as a beige, ersatz suburban soundtrack, honky-tonk culture faded.

Ginny's consists of a long bar bracketed by a pool table and a minuscule dance floor. In between are a dozen or so Formica tables. The music emanates from Dale Watson and his Lone Stars. There's no stage; while I can hear Dale – voice smooth, guitar ringing – I can't see him, obscured as he is by couples dancing two-step, eloquently avoiding crashing into one another. Dale sings honky-tonk standards and his own songs, which have an eloquent, timeless feel, while the clink of beer bottles and the murmur of voices ripple and feed into the music. We start chugging Lone Star, the long day's drive having given us a thirst, admiring the barmaid – a long, tall woman with purple hair and one arm sleeved in tattoos – and talking to the Texans who pack this place. Ginny, a stoic, grey-haired matriarch, shoulders her way through the crowd, collecting empties, upturned Stetson in hand, obliging punters to drop dollar bills. 'For the band,' she says, and no one refuses. I get invited to learn how to two-step by Jenna and am soon moving among bodies, pulled this way and that by a steel guitar's liquid musical tongue. An Asian beauty, who must have been poured into her Levi's, is tonight's honky-tonk queen, taking turns with various Stetson-wearing males to spin across the dance floor. And when she's exhausted the men she teams up with the barmaid, who bends low and off they move, hips snapping to 'Fox on the Run'.

Photos of players and patrons decorate walls and tables. Fans blow from corners but heat and smoke overpower everything. I request a pale ale and get told, 'You have the choice of Lone Star or Lone Star.' Dale even advertises the state brew between

Honky-tonk heaven: Dale Watson at work, Austin, TX, 2006

songs. Unfortunately, it's a pretty mediocre lager. Still, Ginny's is the kind of joint where the walls sweat so Lone Star serves its purpose. Dale's guitar is covered with quarters, nickels, dimes. He strokes it and sends forth a volley of tender, tough notes. Jenna mentions to Dale there's a Kiwi on the dance floor and he asks 'where 'bout in New Zealand?' 'Auckland.' 'OK, I've played Auckland.' He smiles a sad smile and starts picking the introduction to 'Country My Ass', his anti-Nashville anthem. 'They always liked this one in Auckland,' he says, and by the time he hits the chorus all of Ginny's is chanting along with him. When his anthem's over everyone cheers and Dale offers a quizzical smile – aware the honky-tonk country music he was raised on and plays so well is now an endangered sound – then announces a break.

I navigate to an American rarity – a grotty toilet – then wander outside. Dale's leaning against a beautifully maintained Indian motorbike, chatting with friends. He's a small, compact man, heavily tattooed, mid-forties, life on the road lending grey to his hair and lines to his face. I wander over and introduce myself as both the evening's Kiwi and the writer who contacted him from London. He considers this, says it's an agreeable combination, then suggests I might as well start firing questions now. I'm greasy as hell and full of Lone Star but possess notebook, pen and a head full of country music: what shaped Dale Watson, Country Singer?

'Born in Alabama, raised in Pasadena, Texas. My father's from Hazard, Kentucky, and was in the Marines. He always sang country music. My older brothers formed a band and had no one to sing so I was drafted in. We played truck stops, bars, honky-tonks. Pretty much done music ever since. Ginny's is the real thing, a genuine honky-tonk. I grew up in 'em. The first place I played when I was fifteen the band would play behind chicken wire. As a kid you could get in beer joints – ice houses, we call 'em 'cos they had to ice down the beer to keep it cold – but regular honky-tonks was where all the fighting went on. Then around 1977 music went disco and they just became pick-up joints playing pop junk. There's not too many honky-tonks left. Most of them have given way to rock 'n' roll places.

'I got signed to Curb Records and cut two singles. This was at the time when country music was very anti-anything to do with honky-tonks or drinking. Just snappy, poppy guff. One of my songs was called "You Pour it On, I Pour it Down". The reaction was "no! no! no!" There was a time I tried to leave the music. See, my dad died and at the same time I met the girl who would become my second wife and she got pregnant so I thought I should get serious so took a publishing job in Nashville and it was pitiful, paid nothing. Paid so bad I was on welfare. Working for free. That's Nashville for y'all, exploiting people who want to break into the industry. I went to LA and the music scene out there was so open. Met River Phoenix through a friend of mine and he was working on a movie, *The Thing Called Love*. He got the director to give me a job. River said he'd get me jobs in two more movies and then he went and died and there was an earthquake so I shifted back to Texas where the earth don't shake. River was great. He wasn't a drug addict but he was the type of guy who would do whatever everyone else was doing just to make them comfortable.

'I came to Austin with the idea of opening a motorcycle repair place and playing music at the weekends. Cut two albums for a label who gave me a chance. I'm grateful they were there, but angry they screwed me. Learned the hard way. Now I own the masters and cut different deals around the world. I've devoted myself to life on the road. Not just the US. Europe. Australasia. I realise I'm never going to get on country radio so I take my music to the people. Even back home in Austin I play out four or five nights a week.'

Austin's a legendary music city: why does Dale think this is so?

'Willie and Waylon made it the place to come and do your own thing. It's conductive to originality, which is rare in this state.'

What is it about honky-tonk country music that makes it, all nasal voices and weeping steel, so damn soulful?

'Country music, as I know it, is definitely the white man's blues. Back then it really defined the white working-man's experience. Just as blues defined the black man's experience. These days... these days we ain't got country and they ain't got blues. What we got is we all share the same blues. To survive as an ordinary American today is tougher than it's been for decades. 'Cept for those who've all the money.'

Time for Dale to return to work. We troop into Ginny's and order more Lone Star and Dale croons Merle Haggard's 'I'm Always on a Mountain When I Fall'. The band up the tempo, Dale's guitar dancing around the lap steel, the fiddle plays a jig and honky-tonk spirit spreads across the Long Horn Saloon. A heavily moustachioed Virginian gets up on a fast fiddle tune and performs a spectacular 'flat foot' (an Appalachian dance), arms folded tight, left leg bent, right leg straight out, bouncing across the dance floor like some mad hillbilly hobbit. When he finishes, sweat pouring from beneath his wide-brimmed hat, everyone – including the band – cheers. There's a real sense of community in the music, the musicians, the audience, an oasis of good sounds and good vibes. Dale jokes between songs, chats to patrons and sings graceful songs that hint at all the pain – two failed marriages, daughters he rarely gets to see, poverty's ever-present shadow, a beloved girlfriend killed in a car crash, overwhelming grief ('put me in the nuthouse') – he's known without ever descending into singer-songwriter exegesis. Laconic, blue, loving, happy, pissed-off, humble songs. *Country songs*. I get drunk and dance and dance and dance. Lee gets drunk and smokes and smokes and smokes. Toast one another with endless bottles of Lone Star: from LA to Austin in six days... over two thousand miles covered... *whooo-heee!* By 1 a.m. the crowd is thinning and the band relaxing, stretching out, chasing blue notes into the early morning air. By the time Ginny's winds down at 2 a.m. Jenna's long vanished, as has the honky-tonk queen, and Lee and I are too intoxicated to do anything resembling driving. Back outside and no neon 'motel' signs light up the night. We spent all damn day in the car so – *fuck it!* – we'll sleep in it too.

chapter 13

Austin: Waving at the Train

Woken by Austin's early morning humidity, I crawl into the car park that's our first Texan residence, tongue swollen and brain cloudy, desperate to pee. Lee looks like he's up for sleeping till noon, belly swelling and rumbling. 'Lee,' I say, '*Lee*. C'mon, wake up. We need coffee.' And air conditioning: it's not yet nine a.m. but my clothes are damp with sweat. By midday this city will be broiling in 100-degree heat.

Dunkin' Donuts provides breakfast and bathrooms but accommodation proves impossible to find as the Austin City Limits Music Festival – the reason Lee wanted to land here – begins today. We head out of central Austin and find a motel off the interstate with icy air conditioning and a dinky pool: the outside temperature's already so extreme swimming times hover around pre-breakfast and post-dinner. This makes Lee reconsider whether he wants to spend all day at an outdoor music festival. 'What ya got planned, buddy?' Relax a little then have a late lunch with Alejandro Escovedo. 'What da hell,' he says, 'is dat?' Alejandro, I answer, is, maybe, the finest American contemporary singer and songwriter working. 'Ain't never seen him on *Saturday Night Live*,' sneers Lee. OK, suit yourself. He flops across a bed and considers options. Kell fascinated him, a hard-drinking cowboy being exactly what he imagines poets to be. A'right, he says, tell us about this Al-eee-ban-jo dude.

Alejandro Escovedo's music meshes old and new West, Anglo and Mexican cultures, the artist both pioneer and underachiever, his shadowy legend carved out across three decades. Born 10 January 1951, just outside San Antonio, Texas, he comes from a musical family: older brothers Pete and Coke became mainstays of Californian Latin rock and jazz while his niece is funk percussionist Sheila E (a Prince consort in the eighties). Shifting to southern California when he was seven, Alejandro grew up surfing and witnessing every great rock 'n' roll band going – from Love and Buffalo Springfield to The Stooges and New York Dolls – then formed Chicano punks The Nuns (who supported The Sex Pistols at their last stand in San Francisco, January, 1978). While The Pistols imploded Escovedo set about developing his songs, voice and vision: co-founding cow-punks Rank & File, he relocated to New York, then Austin, formed True Believers and lived what fools refer to as 'the rock 'n' roll lifestyle'. The 1990 suicide of his estranged wife Bobbie shocked Escovedo into heading out solo, his behaviour and music now reflecting gravitas. Across the nineties he developed his sound – blending rock and country, Mexican and chamber music – and songwriting, never selling many records, always (as he would write) experiencing more miles than money.

As a child of immigrants, Alejandro's a perceptive writer on the travails of those who attempt to become Americans, the songs he wrote for theatre piece *By the Hand of the Father* matching

'A new language, a new everything': Alejandro Escovedo, Austin, TX

Woody Guthrie's best efforts. When he sings *the sun's not bright here unless you have golden hair* in 'Wave' I can see a Chicano youth trying to find his way among hostile Anglo eyes. He finally reached the UK in 2002, his startling London Borderline performance confirming the promise of his album *A Man Under the Influence*. Covered in critical accolades, Alejandro looked to be winning a wide audience yet collapsed in 2003, struck down by a debilitating bout of hepatitis C. Since then he has been slowly rebuilding his health and career.

Sufficiently impressed, Lee says, 'Let's go meet Mr Alee-banjo.' As we set the Hyundai on to the motorway towards central Austin I ask Lee what he knows about Austin. 'Stevie Ray's from here. An' Jimmie Dale Gilmore. An' that asshole who currently runs the US. That about it. What else I need to know?' Recalling how Texas executes more prisoners than all other US states combined, I can only suggest that if he gets in trouble with the law they might fry his ass. 'Remind me before I get too drunk tonight,' says Lee, and we start yakking on all the great music this city's produced. While Dallas and Houston are oil cities, metropolises that stand as monuments to corporate values, Austin is famously freewheeling, its university, bars and clubs making it a Mecca for many a cosmic cowboy. Back in the 1960s it existed as San Francisco South, home to psychedelic jug band The 13th Floor Elevators and Townes Van Zandt's Gothic country muse. By the early 1970s it was attracting Willie Nelson and Waylon Jennings. Jerry Jeff Walker, the New York folkie who wrote 'Mr Bojangles', set up base here as Captain Gonzo. San Antonio Tex-Mex rocker Doug Sahm arrived via San Francisco while Lubbock natives Joe Ely, Butch Hancock and Jimmie Dale Gilmore came to stay, bringing a touch of country Zen. Dallas natives Stevie Ray Vaughan and The Fabulous Thunderbirds shifted here, providing tough, deeply felt blues-rock. Even Daniel Johnston, the schizophrenic singer-songwriter championed by Kurt Cobain, chose Austin as his base. The city's music scene became internationally celebrated and Austin now hosts South by Southwest music expo, a launch pad for many UK acts into the US market, and the South by Southwest film festival (director Richard Linklater is a native son). More than anything else, Austin's development as a computer software centre has found it experiencing rapid population growth. Like Las Vegas and Phoenix, Austin is part of the new South-west, wealthy, fluid and increasingly liberal.

All this may be good for local commerce but not for traffic: we crawl towards the centre, marooned in a sea of vehicles joining us from what's now known as 'boomburbs' and 'zoomburbs'. Sure enough, in the distance all one can see is an endless grid of roads, housing and golf courses. Finally we're at Curra's Grill on Ortlof, a Mexican diner with bright orange walls. Turns out Alejandro is running late: he now lives in the hill country outside Austin and, hey, is stuck in traffic. Beer and burritos are ordered and, eventually, a skeletal Mexican male walks in. *Jesus, that's Alejandro*? In London his Mayan bloodlines and fine features suggested a Latin matinee idol; here he's gaunt, skin a malarial colour. Alejandro apologises for his lateness, refuses food, orders mineral water, all in a voice I recognise from listening to him sing: smooth, expressive, questioning. I enquire as to his well-being.

'I went through nine months of treatment for hepatitis C and it totally kicked my ass. I was set to take it for another nine months and then the medicine began to work against me and I got sick and had to stop. Funny thing is, I'm feeling much better now I've stopped and the last time I did a blood test the disease was totally undetectable. I'm hoping it'll stay that way. It's up to the Buddha, I guess.'

Like many musicians, Escovedo lacks the private health insurance necessary for US hospital treatment. This leaves him reliant on the largesse of friends and admirers to help cover medical costs.

'Health insurance, it's unaffordable for most people,' he says, 'whether you're a musician or not.'

Alejandro explains that behind *Por Vida* (a recent double CD of artists covering his songs) there was 'the concern of addressing universal healthcare rather than simply paying tribute to me'. One in three Americans under sixty-five went without health insurance at some point during the past two years; Alejandro's just one of 8.5 million Texans – 43.4 per cent of the non-elderly population – lacking health insurance, the highest proportion in the US.

Curra's Grill is a bustle of Mexican-American energy, English and Spanish both native tongues here. The food is heavy and tasty, the salsa spicy, the vibe good. Things have changed, I suggest, since you were a kid in Texas? Sure, says Alejandro, a lot. Go on, I cajole, tell me something about growing up Mexican-American, how it comes into your songs, lives in your music.

'My father,' says Alejandro, 'it's his story. See, when he was twelve years old in southern Mexico, living with his grandmother, his cousin, who was sixteen, told him they could find his parents if they just boarded this train. So he does it, not telling his grandmother, and she's sitting there waving at the train and he's waving goodbye. That's the song "Wave". He went in search of his parents in Texas. They were working as migrant workers and he found them in this little town. The songs for *Hand of the Father* came out of considering my parents' experience. We were living outside San Antonio and it was just like Mexico, everyone spoke Spanish. Then one day we left for California. Left my horse, dog, cat… everything. I've always been moving. It's part of my family history, constant motion.

'You know, when we left Texas it was under the guise of going to visit relatives in California but it wasn't till my father passed away that I heard the true story and it was this: my mother was running away from my father and had everything packed up and the night before we left he turns up and invites himself along on the trip. So that's how we ended up in California, living with relatives. He didn't have any money so we lived in these workers' quarters on a big orange-grove plantation. I had to learn to speak English extremely quickly. A new place, a new language, a new everything. Here was this paradise – we went to beautiful beaches for the first time; lived around orange and avocado orchards – but the trains still carried hobos who camped out in the groves and all our furniture and everything remained in Texas.

'It's funny, my father, he never had to find his identity. He was Mexican. A good singer. A union guy. One of the reasons we left Texas for California is that Texas is a right-to-work state while California has unions. So as young kids we would go to all the strikes he was on. We learned to raise our fists quite early. But, growing up in California, we listened to surf music and English rock and were so immersed in this new culture and it was hard to find your identity. It was frowned upon in school. Now it's encouraged and that's because of what happened in the 1960s.'

You're talking about the efforts of Cesar Chavez (1927–93), the union organiser who fought against the exploitation of Mexican agricultural workers in California?

'Absolutely. Every Mexican family in southern California had a picture of Cesar Chavez opposite one of John F. Kennedy on either side of the Virgin of Guadalupe. He was calm, strong, a man like Gandhi, a very important figure for all of us growing up.'

Does your success and that of Austin rockers Los Lonely Boys represent a breakthrough of sorts for Mexican-Americans?

'We've made progress but we're still ghettoised. We certainly haven't infiltrated mainstream America. Radio programmers

Mural man: Cesar Chavez remembered

have told my record company 'we can't even pronounce his name – how do you expect us to play him?' That kind of everyday racism holds people back. One of the points we try to make in *Hand of the Father* is what went on in the South also happened in the South-west but wasn't as evident to the public eye.' Alejandro falls silent then adds, 'To be honest, I'm trying to get beyond race, just trying to be a better human being.'

OK, let's talk about the Austin music scene you became part of.

'Austin's a wonderful place. For me more than anything else it was here I met all those great songwriters. Townes Van Zandt, I don't think people really realise just how great he was, the depth of his songwriting, the poetry that poured out of him. Eventually other things took over and he lost his way as far as the songs go but he was unique, he never compromised, and he was so young when he wrote so many great songs. Doug Sahm, well, we shared a passion for a San Francisco baseball team and he liked to smoke pot and so did I so we'd get stoned and talk baseball for hours. He was a great guy, a lot of fun. Joe Ely, I learned a lot from him because when I first started off solo I toured with him, both of us playing acoustic, on one of what Joe calls his "Tours of Texas", and as far as taking it to the stage and really performing your songs, he's a master. He's one of the guys who has really, really lived it.'

Van Zandt and Sahm both died in the late-nineties, wrung out by a lifetime of hard living. Ely remains on the road, performing superbly if never quite matching the promise he showed in the mid-seventies. And Escovedo, a man who found his voice only after swapping several cities, wives and bands, is trying to explain how he hates being labelled, especially as 'alt.country', the mid-1990s tag given to an explosion of interest in country-flavoured music.

'Words are important to me. That's one reason I didn't join the typical Latin dance band. I want people to pay attention to my songs. The storytelling, guitar-oriented songs of rock 'n' roll fit with the Mexican *corrido* tradition which I was exposed to by my father and relatives. My parents would have barbecue parties and after they'd had enough beers, they'd break out guitars. My aunt would start singing and they'd all start crying. That's where I'm coming from. Alt-country, to me, is Ryan Adams prancing around pretending to be Elton John. That's garbage.'

Escovedo's music possesses an emotional eloquence rare today. '*What kind of love/destroys a mother?*' he sings of his wife's suicide and it is his ability to convey lived experience which gives his songs such resonance.

'I never thought of myself as a great lyricist but I want to get the emotion of a song across. That's always what I've loved. The songwriters that I love, I always get the impression I know them, that I've had a conversation with them once I finish listening to their music. With the death of Bobbie there was a lot of emotional blockage, trauma. I had to get it out somehow. If I hadn't had the voice in music I don't know what I would have done.'

I mention how I'm heading to San Antonio to interview Tex-Mex legend Lydia Mendoza. Alejandro smiles and recalls his parents playing her 78s.

'We grew up listening to Lydia, to Los Hermanas Mendoza, a lot of *norteño* and *rancheras*, a lot of the cowboy singers. Both my mother and father loved this music called trio – three guitars, Spanish guitars. That song "Rosalie" is kind of a tribute to that music.'

Now in his mid-fifties does he feel his musical journey, from Tex-Mex through punk rock into Austin country (and beyond), makes some kind of sense?

'I'm generally very insecure and lack a lot of confidence. It took me a long time to mature into a bandleader. I was the guitar player with the good haircut and the good trousers. That was my thing, and I thought if I can see the world then that's fine. But at the same time I was always writing, things were wanting to come out. But to write your first song at the age of thirty, that's a difficult thing. It was painful, it wasn't easy. One thing I've got to say is that a lot of the fans have grown up right along with me. Rank & File's *Sundown* album was '82. *Gravity*, my first solo album, was '92. In between those times people started families and such but our values didn't change radically. And now... and now I've got to go and pick up my kids.'

Early evening and we're forlornly wandering around downtown Austin. This grid of seven streets (commonly known as '6th Street') dedicated to alcohol consumption is promoted as one of the great American hot spots for live music yet drifting past ugly bars (Iron Cactus, Coyote Ugly) selling ugly T-shirts/ bumper stickers (*Fuck Y'All, I'm From Texas*; *Texas is Bigger than France*), dried puke patterns baked on to the sidewalk, is depressing. Alejandro recommended Las Manitas ('Little Hands') – a café celebrated for serving the best Mexican breakfast going and hosting many a Tex-Mex visionary – as his favourite Austin institution, one now threatened by the economic boom engulfing the town: planned redevelopment will demolish the café to make way for a hotel chain. 'Keep Austin Weird' is a slogan popular with locals, but saying so today feels as archaic as speaking Latin: downtown Austin is fast becoming an extension of the zoom/boomburbs.

Las Manitas is closed for a private function and we find ourselves among crowds of archetypal American males –'frat boys', they call these loud, boozy young rednecks – who laugh and shout and shout and laugh, intoxicated by Friday night's seemingly limitless possibilities. No need to eavesdrop, these future Lords of Texas communicate at max volume: babes, booze, SUVs, The Dallas Cowboys. Thirty-something years ago George W. Bush and buddies surely strode these same streets declaiming on similar subjects. Wonder whether Bush – who should know Austin well seeing as how he was governor of Texas for two terms – ever checked out Austin's honky-tonks, got drunk with the local longhairs? Alcoholism destroyed Austin music stalwarts Townes Van Zandt and Blaze Foley so Bush may well have once enjoyed their company. He likes country music and reportedly has Alejandro on his iPod. Tonight his progeny are necking shots of beer topped with a flaming liqueur, hoofing and stomping and backslapping and burping, faces bright from alcohol and sun, innocent and ignorant. 'Shall we?' I ask Lee. 'Yeah.' He nods. 'Let's get da fock outta here.'

We head past the state legislature, waves of bats riding the evening humidity, then turn south, aiming to cross the river. I mention how a statue of Stevie Ray Vaughan's located along the river and Lee reasons it might be worth finding to tell the boys back east. I encountered Stevie Ray twice in New Zealand – initially, he resembled a dead fish, poisoned on alcohol and cocaine, a ghost in the making; two years later we met again and he was pink and fleshy, love and rehab having cured him of the self-destruction blues. A gentleman and an extraordinary live performer: my hair stood on end when he dug deep into his guitar at Auckland's town hall one Friday night. Lee nods, announces Stevie was a badass blues guitarist, then declares he don't need to search out no monument as 'it's just a fockin' statue!' We drive on down South Lamar Boulevard, pulling over when we see signs directing us to the self-proclaimed 'last of the true Texas dancehalls'.

The Broken Spoke is a large, barn-shaped venue. Opened in 1964 by James White (he smiles out of many framed photos, often hugging a country star), everyone from Bob Wills and Ernest Tubb – Texan icons who started singing in the 1930s – to Willie Nelson has since taken the stage here. Friday night finds the Spoke ($5 entry) filling with an amiable crowd, not as raucous as in Ginny's saloon yet free of frat boys. Tucked away down one end a band play competent, if uninspired, country. Couples dance on a concrete floor, skirts spinning and Stetsons shining beneath the bright lights. Everything feels a little like *Back to the Future*, a replay of a more innocent America and how they let loose on the weekend. We start demolishing a pitcher of beer then Lee spots a photo of the proprietor hugging George W. with a message stating 'thanks for the good times'. This answers my query as to whether Bush ever spent time in Austin's honky-tonks while Lee announces he ain't drinking in no damn Republican bar: time to return to Ginny's Little Long Horn Saloon. Here Dale's band are storming through another set of standards and originals, the dance floor's packed, air thick with smoke, atmosphere's sweltering and purple-haired bartenders serve up Lone Star to XXXL men sweating beneath Stetsons. The joint is jumping as Texan honkytonks have done for more than a century. Friday night fever, this is what we're after. Make a pact not to lose control; don't want to end up sleeping in the car again.

Townes

chapter 14

San Antonio: All Parts from Mexico

Saturday morning: we rise to a fierce sky and a road calling us south. 'Mexico's a few hours away,' I say to Lee, 'want to break for the border?' 'Like *The Wild Bunch*?' he replies, adding that coffee and a cigarette are priorities right now. Off we go, in our filthy Hyundai, interior and exterior coated with dust and ash, hunting for that most rarely realised of desires: the great American breakfast. Las Manitas tempts us but it means having to drive and park in central Austin; it'd probably be lunchtime before we ordered. Staying in motels off interstates, your eating choices are limited to clusters of fast-food franchises inevitably built around a gas station. The food, the ambience, everything is flattened, lacking beauty and pleasure. By now, after criss-crossing the South-west for several weeks, I'm sick to hell of McDonald's, Taco Bell, Denny's, Burger King and the rest. The rare opportunities that allow food to be consumed in a non-chain diner or restaurant only serve to underline how many of the simple pleasures in America have been extinguished. *Think about it*: the joy of dining out reduced to choosing between this and that corporate food chain, eating turned into stuffing wretched, processed foods into your face as quickly as possible. Hell, considering the queues of cars outside franchise restaurants many Americans don't even leave their vehicles, preferring to pump out exhaust fumes while waiting for dog burgers. Well, that's my diatribe to Lee as we digest Taco Bell on hard plastic seats.

On the interstate south and Townes Van Zandt, a man who preferred whiskey to food, is our soundtrack. Inspired by Dylan and Lightnin' Hopkins, the teenage Townes set about becoming a singer-songwriter and quickly established himself as an original voice. His best recordings – '68 to '73 – consist of mournful songs that appear weightless, beautifully bleak and full of gravitas, a Gothic country muse quite unlike any before or since. Those who champion Van Zandt often paint a picture of a man consumed with being free yet the reality is of a manic-depressive alcoholic who abandoned everything: wealthy family, wives, children and, inevitably, his talent. Kell knew Townes and described him as 'all bones, no meat. Fragile.' Which sounds near enough to the Townes I met in Auckland. Lee presses for recollections but I can't think of many: he was on the wagon so largely silent – unlike at his most feted live concerts where, liquored up, he merrily told corny jokes – his face etched with suffering, black eyes mournful. Our conversation came alive only when I mentioned fellow Austin casualty Roky Erickson. 'What you heard about Roky? That he done lost his marbles?' quizzed Townes. 'Something like that,' I agreed. A wry look crossed Townes's face before he added, 'Roky just done got himself a whole new set of marbles.' Good answer but bullshit. Roky became a toothless, homeless wreck, saved from a pauper's grave by his brother's intervention – this involved putting him on the correct medication – so allowing Roky to join Brian Wilson on the casualty comeback circuit. Townes might have joined them had not alcohol and depression chewed him up, the fifty-two-year-old emulating Hank Williams by dying on New Year's Day, 1997.

Austin quickly becomes suburbs, bungalows with cactus gardens, then the highway opens up and we're cruising through Texan desert, billboards stuffed with Gun Show September 25–28 and which turn off to take to get turned on at Adult Video Megaplex. Soon San Antonio spreads, blond and humble, in front of us.

San Antonio: those five sensual Spanish syllables herald the city where 189 Anglo and Mexican settlers held out for four days against 4,000 Mexican soldiers at the battle of the Alamo in 1836. The settlers lost but the sense of Texan identity as rough, tough and refusing to surrender quickly took shape. By 1837 the state had fought itself free of Mexico, existing for four years as the Republic of Texas, something certain Texans remain volubly proud of while tending to overlook how the Mexican government's banning slavery fuelled secessionist sentiment. Indeed, for a long time Texas was not a good place in which to be an ethnic minority, the Texas Rangers being notorious for their brutal, often murderous, treatment of blacks, Mexicans and Natives. A much stronger reason to have pride in Texas is the state's magnificent music: seminal blues, soul, country, rock 'n' roll and much Mexican-American music – Tex-Mex to Anglos, *norteño* to Mexicans across the border, *conjunto* to Mexicans this side and, more recently, tagged '*tejano*' (Mexican music made in Texas). Whatever you call it, there's no greater Mexican-American musician than Lydia Mendoza.

If the Alamo is San Antonio's most famous attraction then Lydia Mendoza is the city's greatest star. Attending a film-club screening of Les Blank's *Chulas Fronteras* (*Beautiful Borders*) in the 1980s, I was introduced to Tex-Mex music and Lydia. I then came across her music through Arhoolie Records' reissues of Mendoza's historic recordings (1930s–1950s), alongside two superb eighties albums *La Gloria de Texas* and *In Concert*. Lydia's bell-like voice and fluid twelve-string acoustic guitar picking demanded attention and I've been a fan ever since. As Lydia made her most famous recordings in the 1930s I felt she surely must now have left this world. Interviewing Mexican cabaret diva Astrid Hadad in 2004, I pestered her for tales of Mexico's many musical legends. Astrid surprised me when she said, 'Lydia's had a stroke and isn't playing music any more but beyond that I hear she's well.' My heart skipped a beat.

We turn off the highway before reaching central San Antonio, Lee negotiating our way through sun-baked suburbs, running smooth towards Laurel Heights Nursing Home. Via Arhoolie Records (the Bay Area label that brought Lydia to wide prominence) I've arranged to interview Lydia through her daughter Yolanda Hernandez. Lee's never heard of Lydia, yet whenever I mention her name in the South-west people light up: Alejandro recalled his parents playing her records, an uncle dating her sister; Kell whooped, declaring, 'I saw her play one time in the 1950s, alone with her guitar. She was spellbinding and very beautiful.' Freddy Fender, the Mexican-American singer who enjoyed great crossover country and pop success in the 1970s, once noted, 'I would hear her from every window in our San Benito neighbourhood while I staked the wire of my mother's old radio into the ground and my mother sang along in the house. She was such a powerful singer.' Lee wants to know more. OK, I say, it's an epic American story.

Lydia Mendoza was born 21 May 1916, in Houston, to a Mexican family who had fled the chaos of the Mexican Revolution. Her grandmother and mother Lenora were both musical and from early childhood Lydia and her siblings were taught a variety of musical instruments. This training was anything but a luxury – the Mendozas were impoverished migrant workers and the family's patriarch, Francisco Mendoza, forced his children to play music on the streets. Lydia never went to school; prowess at singing and playing the twelve-string guitar found her designated the family's principal earner. The Mendozas regularly moved between Texas and the northern Mexican city of Monterey; when the harvest season was under way they travelled across the Rio Grande Valley, town to town, playing in restaurants, barbershops, even going to the fields and serenading the workers, gathering pennies, nickels and dimes. Hunger and the threat of eviction were constant.

In 1928 *La Prensa*, a popular local paper, announced Okeh Records were holding auditions in San Antonio. Francisco convinced a friend with a car to drive the family to the auditions and the twenty songs they recorded won them $120. Before their 78s were pressed the family left for Detroit, seeking work picking sugar beets. Francisco quickly tired of farm labouring, forcing his family to play on city streets and at migrant worker camps. In 1930 the Mendozas returned to San Antonio, where they became fixtures in the city's old public market. It was here in 1931 that a broadcaster heard Lydia sing and invited her to guest on his programme.

As Lydia's popularity rose she began getting restaurant and tent-show bookings. An unscrupulous agent held on to most of the fees, forcing Lydia to continue entering talent contests (which, naturally, she won). In 1934 Blue Bird Records came to San Antonio. Lydia auditioned and recorded four songs for $60. Two months later her first 78, 'Mal Hombre' ('Evil Man'), became a huge hit across the South-west. Blue Bird offered to sign Lydia to a contract guaranteeing royalties but Francisco insisted she receive the fee of $40 per two songs recorded. Lydia recorded hit after hit: in 1935 she received a demand for $30,000 in taxes. Blue Bird dealt with the tax authorities, her family realising only decades later that Lydia had lost a fortune in royalties. To her fans Lydia was 'La Alondra de la Frontera' ('the Meadowlark of the Border') and 'La Cancionera de los Pobres' ('the Songstress of the Poor'), the singer who gave voice to the Mexican-American experience.

In the 1970s Arhoolie Records began reissuing albums of Lydia's pioneering recordings. This introduced her to a younger audience and she continued to tour until a stroke in 1988 curtailed her ability to play guitar. Which is why our destination is a nursing home. Arriving, we wander through a bright if depressing old folks' home/ hospital, eventually stumbling upon Lydia's daughter Yolanda and her husband Ricardo. Lydia has, says Yolanda, experienced five heart bypasses, broken both hips and a leg and, earlier this year, experienced a hernia. 'Man,' says Lee, 'she's a survivor.' Yet infirmity charges a high price and when I meet the pale, silver-haired woman in a wheelchair she doesn't resemble the Lydia I'm familiar with from CD sleeves and *Chulas Fronteras*. At eighty-nine years of age Lydia Mendoza is confined to the wheelchair, very thin, the wide smile and laughter that once accompanied her every gesture now silenced. Wrapped in a black shawl – rouge on cheeks, gold rings on fingers, nails painted a colour as fierce as her lipstick – she remains, undoubtedly, a queen. Introductions are made and I quickly realise that Lydia, although having lived her entire life in the USA, has never learnt to speak English.

'The doctors are surprised Lydia has healed so fast,' says Yolanda of Lydia's recent hernia operation. 'I put it down to her cooking with a lot of garlic and chilli.' While Lydia retains her health she's now too fragile to make music. Does she, I enquire, miss making music?

'That's why I'm dying here because I miss my music so much,' is the blunt reply. I mention Kell saying how he fell in love with her upon seeing her play. 'Where is he now, then, when I need him?' she says. Good to know she's not lost her wit. Lydia pulls her shawl tighter and gives me a fierce look. OK, next question: what does she recall of San Antonio in the 1930s?

'We finally got started here in San Antonio, in a huge open-air market,' says Lydia. 'In the evenings from midnight on it was the market where all the produce trucks from the Valley and everywhere would arrive. This went on from midnight until about ten or eleven a.m. Then around seven in the evening all the people who were going to sell food there would come in and set up restaurant tables. Each stand would set up its tables and sell chilli con carne, enchiladas, tamales. There were a lot of them and there were a lot of groups singing there. It was around this time that I started to sing solo. I asked my mother to give me the guitar and I'd sing. People started to hear my voice and like it. That's how a radio announcer came to hear me.'

The announcer, Manuel J. Cortez, fronted San Antonio's only daily Spanish-language programme – *La Voz Latina* ('The Latin Voice') – and invited Lydia to sing on the programme. Lenora was initially reluctant to let Lydia go as it meant giving up valuable earning time but Lydia insisted. She sang two songs and returned to the Plaza. Back at the station, phone lines lit up. No wonder: Lydia's yearning voice and fluid guitar transformed folk songs sung in fields, mariachi movie tunes, border radio hits, into a new American music. That she was a cherubic sixteen-year-old who bossed a big, twelve-string guitar with the ease of a veteran bluesman made her irresistible. Yet before Mama Mendoza would let her leave the Plaza to sing on the radio again she insisted Lydia get paid. An advertising sponsor was found and Lydia sang two songs every night of the week for $3.50 a week.

'Well, with that three-fifty, we felt like millionaires,' recalled Lydia in *A Family Autobiography*, the oral biography Chris Strachwitz compiled. 'Now at least we could be sure of paying the rent. Because to get the rent together, which was one dollar

Lydia Mendoza, San
Antonio, Texas, 2006

and twenty-five cents a week, we had to play... two days. We
had to play Saturday and Sunday to put together the rent. And
sometimes we didn't even get it together. Now with three-fifty, we
had the rent for sure.'

By 1936 Lydia was enjoying hit 78s across the South-west,
married, a mother and managed by Antonio Montes. Francisco's
alcoholism worsened so Montes banned him from coming on
tour, paying him to stay in San Antonio and drink. Your dad, I
say to Lydia, he was a handful. She nods, reflects on the past and
mentions it was Mama Lenora who taught them how to make
music when they were children. They toured Colorado, Arizona
and California, time and again were refused theatres, hotel rooms
and restaurant service: 'No Dogs Or Mexicans Allowed' was a
familiar sign. The Mendozas travelled with cooking equipment,
sleeping in Catholic church halls.

'Things are better today,' says Lydia when I ask her about life then and now. 'Today we have so many good highways and it's so easy to get around. Back in the 1930s driving long distances was always very difficult.'

This answer sideswipes me: I'd expected her to suggest the lessening of discrimination or the strengthening of her community's wealth and status but, understandably, the combustion engine and the highway allowed Lydia to stay in motion, earn a living. Her autobiography chronicles vehicles breaking down, tyres puncturing, several crashes (one killing her sister), lives in motion, always more miles than money...

In concert Lydia mixed songs from Argentina, Cuba, Colombia and Spain with her vast repertoire of Mexican *rancheras*, *corridos*, boleros, *huapangos* and *canciones*. And as border radio stations began blasting Lydia across the USA – one even had a woman pretending to be Lydia! – her fame grew. Why, I enquire, do you believe you became the first Mexican-American singing star?

Lydia looks at me as if making a silent judgement, then says, 'Whether I was singing a bolero or a waltz or a polka it didn't matter. When I sang it felt like I was living that song. Every song I ever sang I did with the feeling that I was living that song.'

Songs of heartbreak and hunger, songs of bad men and unfaithful women, of heroes of the Mexican Revolution and those Anglos across the border who treated Mexicans with such contempt, Lydia sang the blues for a Chicano populace considered little more than mules – 'bean eaters' – by Anglo-Americans. No Statue of Liberty welcomed them as they crossed the Rio Grande into Texas. Yet in Lydia this scorned, impoverished community heard their own voice, knew their culture worthy of celebration. Post-WW2 Lydia would become a huge star in Mexico, Colombia and pre-revolutionary Cuba. Anglo-America, long oblivious to the Tex-Mex icon, began offering recognition. A play about Lydia toured Texas. Books celebrated her life. She sang at President Carter's 1977 inauguration, in 1982 became the first Texan to receive a National Endowment for the Arts Heritage Fellowship, and in 1999 received the National Medal of Arts at a White House ceremony.

'It was a great experience to get the award from Clinton,' says

Yolanda. 'I went along with her and she was very proud to be honoured.'

'I was touring, playing Lubbock, Texas, when President Kennedy was killed,' adds Lydia, alert to the conversation. 'They cancelled the concerts and I remember they quoted me saying how terrible it was in the local newspaper.'

We chat about the Mexican musical legends she knew: Pedro Infante, Jose Alfredo Jimenez and Kell's favourite, Lola Beltran ('we met but weren't friends'). I ask how Lydia came to play twelve-string guitar; she recalls first hearing it played by men in San Antonio's Plaza: 'I always loved the sound of it.' No, she hasn't heard any contemporary music that she likes. Yes, she still loves mariachi, *ranchera* and *conjunto*. Age has not withered Lydia's mind but by being unable to do the one thing that's always sustained her – *make music* – she feels imprisoned. *Think about it*: a woman soaked in song, singing for a public since childhood, now unable to do so. 'Lydia,' I say, crouching before her, *'gracias por todo la música.' Thank you for all the music*. Lydia nods, replies, 'I'm proud people still like my music and know who I am.'

Don't fly too close to the sun: doomed Tejano icon, Selena

chapter 15

Gruene: Honky-tonk Masquerade

'*No Smoking, No Weapons*' says the sign as you enter the Alamo. This makes me smile when considering the building's original inhabitants. The interior's thick walls offer a welcome relief from the heat. A large tree spreads branches across the Alamo's forecourt offering a genuine sense of green peace. Lee suggests it's time for our first beer of the day. Instead, I offer, let's work up a thirst by exploring San Antonio's river walk. San Antonio was founded because of the green waters that rush through this part of southern Texas and, fortuitously, wise town planners chose to incorporate the river into the city rather than burying it. A sidewalk follows the river, initially passing through malls, barge tours, restaurants, bars, gift shops. Flocks of tourists throng the lower part of the river while farther along the crowds thin and the river walk reverts to San Antonio's citizens. A banner overhanging the river advertises a watering hole called the Esquire, and as our thirst is now mighty we climb the iron stairwell, entering a saloon bar with slow whirring fans hanging from a high, wood-panel ceiling and a long, sleek bar free of seats: you stand against it with a bronze bar at ankle level to rest your boots against – thus the term 'bar' for US drinking establishments – while wooden booths with leather seats and a dark table offer drinkers the kind of privacy you rarely find these days. A silent TV in the corner projects American football while a chrome jukebox blasts Patsy Cline's 'I Fall to Pieces'. The staff and clientele are Mexican, the one exception being a tiny Anglo waitress. She approaches us and when asked what's on tap advises Shiner Bock. 'Is it good?' Eyes blank and resigned, she shrugs. We order and she delivers two tall glasses filled with dark beer. Icy cold, fabulously tasty. *Salud!*

Mexican American musicians, Taos, New Mexico, 1940

The jukebox has swung to an Isidro Lopez *tejano* number, all horns and Lopez's big, smooth voice. Lee and I soak up the Shiner and order two more. The jukebox keeps feeding great songs – Ray Price, KC & The Sunshine Band, Sunny & The Sunliners, Stevie Ray Vaughan, Sonny & Cher, The Rolling Stones, Los Tigres del Norte, Otis Redding, Little Joe, Chalino – and I think of Kerouac saying (of New Orleans) to Burroughs *'there must be some ideal bars in this town'* and loathsome Bill replying *'the ideal bar doesn't exist in America'* before decrying all that was wrong with US drinking establishments. Obviously, he'd never been to the Esquire. Then the jukebox plays a *tejano* pop number sung by a young female voice and the bar's energy shifts, people raising glasses, shouting. 'OK,' I say, 'it must be Selena.' Lee looks blank so I rise and check the jukebox. The tune is 'Como La Flor' and the singer is Selena.

Hugely popular across the South-west, Selena has a story eerily similar to Lydia's: a despotic, impoverished father forces his children to sing and perform. Nine-year-old Selena is quickly recognised as a potential star so pulled out of school to sing in plazas, fairgrounds, weddings and parties across Texas. Aged sixteen, she wins Female Vocalist of the Year at the 1987 Tejano Music Awards. Grammy awards, film roles, Coca-Cola tie-in deals all follow Selena's rise to Mexican-American superstar, her hiccupping voice riding hit after hit while Native and Spanish bloodlines find the girl growing into a sensual mestizo beauty. She begins singing tentatively in English and opens Selena Inc.

clothing/beauty boutiques in Corpus Christi and San Antonio. Then, on 31 March 1995, Selena confronted Yolanda Saldivar, president of her fan club, in a Corpus Christi motel over financial irregularities. Yolanda pulled a pistol and shot the twenty-three-year-old dead. Lee shakes his head, says, 'Crazy fockin Meskins.' Well, sure, but Selena's South-west tale – money, miles, motels, music and murder – is a quintessentially American one, making me wonder whether Sandra Cisneros, San Antonio's most celebrated author, will ever turn Selena into literature. Cisneros reportedly lives in a bright purple house and once wrote *All Parts from Mexico, Assembled in the USA* among other fine things on being Chicana.

'Guess Lydia never got to make Selena-style money,' ponders Lee, 'but least she got to live.' Amen to that. Was meeting Lydia, asks Lee, what you expected? No easy answer springs forth. I mean, what *did* I expect? Obviously, not the character I saw in *Chulas Fronteras* from some thirty years ago. But perhaps not someone quite so frail, battered by life. Try to reply by saying how often do you get to sit with someone who started recording in 1928? How often do you get to sit with an American music pioneer? Lydia took an oral music and helped shape it into a definite twentieth-century sound. I rank her alongside Louis Armstrong, Jimmie Rodgers, Bessie Smith and Robert Johnson. *Hey, Robert Johnson's first recording session was in San Antonio in December 1936!* What young Robert made of this city is unknown yet here he cut 'Crossroad Blues' and 'Come on in My Kitchen'. Lydia was recording here then and this gets me to thinking of the two inadvertently meeting at a recording session and trading guitar licks. Country music pioneers the Carter Family were based in San Antonio through the late 1930s, working the border blasters. *Imagine Lydia and Maybelle Carter making music together!* Surely they heard one another but language and culture kept them apart. 'Hey,' says Lee, 'reckon Lydia played this bar?' Possibly, quite possibly.

A mariachi trio, featuring two middle-aged men on guitar and violin and a moon-faced youth on guitarron (a fat-bodied

Mexican six-string acoustic bass), enter wearing black slacks, short-sleeved white shirts and embroidered vests. They launch into a tune, drinkers nod appreciatively and the jukebox gets unplugged. *Ooh, it's lovely!* This mournful old Mexican blues, deep and rich and resonant. Three cholos (greasy hair/jailhouse tattoos) take turns at standing, pulling out dead presidents and dropping them on a small table in front of the musicians. When other drinkers aren't fast enough to accommodate the mariachis one of the cholos, a guy whose raw features suggest a good future in Robert Rodriguez films, stands and starts barracking drinkers, 'Give 'em a fuckin' dollar! C'mon, they're playin' for ya!' Soon everyone is ripping bills out of trouser pockets and bra cups. An Anglo couple enter the Esquire the same way we did, both dressed in the loud jackets favoured by Americans on vacation, glance at the clientele and immediately exit.

The mariachis keep singing, voices high, gorgeous and fabulously lonesome. The youth pulls lovely deep ripples out of the guitarron. The guitar keeps rhythm, a steady, strolling groove, and sings high, keening tales of border pathos. The violinist, face creased, eyes wistful, bends towards his instrument. Everyone claps after each number and the musicians nod, polite smiles on their lips, then strike up another number. The patrons' voices return to a low rumble, careful not to drown out this old Texan soundtrack. Lee, I say, check how the violinist carries his sad, sweet self like many a Balkan Gypsy violinist, such raw, tender notes pulled from this most fragile of instruments. All is good, all is peaceful, but as the shadows lengthen a uniformed security guard makes his presence known, striding the length of the bar, holstered 9mm on hip. The mariachis take this as a cue and disappear down the iron stairs and the jukebox returns with a heavy blues that could be Albert Collins. 'Another beer?' asks Lee. No, let's go in search of the oldest dance hall in Texas.

Outside and the Esquire makes sense: the river walk is only metres below but the Esquire exists in the barrio. Shops wear metal shutters, pawn and liquor stores predominate, golden youths stroll the street, two teens gang up on another who stumbles backward.

'Pussy!' they shout. He turns, squeals, 'I'll get my boys,' flees. A low-rider rolls past pumping *tejano* tunes. Lee suggests twilight's a good time to, y'know, return to the ever secure Alamo.

In the plaza outside the Alamo Saturday evening activity is beginning with jugglers, mariachi orchestras and caricaturists, all continuing Lydia's street entertainment tradition. A black man stands atop a box and starts delivering hoarse sermons, serving the usual blend of hell, damnation and eternal sunburn. No one pays him any attention, concentrating instead on consuming burritos and frosted doughnuts, teenagers flirting, people promenading. Beauty is everywhere – tan skin, black hair, a lush yet shy South-western sensuality – *imagine it, a city of Jessica Albas! Oh, chiquita!* I recall Jack and Neal having a similar epiphany upon reaching San Antonio: '*It was fragrant and soft – and dark and mysterious, and buzzing. Sudden figures of girls in white bandanas appeared in the humming dark.*'

Back on the highway, night settles and traffic moves in great waves. We exit into the Texan hinterlands, slipping through radio stations where Baptist preachers are in full swing, calling upon God's theocracy. I listen to them honk, these cheerleaders of the apocalypse, then lean out the window and turn my head towards the heavens. Stars are appearing in the night sky. Oh, universe of infinite possibilities, what do you say to these dull Texan braggarts who bash such tired texts? Nothing, of course, nothing. Exactly what Townes Van Zandt suggested was waiting for him in one of his last, bitter songs. Nothin'.

Gruene, thirty miles north-east of San Antonio, is home to Gruene Hall, the oldest functioning dance hall in Texas. Gruene was once on the main stagecoach route between San Antonio and Austin, but as the automobile became king the town faded until Gruene Hall ended up resting empty, a big, derelict honky-tonk that once hosted Bob Wills and Lefty Frizzell, Hank Williams and Johnny Cash. Gruene's faded beauty was reinvented as a 1980s vacation hot spot, old shops refurbished with expensive produce and old houses turned into B & Bs. The dance hall reopened, and as we pull up I can hear a guitar being strangled. Not a welcoming sound from a place reputed to be honky-tonk heartland but let's see: the woman on the gate says tonight's attraction is Larry Joe Taylor. I've never heard of him. 'He's got a strong following around Galveston,' she states, relieves us of $8 each and through the gate we pass.

Gruene Hall appears unchanged by time. A prominent sign reads *'We reserve the right to refuse service to anyone. We don't care who you are, who you think you are, how much money you have or who your daddy is.'* For a Saturday night the hall's sparsely populated. A solitary black guy shoots pool. Most people sit on long wooden benches, resting against venerable trestle tables decorated with carved initials. The walls are covered in B & W photos of the good, great and forgotten who have played the hall. Spacious and airy; the sense of dead voices singing resonates. The bar is cash only and serves both Bud and Miller. The toilet is wrecked. Being a functioning live music venue means the hall should be filled with Saturday night fever. Instead, a weird despair hangs in the air. Understandable: Larry Joe performs a dire Springsteen imitation with added guitar wank. The dance floor, worn smooth by decades of couples waltzing across Texas, stands empty. Yet the tubby man in a garish Hawaiian shirt at the centre of this tempest appears unfazed, a ham actor in love with his lines. Joe Ely once sang of a 'Honky-tonk Masquerade' and tonight Gruene Hall is just that.

Nine a.m. and the phone in our desolate New Braunfels motel begins belling and won't stop. The motel's manager is giving us an unrequested 'wake-up call' and suggesting he wants the room empty like, hey, right now. Where to? Well, the only place with a variety of decent eating places in the vicinity is, of course, Gruene – if gentrification ensures one thing, it is decent coffee. Returning to this quaint hamlet in the daylight I'm immediately impressed by a sense of space; big wooden buildings, weepy willow trees and a venerable water tower lend charm and nostalgia. Founded in 1878 to serve families working on cotton plantations, Gruene's now a boutique town with a Sunday market selling luxury soaps and organic jams.

Passing Gruene Hall we hear musicians setting up and Lee suggests a beer for breakfast. Well, it *is* hot. Inside, Gruene Hall is lovely and cool, the building's wooden structure more effective than air conditioning. An acoustic guitarist and double bass kick off the kind of hillbilly twang Gruene Hall was built to host and a demure blonde in tight pink dress starts strumming a mandolin and singing. Within sixty seconds we're won over and Brennen Leigh, as it turns out this morning's bandleader is called, takes slugs from an alco-pop, smiles slyly, positions her mandolin to project her breasts forward and introduces her musicians. Brennen's performance is played in front of the bar (rather than on the main stage) and full of Texan charm. She advertises her CD, aptly titled *Too Thin to Plough*, and Lee lays down the dead presidents.

A board outside advertised the event as *Dance Hall Sunday* and Brennen sings several Appalachian gospel songs, mournful in their intensity, yet manages to make the Louvin Brothers' 'The Christian Life' sound, well, *sassy*. Which is appropriate: Brennen's attire and attitude suggest more a honky-tonk angel than the kind Southern Baptists pray to. 'We tune because we care, folks,' she says before launching into a song about a girl whose soldier boyfriend goes to Iraq and never returns home. As Brennen sings of youths dying for George and Dick's business interests we exit to find outdoor temperatures rising to Baghdad levels. Time to return to Austin, Brennen having restored my faith in Gruene as a town offering genuine musical treats and in the legend of Texas being the land of big-boned blondes. I mention this to Lee and he says, 'Man, you could fry an egg on her G-string!'

Lee drives while I study church billboards: *Sin Fascinates You. Then it Assassinates You*; *The Wages of Sin Demand Unpayable Interest*; *Fear the Wrath of God*; *God Bless Our Troops*. Within ninety minutes we're in Austin, cruising straight to Ginny's. Inside Dale's playing with fluid grace and a mixture of locals and tourists pack the greatest little honky-tonk in Texas. During the afternoon a large board marked out with numbered squares is placed across the pool table and a plump rooster is sat down.

Everyone watches the cock strut back and forth, oblivious to honky-tonk mayhem, picking at grain. Finally the cock drops his load on number 21 and everyone cheers, this being Chicken Shit Sunday. Numbered tickets had been sold for $1 a piece and the winner collects a cool $100, which at Ginny's buys a lot of beer. The event is repeated over the course of the afternoon with free hot dogs and chilli provided for revellers.

Stepping outside for fresh evening air, I notice Dale standing alone so regale him with tales of San Antonio and Gruene Hall. His response to the artists I encountered goes something like: Lydia ('a Texan legend'), Brennen ('she's great. We've talked of cutting a duets album') and Larry Joe ('the worst!'). The weekend's nearly over, I've a night dog to ride to Nashville while Lee has a morning flight east. We covered a lot of ground in eight days. Not bad for two strangers to each other and the South-west. 'If in London,' I say. 'If in Philly,' he replies. '*Hasta la vista*,' I offer, and Lee shrugs, opens a beer for the road, says, '*Vaya con dios*. Or some shit like dat, yeah.'

'Lord, it's a bourgoise town': Gruene, TX

BILLION-DOLLAR BAPTISTS

Nashville, Memphis

Memphis was the worst town you ever seen. If you could make it in Memphis you could make it anywhere. If you come out of Memphis, you was alright.

Honeyboy Edwards

I was talking with a friend of mine about this the other day, that country life as I knew it might really be a thing of the past and when music people today, performers and fans alike, talk about being 'country' they don't mean they know or even care about the land and the life it sustains and regulates. They're talking more about choices – a way to look, a group to belong to, a kind of music to call their own. Which begs a question: Is there anything behind the symbols of modern 'country,' or are the symbols themselves the whole story? Are the hats, the boots, the pickup trucks, and the honky-tonking poses all that's left of a disintegrating culture? Back in Arkansas, a way of life produced a certain kind of music. Does a certain kind of music now produce a way of life? Maybe that's okay. I don't know.

Johnny Cash

Nashville Babylon: Hank Williams and friends

chapter 16

Nashville: Getting Ready to Go Crazy

All Texan bonhomie vanishes at Austin's bus station, replaced instead by the surly service characteristic of Greyhound employees. Bags are thrown, not tossed but flung hard, into the bus undercarriage. Take a deep breath- no, *don't*, the air is thick with exhaust fumes. OK, relax, say a little prayer, meditate... whatever. I'm going to ride this dog night and day through what's called 'the Bible Belt'. James B. Davis, founder of South Carolina gospel sensations The Dixie Hummingbirds, once exclaimed '"The Bible Belt!" That's what they call it. I'm so sick of that I don't know what in the world I'm going to do. Those "Bible Belt" people, they'll hang you before you can bat an eye.' Davis was referring to the Southern states where Protestant fundamentalism rubs uncomfortably up against liberal democracy; these states tending to scare not only black Americans but the world, securing George W. Bush the presidency and promoting creationism as a legitimate science. *The Bible Belt...* maybe I should be joining Lee on a flight east.

My nerves are frayed, the constant driving and drinking and honky-tonkin' burning me out. I feel uncertain as to whether I should get on this bus. Then the Frost dictum of best-way-out-is-through replays deep in my tired mind (*a quest, remember; you can't quit a quest*), so I take a deep breath and force myself on board, grabbing a window seat. An obese Mexican male then sits alongside, his bulk flowing on to me as he settles into a seat not designed for XXXL. A beautiful young woman, hair the colour of corn, takes a seat right opposite: the luck of the long-distance traveller, stuck with the beast when it could have been beauty. And what's she doing riding the dog? Greyhound is a true leveller,

America's great unwashed rubbing against one another. Literally: Mr Blobby dozes off as soon as the bus hits the road and, as the miles click past, starts using me as a pillow. He snores, I read, struggling to re-engage with Henry Miller's air-conditioned nightmare as mine gets under way.

Last time I read Miller was in Grants, a town that in *Buffy the Vampire Slayer*-speak would be called a 'hellmouth'. Pick up where I left off but trying to focus on Hank's dense, hyper prose is no easy task. The Brooklyn bard's *Tropics* novels remain among the funniest, most life-affirming prose I've ever read, but when WW2 chased Miller home from Europe he appeared not simply old but grumpy, so uncomfortable was he with being back among Americans. A road trip did, admittedly, allow Miller to act as a prescient critic of US exegesis – the ruthless laying waste of urban and rural space in the name of quick profits – and I've underlined a passage, *'everybody's getting ready to get raped, drugged, violated, soused with the new music that seeps out of the sweat of the asphalt... Down further, towards Mobile, they're practicing the St Louis Blues without a note in front of them and people are getting ready to go crazy when they hear it yesterday, today, tomorrow'.* I chew on this and wonder whether Hank was prescient to the sonic voodoo then percolating.

Tiny print and dense prose soon force me to swap book for CD Walkman. I shuffle through discs I've played too often, aware I must invest in an MP3 thing, whatever they are. Always last to master new technology, that's me. Tonight's road music is the *Anthology of American Folk Music*, that proto-mix tape American magus Harry Smith compiled out of forgotten 78s in 1952. The *Anthology*'s recordings were from the 1920s and early 1930s yet sound ancient, verses often literally adapted from folk songs that arrived here with migrants. 'Old Timey' was what the musicians (and those who marketed their music) called Southern white rural music, old timey because many of the songs dated back centuries. American music gained flesh and blood, its own identity and language, as these recordings were being made – Harry Smith ignored contemporary recordings by the likes of Louis

Armstrong, Bessie Smith and Jimmie Rodgers, all too successful, too confident, for his primeval quest. Old timey represented, to Harry, America as another country, one removed from the urban-industrial juggernaut the nation had become well before WW2. I flick through *Anthology* tracks, replaying the Carter Family and Uncle Dave Macon, both of whom inadvertently helped build the metropolis I'm heading to: a muggy city in east Tennessee that became the hillbilly Hollywood, Nashville.

Old American music in my ears, I stare at the highway, a constant flow of cars riding south, headlights blazing, lone travellers and couples, families and friends, the optimistic and the desperate, packed into plastic and metal shells, combustion engines firing, crossing this vast and fearful land, chasing all kinds of American dreams. At Dallas South Blobby wakes, yawns, disembarks. Standing outside, trying to loosen limbs, I overhear a Mexican man politely ask the black bus driver as to what time this dog lands in Little Rock. He receives a vitriolic reply that ends with the accusation 'you people who can't even *speak* English!' 'But I *only* asked you a question,' says the Mexican – again in perfect English – shocked at such treatment. 'Ask in there,' says the driver, pointing to a small, neglected office, his gnarled features making him resemble Chuck Berry at his most crazed. And I'm riding all night with this guy at the wheel...

Back on board I hope to have both seats. No such relief; I'm joined by John, an Indian from Madras who has lived for nine years in Dallas; in that time he's converted to Christianity. And now he wants to convert me. The barely air-conditioned nightmare continues. We stop regularly – smokers gathering in a huddle, Mexicans circling to chuckle in Spanish – most eager to get off the bus. People are friendly but there's one guy, a white male, louder than the rest. He's late twenties, cropped, muscular, small, mean eyes, wearing combat pants and a singlet that advertises a serpent tattoo spiralling across shoulders and curling around biceps. His tattoo – indeed, his entire vibe – exudes aggressive unease reminiscent of the Grants biker bar. He's also demonstrating a loud interest in Ms Midwest. And she... well, she is looking nervous. Being one of life's natural cowards I normally give short shrift to helping the vulnerable but she is surely the only innocent on this damn bus. And he… he looks like he took several hits on a meth pipe before getting on board. Rather than confront him – which would only end very badly for me – I strike a conversation with her in a convenience-store queue. She sticks close as we step outside, the crankster glaring, eyes suggesting bad things, mouth moving as if to bite her.

Janie, as she's called, is heading home to Chicago after having spent the weekend visiting a San Antonio-based boyfriend. Turns out they met several years ago via a teenagers' website, initially communicating through e-mail, then phone. When she suggested they should meet he told her he had something to confess – he was Korean. 'Is that a problem?' she asked, and they've been an item since. 'We're so happy together,' she announces with a radiant smile, and I believe her; lots of emotions can be faked but world-conquering love is near impossible. 'I want to teach high school when I finish studying,' Janie adds. 'People say it doesn't pay well and is hard work but I really like the idea of teaching.' Good on you, Janie, for finding happiness, for believing in an America that you engage with, not just take from. At the next stop we again stand together, Janie expounding on American dreams that taste real, make sense, the crankster shadowing us, a bad smell, a malevolent spirit. Recall a Doors song about a killer on the road – '*brain squirming like a toad*' – and feel uneasy.

John exits in Texarkana, Arkansas. Marvin, my new travelling partner, is a laconic black man who announces he's returning to Little Rock to 'collect my thirteen-year-old daughter – her mama's unfit to keep her'. Is, I wonder, Marvin looking forward to raising his daughter? 'Hmmmmm,' he says, as if thinking about it for the first time, 'should be a'right. I been married three times, fathered six – no, seven – children. Never again, I swear.' Marvin exits to find his daughter in the middle of the night and finally I have two seats. Wish I could sleep but, no, impossible on buses and planes. Especially on a bus like this one, shake-rattle-rolling its way down the highway. Listen to fellow passengers snore, their babies wake and cry, air tepid and sour with sweat. There's a weird drone I imagine to be the crankster grinding his teeth but when I look for him at an early morning stop he's vanished. Surely soon to be found in a state penitentiary.

We cross the mighty Mississippi river around dawn, sunlight illuminating small towns and lending plantations a pastoral hue, landing in Memphis around midday. Janie's riding on all the way to Chicago while I'm changing bus. 'Thanks for talking with me and not leaving me alone with that scary guy,' she says. My pleasure, Janie, my pleasure. Two stocky men, one black, one white (biceps pumped, heads shaven, strapped with large-calibre pistols), stand by as baggage is shovelled out, directing a large Labrador on a leash. The dog sniffs our dented luggage, looking for product from across the Mexican border. Welcome to Tennessee.

I shift into the Nashville queue for more rough baggage handling and a metal detector swipe. We're soon heading out of Memphis, past the city's glass pyramid casino, over the Mississippi and rolling down Music Highway. Note the Tina Turner–Isaac Hayes Rest Area. Another stretch of road calls itself the Carl Perkins–Casey Jones Highway. As we pass the Shiloh National Military Park – site of the Civil War's bloodiest battle: 20,000 men slaughtered, fields littered with corpses and carnage – I wonder about the ancestors of the Shiloh soldiers, guessing some are now in Afghanistan or Iraq, still fighting futile wars. We pass the Nathan Bedford Forest Memorial – Nathan being the KKK's founder – and cross the Tennessee river's calm waters. A hand-painted sign reads 'Jesus Loves Babies' while a church billboard reads 'Don't Give Up: Moses Was Once a Basket Case'. The towns start to get bigger, the suburbs swell and after almost twenty hours arrival is imminent in Austin's supposed antithesis, Nashville.

Greyhound's charm offensive continues, 8th Street in Nashville being seriously seedy. Sweltering temperatures and an atmosphere of exhaustion and foul tempers prompt passengers to collect luggage and flee. I imagine all the hopefuls who have dismounted

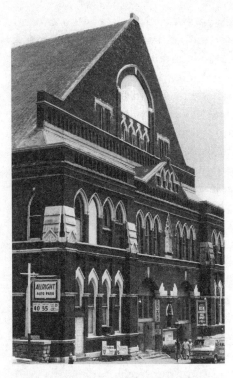

House of the holy: the Ryman Auditorium

at this same station, guitars in hand, heads full of hope: somehow it's appropriate that Greyhound are the first to dash their dreams. I start to walk towards downtown but the early evening heat chews on me. Where Texas heat was dry and hard, Nashville is tropical. I've barely slept these last few days and feel impossibly grungy, so head towards the first motel sign flashing 'vacancies'. I didn't aim on finding the worst motel in town but for $39.99 I appear to have done so. The room's as expected: a zombie coop, too shabby even to shoot a porn video in, the perfect location for conducting drug deals. A dead cockroach, feet stiff in the air, lies beside the bed, making an interesting alternative to chocolate on the pillow. One bare light bulb illuminates a crepuscular room. Shower until I've washed all those miles out of my skin and then crash out, dreams full of Hank Williams and other nice things.

Rise late for cups of tepid coffee and pancakes soaked in syrup and butter (sides: bacon rashes, grits, fried eggs and hash browns). Deep South food, Elvis food. Out on the street obese men and women wobble past, people who tackle a breakfast like mine daily, movable jellies with tiny limbs and cupcake heads. What kind of culture employs food as a self-destructive sedative? One where money and fear mark too much of adult existence. Think of Janie – by now in Chicago – and hope money and fear never dominate her adult life. San Antonio to Chicago by Greyhound: true grit worthy of a country song.

Back outside and the heat threatens to unravel my senses; time to take refuge in a museum that celebrates Nashville, the Country Music Hall of Fame. The CMHOF's impressive structure resembles a gigantic bass clef. Such architectural daring is radical in a city where every other building appears to be either mock classical or built with less imagination than your average car park. The CMHOF cost an impressive $32 million and today charges a steep $16 entrance, such expenditure emphasising how country music remains Nashville's proverbial gold mine. A gold-plated Cadillac once owned by Elvis and lots of ornate rhinestone cowboy suits are the museum's star attractions. As ever with American institutions, the air conditioning is cranked up to Antarctic levels.

Back on Broadway I head to Ernest Tubb's Record Shop. Tubb, from San Antonio, helped pioneer what's now called 'honky-tonk', bringing electric guitar into the music and writing a classic of the genre with 1941's 'Walking the Floor Over You'. His nasal voice and limited range – 'dejected' would be a good description of Ernest's prevailing emotional temper – was more than made up for by a work ethic (over two hundred gigs a year) and understanding of promotion: Tubb opened this store in May 1947, to sell recordings and trinkets. He performed a weekly Saturday Midnight Jamboree from here; this helped keep his name in lights even after the hits had long stopped coming. Tubb died over twenty years ago but this shop and another with a theatre connected (to keep the Midnight Jamboree alive) still exist. Only just. Today Tubb's offers a motley selection of CDs alongside old vinyl, cassettes, curling B & W photos of seventies country stars, decrepit souvenirs and antiquated songbooks. A layer of dust covers merchandise while a showroom dummy holding a stuffed guitar and wearing a polyester suit and hat stands in for Ernest.

Exiting Tubb's, I cross the road and head to the Ryman Auditorium: if any one building can be cited as the heart of Nashville it's the Ryman, home from 1943 to 1974 to the Grand Ole Opry, the Saturday night radio broadcast that championed country music, broadcasting to millions of devoted listeners across North America. While the Opry – named after a presenter's play upon 'grand opera' – first took shape in 1925 (and was officially christened TGOO in 1927) when National Life & Accident Insurance set up a weekly radio barn dance, the Ryman is where TGOO developed into an entertainment powerhouse, breaking new talent while establishing a template for country music performance and stardom. The Opry's success attracted recording companies and music publishers to set up in Nashville. *Think about it*: around an old-timey radio show set up to sell insurance to Southern Baptists a multibillion-dollar industry has grown.

The Ryman Auditorium, built in 1892, is a solid, red-brick building, its exterior still that of a nineteenth-century tabernacle. When the Opry left (in 1974) for the Opryland complex in East Nashville, the Ryman initially fell into disrepair before being renovated as a concert venue. During daylight hours $8 lets daytrippers in. Feels odd paying to enter a venue with nothing onstage. But as that stage hosted Hank Williams when he first tasted fame on 11 June 1949, it's part of the pilgrimage. Studying the Ryman's history, I realise Hank wasn't the first icon to tread the boards: although built as a church, the Ryman quickly developed into a theatre, and the likes of Booker T. Washington, W. C. Fields, Charlie Chaplin and The Fisk Jubilee Singers all appeared here before Hank. Seating remains provided by pews. An odd touch today but, I guess, in keeping with the Ryman's calling card as 'the mother church of country music'.

Kick back in a pew and let my mind wander. Imagine all the giants who took this stage. And imagine those days when

Americans gathered around their radios, investing joy and dreams in the sounds emanating from here. Even more so than the Apollo in Harlem, the Ryman served as musical oracle, a place where homespun philosophising and deceptively simple music emanated every Saturday. The Opry was a starmaker with ringmaster Roy Acuff ensuring performers adhered to a squeaky-clean grand design. Considering most country musicians came up the hard way, playing skull-orchard bars, existing on a diet of whiskey and amphetamines, this led to plenty of conflict. Hank was fired in August 1952, for his habitual inebriation. Johnny Cash had his drummer banned ('too nigger sounding') in 1958; a decade later, all speed-freak fury, he kicked out the stage lights. Patsy Cline, literally sewn back together after going through a car windscreen, returned to sing 'I Fall to Pieces' before getting on that doomed flight. The Louvin Brothers harmonised here on 'The Christian Life', Ira Louvin's clenched jaw and popping eyes hinting at a man riding the highway to hell. The Flying Burrito Brothers also sang 'The Christian Life', Gram Parsons both ironic and earnest, while the audience taunted them as 'squirrels' owing to their long hair. Loretta Lynn preached hillbilly feminism. George Jones, possessor of the most beautiful voice in country music history, took the stage so cocaine-blasted he sang chipmunk style. Tammy Wynette purred about standing by your man even though she left a bunch of 'em. That said, Tammy did stand by Alabama's segregationist governor George Wallace over the years. The seventies found Kinky Friedman's Texas Jewboys and James Brown playing the Opry but the eighties rendered the Opry superfluous – who needs a Saturday night radio show when you have 24-7 CMTV (Country Music TV)?

A man walks across the stage, adjusting monitors and interrupting my reverie. The high church of country music may have been run by those who adhered to the worst hypocrisies of Southern segregation but... *but the sights and sounds this venue has seen and heard...* much American beauty flowed from here and musicians from many backgrounds drew upon the reservoirs of music that flowed from the Ryman. In 1974 the Opry left the

Ryman, its exit a coda of sorts. American culture was changing and today the Ryman stands like a Medici tomb, a reflection of when the music had grit and life appeared simpler, less veined with uncertainty.

When the Opry left the Ryman it headed to Opryland, a purpose-built entertainment complex on the outskirts of the city's eastern borders. The Opry was never, as has been suggested, Nashville's heart but more its face, reflecting stars and fashions; appropriate, then, that as the decline in country music artistry became visible – the likes of Garth Brooks and Clint Black began selling millions of albums in the early nineties like no Nashville acts ever before – the Opry became easily forgettable. No need for me to visit Opryland, then. Yet I admit to a certain fascination and, as it happens, I've been offered a lift there by an East Nashville resident who happens to be a rising talent: Diana Jones.

Most of the music I write about comes through reading or being sent a CD or stumbling across it while travelling. My connection to Diana is simpler: a Czech friend, Lenka, hearing I was heading to Nashville, had suggested I look up her sister-

'Everything began to make sense': Diana Jones, Nashville, 2009

in-law (who happened to be a country singer). Finding Jones had a new album out, I purchased *My Remembrance of You* and found a singer and songwriter whose music echoed old-timey mountain music, sounds the Opry was founded upon, yet written with a keen, contemporary eye. *My Remembrance of You* is a quiet album – songs like 'Pretty Girl' and 'Pony' could have been written a century ago, while conveying a restless, dislocated quality, very twenty-first century. Lenka provided a phone number and, after yesterday afternoon's ramble around downtown, I found myself in the audience at the Bluebird Café, Nashville's leading acoustic music venue. The Bluebird featured heavily in River Phoenix's final film *That Thing Called Love* and photos of country stars who once played here cover the walls. Jones, accompanying herself on acoustic guitar, held the audience as she strummed and sang in a keen, yearning voice. Her songs appear timeless and, dressed in vintage clothing, she resembles the women in Dorothea Lange's photos. Considering the response she received, Jones's photo will surely soon join those on the wall.

Now, in the East Nashville sunshine, she's wearing jeans and T-shirt, her conversation pithy and wry. I'm a little surprised by the neighbourhood's tranquillity; reports had suggested East Nashville's entire economy revolved around biker bars, burglary and drug deals. When the likes of Steve Earle wanted to score it was to East Nashville they would head. Well, that was then. Gillian Welch and David Rawlings – the Gothic, cerebral Boston musical couple – shifted here in the nineties, purchasing a recording studio and house, and many followed in their wake. Today East Nashville's shotgun shacks and wood villas have been restored and the neighbourhood's spacious, old-fashioned ambience is very appealing. Diana says she purchased her former shotgun shack for $39,000, adding 'quite the bargain'.

Diana takes me to her favourite health food shop and the best café in East Nashville (lots of soy milk and decaf drinks available). She says East Nashville once had a bad rep but today is being gentrified. 'I lived in Austin previously, played music there. Great city but crazy expensive. Nashville's so much cheaper to live in and East Nashville's just full of musicians. It's ideal.' East Nashville is, I suggest, like an Austin adjunct to downtown Nashville? Diana thinks about it and says, 'Yeah, maybe something like that.' I compliment her on a great debut album and Diana fesses up that she cut two previous albums but both were more 'folky-singer-songwriter'. Via Lenka I'm aware Jones has lived in several cities before Nashville, including a spell in London ('Croydon, actually'). Turns out she was adopted and raised in the suburbs of New York, knowing nothing of her parents yet feeling an attraction to country music. Tracing her birth mother, she discovered her origins were in Tennessee.

'Maryville, Tennessee, in the Great Smoky Mountains. It was like the Waltons: fourteen cousins, four aunts, great-aunts and uncles – and my grandfather.'

Her grandfather, Robert Lee Maranville, had been a musician who'd played old timey as a youth before quitting music for a factory job. When long-lost grandchild Diana turned up with a guitar and mandolin, Robert started playing again, sharing musical secrets he had learnt decades before.

'My grandfather turned me on to all that mountain music,' she says. 'His favourite was "Will the Circle Be Unbroken". I ended up singing that at his funeral. Through him I began to make a deeper connection with the music, with my roots, and everything began to make sense: the way I look, my mannerisms, speech, taste in music. It took me a while to shift here but I really believe I'm home now in Tennessee, my ancestors have lived and died here for generations. There's definitely a connection here that I never felt back East.'

New York and Austin are also difficult places to build a career in country music: Nashville remains the music's epicentre and I wonder aloud why.

'Look at where Nashville is on the map,' says Diana. 'You can get to concerts across the South, the East, North, into the Midwest with a max of twelve hours' driving. You can cover the core region that supports and nourishes country and bluegrass and get back home – or to the Opry as Hank and a lot of the old school had to every Saturday night – without too much travelling.'

Diana points out a spectacular house now owned by her estate agent ('she's made a million from getting in on the East Nashville boom'), then suggests we head to Opryland. As Diana drives I ask about 'Pony', a song from *My Remembrance of You*: sung in the first person of a teenage Native female placed in a state boarding school. She sings, 'They cut my hair and changed my name.'

'OK, I based that on what went on in the late 1800s and into the 1900s when Native American kids were rounded up and put in these schools,' she says. 'The educational thinking then was to remove them from their families, their tribes, and hope they would grow up just like white Americans.'

Same thing, I offer, happened with the Aboriginal children in Australia.

'Really? That's so sad. See, I know what it's like to be taken away from something, to not know where you're really from. That gave me the idea to write "Pony", provided the song's soul, but to tell of the experience through someone else's story. People seem to respond real strong to "Pony".'

Indeed, the Bluebird Café's audience hushed as Jones narrated the tale, offering fanfare after fanfare when the song ended. 'Songwriting's an adventure,' says Diana, 'I draw from myself, my experiences, but I'm treating the songs as stories, trying to avoid autobiographical pathos that you find in so many singer-songwriters. I guess I'm doing something right when I get a reception like I do for "Pony".'

Opryland spreads in front of us, a sprawling complex best described as 'Nashvegas', surrounded as it is by thousands of hotel rooms and conference centres. An amusement park, complete with roller-coasters, once stood alongside, but flooding from the nearby river, bad management and the launch of Dollywood – Dolly Parton's theme park in the nearby Smoky Mountains – led to its demolition. This leaves only a gigantic mall: while the Ryman represented an American past this is the American future. Situated beneath a huge glass ceiling in a temperature-controlled environment, the Opryland mall, among hundreds of shops, offers struggling country singers the chance to do live spots. At the mall's centre rests a Disneyfied recreation of New Orleans' French Quarter called Delta Island: ersatz weatherboard buildings stand alongside a stream down which you can travel on a boat and learn the 'history' of Opryland.

Buried somewhere among all this is the Grand Ole Opry, an archaic institution within a postmodern structure. I check what's forthcoming at the Opry: this Saturday follows the static tradition of decades, hosted by Porter Wagoner, featuring regular performers Little Jimmie Dickens and Jean Shepherd, square dancers and special guests. The Opry operates as Saturday lite entertainment, as, I guess, it always has. The difference being the Opry once hosted genuinely radical new talent; things are now played very, very safe. Every Saturday there are two shows at six p.m. and nine p.m.; ticket prices for the 4,400-seat theatre start at $30. Diana suggests I'd probably be one of the few in the audience with my own teeth. She's probably right, but if I were in Nashville on a Saturday I'd attend, hoping Porter would still be able to conjure the magic he had in the sixties, that maybe one of the guests possessed some true country soul.

On our way back to downtown Diana tries to explain why she and a growing number of other young musicians are making music that harks back to pre-Elvis Southern music. 'Call it folk or country or old timey or whatever but this is what I feel natural doing. I like its honesty and down-to-earth quality.' You are, I offer, in good company: Old Crow Medicine Show, Uncle Earl, Alison Krauss, Iris Dement – and they're just the most well known. 'It's exciting,' agrees Diana. 'You keep hearing about the music industry having problems with downloads and stuff but on a creative level, well, things are real strong in East Nashville.' I then observe that her neighbours, Gillian Welch and David Rawlings, have made a pretty good go of playing what they call 'American Primitive' music. 'Yeah, they're so inspirational,' says Diana. 'They've shown a lot of us that you can play this kind of music and find an audience. Y'know, you can sing country and not have to compromise to all that pop crap Nashville now produces.' Not that getting heard is easy: country radio having been neutered after 1996 federal deregulation. 'Deregulation brings us Hot New Country radio,' says Diana, 'that plays back-to-back Brooks & Dunn and Toby Keith along with hours of ads extolling Chevy trucks. Luckily, there's lots of festivals and small venues that like the kind of music we make and a big interest across the US among people of my generation.' As we cruise the 40 loop highway Diana slips *My Remembrance of You* into her van's CD player and her voice – high, light, not noticeably Southern – sings

Cradle me, cradle me
in the warm hills of my family

SUNDAY SINGING

The family that sings together: country gospel, 1935

chapter 17

Nashville: Breakin' Broncos and Ridin' Bulls

'Dead Indians. That makes Nashville what it is – the town is built on the graves of dead Indians, and that's what gives the town its soul, its sadness; it all comes from being built on the bones of dead Indians.' John D. Loudermilk, writer of songs for everyone from Eddie Cochran to Norah Jones, once expressed this sentiment in reply to British DJ Nick Barraclough's query as to why Nashville birthed so much fine music. Back on Broadway, I get to dwelling on Native spirits: does genocide haunt a nation even if few acknowledge the crime?

Thousands of years ago the surrounding territory, where the Ohio and Cumberland rivers met the Smoky Mountains, hosted several Native tribes; indeed, the Cherokee gave the state its name when questioned by European explorers as to a certain river. Europeans may have embraced the poetry of the Natives but they were quick to encroach on these most fertile of tribal lands. The forced expulsion of Choctaws in 1817 became known as 'the trail of tears' while 1838's Nunna daul Isunyi ('the Trail Where We Cried') evokes 17,000 Cherokee being driven across Tennessee and Arkansas into Oklahoma, with 4,000 dying along the way. Country music is often derided as 'tear in my beer' songs; considering Tennessee's history this appears apt. Loudermilk wrote 'Indian Reservation' – a 1971 pop No. 1 for the Raiders – about the Cherokee's tragedy, yet I can't think of a single successful country singer of Native ancestry: Johnny Cash once claimed to be 'quarter Cherokee' but later admitted this was, as Huck Finn liked to say, 'a stretcher'. Ethnic cleansing, slavery, the Civil War,

Jim Crow laws, sharecropping's savagery, dirt farming's drudgery: the soil and soul of Tennessee's capital are fertile with suffering.

This all adds to the mystery of Nashville – how did so much musical magic arise from these streets of torpor and concrete? Beyond Broadway the city appears to consist of little more than hyper-Bible emporiums, used-car lots, fast-food joints, motels, gas stations and banks. Even Broadway is overshadowed by towering US Bank and Bell South structures, ugly smoked-glass monuments to corporate capitalism. The old buildings are Protestant plain and functional. The new buildings are Protestant gross, baldly extravagant, pumped up and aggressive. Steroid architecture. Walking also emphasises how Nashville earns its 'Protestant Vatican' nickname; city limits containing over a thousand churches – more per capita than anywhere else in the USA – missionary organisations, Bible publishers, faith-based colleges, religious administrators and preacher-teachers are all based here. Far more shops sell Bible-related materials than musical instruments; even Broadway's tattooist has a sign announcing he's a Christian biker. Nashville's the pumping heart of the Bible Belt; I'm where The Dixie Hummingbirds feared to tread.

If Broadway is where the talent turns up to hustle gigs and drinks, Music Row – two miles west – is where deals are cut, songs sold and records made. Today the buildings boasting EMI, Sony and co. share the crap architectural aesthetic ruling Nashville. RCA's Studio B – everyone who was anyone cut sessions here 1957–74 – is now a museum and retains a functional modernist skin. No beauty, but at least Studio B avoids the vulgar extravaganza that is Gaylord Entertainment's headquarters; Gaylord being the conglomerate owning the Opry. What did I expect to find here? Nothing really, just sniffing after the ash of history, aware that today Nashville constructs country music using a grammar found in advertisements: everything is laid out, no room for surprise or mistake or even the appealingly offbeat. Instead the songs come programmed with cues to hook the listener, push soap-opera emotions and suburban values. Even feisty women like

Shania Twain, Gretchen Wilson and The Dixie Chicks stick to a dispiriting/slick, loud formula.

Country's surviving old school – Merle Haggard, George Jones, John Anderson, Willie Nelson, Dolly Parton, etc. – tend to endorse this view, bitching about how Nashville's lost its roots, gone pop. The executives in Music Row shrug off such complaints, feeling no nostalgia for Nashville's golden age, focused as they are on creating multi-platinum entertainers. In terms of pure commerce the transformation of a rough, regional music into a huge cash cow is a great success, Nashville now vying with LA and New York as the daddy of all US music cities. Over the course of the twentieth century black American music forms (jazz, blues, soul, rock 'n' roll) arose from the South and conquered the planet while country remained an ugly stepchild, a music many sneered at. Today blues, jazz and soul are boutique music(s), largely appealing to middle-aged, middle-class white listeners. Rock 'n' roll is extinct, leaving its leaden offspring: *rock*. Nashville's country stars now often match or outsell even the most popular pop/rock/rap performers, Shania Twain selling more CDs during the 1990s than any other act.

Platinum sales haven't helped make country music fashionable and jokes about hillbillies, incest and folk who manage to make saying 'yeee-haaaa' sound malevolent still abound. Which is patronising but understandable, country music having a strong reactionary streak, reflecting – to some degree – America's white working classes, their suspicion of social change and the conservative values many cling to. It's always been this way, but where the music once had spirit *(white man's blues, redneck soul)*, Hot New Country is insipid, Botox music. Perhaps this flattening of the music is a reflection of how American agribusiness has crushed the family farm; today most country music fans don't live in the country. Even those who do don't endure the harsh challenges small farmers once dealt with on a daily basis. Which, I guess, helps explain why most contemporary country music now sounds closer to The Eagles and Billy Joel than Hank and Lefty. What remains is a taste for sentiment, life simplified into sugary ballads and dumb stadium rock: driving across Texas I heard several 'yellow ribbon' songs, the Iraq invasion presented as platitude (faith, love, small-town community), no questions asked, song narratives receding into patriotic rom-coms. It's not the lack of a left perspective that offends me but the loss of vision and soul in a music once offering plenty of both. America's always been messy, as are the concerns of American music, yet Music Row now ensures songs get flossed, made over until all the dirt, pain and grit are removed.

This is the problem of travelling alone: I tend to start arguing aloud with myself. Can feel more vitriol coming on.

I look around Music Row and shudder: what they now create here is neither country nor good. *Burn it down.*

Back on Broadway a busker offers to play any requests for $1. I toss a bill and request Hank. The busker's raw-boned, surly-eyed, drawling as only small town boys do. 'Hank?' he says – pronouncing it *'Huuunnnnchhhh'* – seemingly surprised. He digs into a notebook, finds a chord pattern and begins singing a very perfunctory 'Cold, Cold Heart'. The spirit of Hank Williams hovers in Nashville's humidity, his nasal voice, stomping songs and magic hooks marking him forever as the man who turned country into something bigger than the sound of the po' white South. Hank, with his damaged spine and weeping emotions, using whiskey and morphine as medicine, stands as one of America's great popular poets, a man who composed songs as he and his band, The Drifting Cowboys, cut from honky-tonk to dance hall, beating rhythms upon a Cadillac's dashboard, knocking out hit after hit, this wild, doomed man whose flair with words and music had him dubbed the Hillbilly Shakespeare during his brief twenty-nine years. The busker finishes and my reverie ends. I'm amazed, I say, that you don't have the Hank songbook memorised. He shrugs, states The Eagles and Pink Floyd as preferences. When even the hillbillies prefer 'classic rock' staples, well, country music's in real trouble.

The warm evening finds Broadway busy, people dipping in

and out of bars and restaurants, hoping to catch a taste of what made Nashville famous. The vibe is similar to that found in Hollywood, the almost urgent expectancy of celebrity and louche good times, except everyone is white and most are over thirty-five. And many are obese. Is there a link with the decline in US Top 40 radio and increasing US bodily corpulence? AM and FM radio once bubbled with both inane songs and wild spectacle, the democracy of American music allowing for the good, the bad and the ugly to get through. This made listening an adventure, a pleasure. Today, popular music radio in America is numbing, the same shiny songs programmed over and over, corporate country/pop/R & B designed to bookend loud, garish advertisements. Fun, imagination, magic, *spirit*: all removed. Less joy in music = less joy in life. Well, worse theories exist.

Shouting and cursing erupt behind me and I turn to find two middle-aged couples brawling on the corner of Broadway and 4th Avenue South. The men (moustaches, tight jeans, big belt buckles) push, pull and swing at each other, aggressive yet stiff, so unlike the fights you see in movies, punches connecting only with air. The women (big hair, pant suits) fight nasty, bashing at each other with handbags, tearing hair. Broadway stops and stares and an obese family I've just stepped around – Papa, Mama, Bubba, Sis – shout the odd 'Whoooo' in support of the free entertainment. Bubba paws fried chicken from a huge tub of KFC Papa's carrying and in between mouthfuls sets up a running commentary, comparing the brawlers to his favourite WWF wrestlers. Unlike WWF brawls this scrap goes on for ever: no police arrive, no Samaritan steps in. A newspaper box gets knocked over. The ferocious four's messy spectacle continues, dead Indians still extracting their toll.

Texan country rocker Joe Ely likes to joke 'what's got five balls and fucks rednecks? The Tennessee state lottery.' To which I'd add Bud and Miller; those scrapping are definitely inebriated. Turning away, I drift into Broadway's honky-tonks. Tootsie's Orchid Lounge offers walls covered in discoloured photos of country stars and faded graffiti. The likes of Kris Kristofferson,

Willie Nelson and Waylon Jennings spent much of the 1960s boozing and songwriting here. Hank Williams would reputedly prop up the back bar between Opry appearances, having only to stagger several metres down the alley and into the Ryman Auditorium when needed. I wonder whether it was Tootsie's whiskey that found Hank fired from the Opry for lack of sobriety in August 1952? Today Tootsie's trades heavily on its past, offering free admission then overcharging for drinks. It has a tiny stage by the Broadway entrance (for solo performers) and a larger upstairs stage for bands next to the Ryman's alley. On a hot Wednesday night a skinny Southern white boy is working the upstairs stage hard. Chris Janson announces he's nineteen and struts to the front of stage, leaps on a monitor and begins to blow tough blues harmonica. He's wearing a faded Kiss T-shirt, filthy Levi's, backwards baseball cap, nothing but rags, skin, bones, teeth and music. As he honks away women old enough to be his mama reach forward. Chris swaggers through bar band standards; on 'Honky Tonk Woman' he focuses his attention on a young woman sitting side of stage and dances the shim-sham-shimmy. She smiles. *Honky-tonkin'*.

If East Nashville is now tame, an evening stroll along 8th Avenue – past my beloved Greyhound station – is urban Nashville's way of putting the frighteners on. I'm attempting to find a Nashville music venue but there's little street lighting and no signs. Walking through inky darkness I grow increasingly desperate. Tourist Nashville is a long way back, and when the road splits into Lafayette Street and 8th Avenue South I ponder the wisdom of continuing – I mean, who knows what lies ahead? *Failed country singers mugging the unwary? Crankster hillbillies hungry for the money and marrow of those lost in the ass-end of Nashville?* Force myself forward; a genuine old-school country legend is playing tonight. The night air has settled at sauna temperatures but I break out in a cold sweat, jumping at shadows, feeling uneasy in the American night. *Why didn't I take a taxi?* Obvious question to beat myself up over. Thing is, the Mercy Lounge didn't appear a great distance when I studied my Nashville map. And being a music venue I imagined it would be surrounded by other facilities. Fat chance. What little I can make out appears to be factories, warehouses, vehicle repair shops... city gristle. Lots of traffic roaring past but none of it stopping. And I'm the only one out walking. *Why didn't I take a taxi?* Funds are running low so I'm back to budget travelling. Scratch that, I'm *always* budget travelling. To travel in comfort? Stuff of dreams. Feel increasingly uneasy, wondering whether I'm actually on the right road, yet the map suggests Cannery Row is somewhere off 8th Avenue South. A brightly lit minivan tears past and then swings a sharp right, headlights illuminating a Mercy Lounge sign.

Sprint up the alley and in front of me a large spacious building squats by train tracks. I catch my breath and breathe a sigh of relief that surely is heard across town. The Mercy Lounge is, obviously, a former factory. High ceilings. Hardwood floors. Pool tables. Pinball machines. Long, curving bars. Vintage couches. Large stage. Atmospheric. One helluva improvement on Broadway's honky-tonks. On stage is Junior Brown, a big man in a suit and Stetson who plays a combination steel/electric guitar, mixing weeping notes with jazzy leads. The sound is extraordinary but it's not Junior I've ventured out for. Tonight's headliner is Billy Joe Shaver, a South-west legend, and the crowd he draws reflects this: Hell's Angels, college students, middle-class professionals, grizzled men who might be ranch hands or truck drivers, and designer cowboys (Stetson, boots, belt, embroidered shirt and trousers). Last time I saw Shaver was at London's Borderline where his band included guitarist Jesse Taylor. That hot summer night they rocked the Borderline like few others ever have. Billy Joe can not only write a great song, he can sing it too. Using my 'journalist/London' ruse I make my way backstage, where a congenial atmosphere finds musicians and friends relaxing, no pre-show nerves. Over in a corner sits a large, grey-haired man reading the Bible. Obviously pre-gig preparation as Shaver is known to pray onstage between songs. 'Excuse me, sir,' I say, approaching him quietly, 'would it be possible to ask you some

'Been busted up so many times': Billy Joe Shaver, Nashville, TN, 2006

questions?' He looks up, broad features creased and lined, black eyes cautious, considers my request, then nods. He gestures with a hand missing several digits. I freeze, a little intimidated. 'You want me to give you a medal?' he growls, then chuckles. *'C'mon!'*

Billy Joe Shaver was born in Corsicana, Texas, in 1939, yet fate almost decreed he would not spend any time on earth: his father Buddy, an illiterate, bare-knuckle brawler of French-Blackfoot ancestry, drunkenly decided he wasn't the sire of his wife's unborn child and set about beating Billy's mother to death two months before their son was born, dumping her broken body in a stock tank. Somehow Mama and unborn baby survived but, after giving birth to Billy Joe, his mother fled sharecropping and a son that reminded her of the psychotic Buddy. He was raised by his grandmother on a dirt farm, and his hardscrabble existence ensured Shaver would try the US Navy, timber mills (the missing fingers) and the rodeo circuit (a broken back) before making his way to Nashville in 1966.

After several years of hustling and struggling, Shaver established himself as a first-class songwriter, won a record deal and in 1973 released his debut album, *Old Five & Dimers Like Me*. Shaver's songs are simple creations, narrative tales that chug along without musical or lyrical adornment, and he sings them as if he's making them up on the spot, jamming a word here and yodelling on a vowel there. Willie Nelson describes Billy Joe as 'maybe the best songwriter alive today', Johnny Cash called him 'my favourite writer', while Kris Kristofferson makes comparisons with Hemingway. I'll add that Shaver is a song poet of the highest order, his direct, eloquent verse both poignant and droll. Few American writers have managed to describe love and lust and the bitter grace of manual labour in a manner comparable to Shaver. He is the poet laureate of honky-tonks and the music he makes – 'hard country', music rooted in soil and lived experience – is inspirational stuff. Alongside Merle Haggard and Tom T. Hall, Shaver's the most consistent hard-country songwriter of recent decades. 'Go on, son,' he gently reprimands, 'ask something.'

OK: what shaped Billy Joe Shaver, Country Singer?

'I started out doing farm work. We lived in a cotton gin town and in summers I would spend time with my uncles, who were farmers. We had three months off school and I'd go live with them on their farms and work my ass off. I got most of my learning done out there. They were real spiritual people, they churched a lot, had to as it's real tough being a farmer in Texas. The weather hits you in the head an' all. I remember one of my uncles crouching and drawing patterns with a stick in the dirt and not saying nothin' but I knew he was thinkin' "what are we gonna do if we don't get any rain?" Man, I got off that farm as fast as I could and I ain't never goin' back! Ain't it strange how people in the town want to live in the country an' vice versa? They say the grass is greener. Well, I done farmed an' I know that ain't true.'

What about riding rodeo? That's real cowboy stuff!

'I broke broncos and rode bulls. Won some trophies but most of the time I seemed to go up in the air and land on my head. Rodeo's hard, man. Gotta be young and tough to wanna do that.'

By the sound of it you were tough, living the wild life, always getting in fights?

'We'd go down to Chicago to these smokers and really hurt ourselves. Smokers were, I guess, a form of illegal prizefighting with people betting on the fighters and they'd let us navy boys participate 'cos they knew we loved to fight. You'd walk away with maybe ten, twenty dollars, nothing, we did it not for the money but for the craziness. And, yeah, I used to fight a lot in honky-tonks but that was me only fighting to stop from getting killed. But I can't fight these days. I've got a plate in my neck, quadruple heart surgery... I've been busted up so many times that I can't go and get hurt like I used to.'

You tried farming, the navy, mill work and rodeos: what made you decide to be a country singer?

'My English teacher at school, she encouraged me [to write]... told me point blank that I was good. And I believed her. When I lost my fingers and broke my back I realised how I must move on. And writing and singing, I'd always been attracted to those two.'

Any musical heroes you care to mention?

'I snuck out to see Hank play in Corsicana when I was a little boy. Got a whuppin' from Granma when I got back but I'm sure pleased I saw him. Grew up sellin' papers an' singin' while I sold 'em. Singin' Roy Acuff an' Jimmie Rodgers. Cross the tracks from where Granma lived there was an African-American family an' they had a stand-up piano an' bottleneck guitar. I'd go an' listen to them play all day. Best music I ever heard. They'd play Jimmie Rodgers songs – they thought Jimmie was black an' so did I 'cos he sang an' played like a black man. Years later one of those guys said to me, "I seen a photo of Jimmie Rodgers an' he's white!" Skin's funny. Ain't nothin' different 'bout it but the colour of pigment an' people make such a big deal 'bout it. That stuff 'cross the tracks was better than anything else. Better than anything I ever heard before or since.'

This makes sense: Shaver's music has a down-home, front-porch, bluesy flavour. Just as Jimmie and Hank's music did.

Having arrived in Nashville almost forty years ago, did Billy Joe feel much affection for the city?

'Nashville back then... it was pretty rowdy... I became fast friends with Tom T. Hall and David Allan Coe, they were both young songwriters new to town. Bobby Bare signed me as a songwriter – God bless him but the deal he cut me has cost me a fortune – and let me sleep on his sofa. After four years I was still sleeping on that sofa so about to quit and head back to Texas. Then Bobby introduced me to Kris Kristofferson and he cut my song "Christian Soldier". Through Kris I met Waylon and Willie an' that Texas crowd. Got to know Johnny and June Cash. But I was wild... didn't make the most of my opportunities.'

Has Music City changed? Tootsie's still exists.

'Tootsie's? Been thrown out of there plenty of times! Back then nobody ripped you off, everyone thought they wrote the best. Now you have to be more careful, people will steal stuff from your songs. They've worked out you can make a lot of money in country music. Today it's a much bigger industry. I lived here from 1966 to 1984. I love it as a city. But I had to leave it as everybody was getting so high.'

Shaver now lives in Waco, Texas. Is Waco as insane as I imagine?

'Every five years something crazy goes off there. David Koresh is the most famous. More recently some guy cut someone's head off and used it as a basketball. See, Waco used to be an outlaw town and the Texas Rangers figured the only way they could control it was to hang everyone. So the Rangers came through and started lynching people, innocent or not. That craziness still comes through. I mean, you don't go to nightclubs there. I just spent fourteen hundred dollars on a lawyer to get my nephew off a murder charge. Some fellow pushed his motorbike over an' while I know that's something you don't do it doesn't mean you have to kill the man. But they shot him.'

For all the violence surrounding Shaver's life he's a gentle bear of a man, never boastful, and very lyrical when recalling the great loves of his life: his grandmother Birdy, mother Victory, wife

Brenda and their one child, Eddy. Birdy raised Shaver and told him as he sang along to the radio that one day he would appear on the Grand Ole Opry. 'That planted seeds. She was a great woman.' His tempestuous relationship with Brenda (the couple married thrice) shadowed his adult life. Eddy joined Shaver's road band aged twelve, developing into a gifted guitarist, playing with Billy Joe over the years. Shaver's mother and wife both passed during 2000. Billy Joe suffered a triple whammy when Eddy died of a drug overdose on 31 December 2000.

'We went from being father and son to being friends 'cos that's the only way to endure one another on the road. An' we were really good friends… the greatest of friends. Eddy did everything… figured he was good lookin'… bulletproof. He fell in with a bad crowd so when he OD'd, instead of callin' 911 they called the drug dealer an' he came around and injected him with some drug an' that's what killed him.'

I'm unsure of exactly what to say next but Billy Joe fills the gap.

'Eddy was an adult. Knew what he was getting into. I'd warned him but I weren't the best role model – when he was a kid I was boozin' an' crankin' an' all the rest…'

He shrugs, mouth downturned, black eyes, *Indian eyes*, stoic yet filled with sorrow.

'I've done plenty of crazy things in my time… fought far too much. But I look back over my life and think [pause] just to survive is great.'

He smiles, a tall Texan tale that keeps unfolding.

'I started off being a cowboy. Still *am* a cowboy. Just moved on a little.'

Stage time: Billy Joe picks up an acoustic guitar that looks to have lived with him for decades, a piece of string as guitar strap, steps up to the microphone, offers some good-natured pleasantries and the band kick in behind him. He sings about being an old lump of coal but, hey, he's gonna be a diamond some day. And he sings about how they don't make men like Jesus Christ any more. He chuckles at his own lyrics, thanks Jesus, and holds the Mercy

Lounge transfixed. Thing is, Nashville doesn't produce artists like Billy Joe these days, his hard-spun wisdom and honky-tonk cantos shining diamond hard. Tonight's a quieter show than when I caught him with Jesse Taylor but he and his band still rock. On one song he sings '*And I just thought I'd mention/my grandma's old age pension/Is the reason why I'm standing here today*' and everyone cheers. Billy Joe, you're the greatest!

'I get real sensitive': Deanie Parker in the 60s

chapter 18

Memphis: The Beauty of Primitive Music

Talk about living the dream: I'm on a South Memphis street and Al Green is walking past. Though 'walking' is inexact as a fleshy circle of bodyguards convey Green towards the stage, the tiny soul man appearing to hover among a movable muscle bulwark. All this is odd – not Al's forthcoming performance, but the security overload, Al long having been a native son, and these surely are his people. What makes Al's behaviour even weirder is there's so few folk – *one hundred? One hundred and twenty?* – relaxing in the early evening sun.

Word of Green's appearance hasn't brought the 'hood out and those under forty don't appear to know who he is. A young black woman wanders past, looks at the stage and says, 'What the fuck they doin' closin' my block?' She shakes her head in despair then adds, 'Lettin' crackheads run all over the place. Sheeee,' and stalks off so I'm left wondering, *Where're the crackheads? Are they out to get me?* But all appears calm; local kids are enjoying having the street to themselves while weary older residents with *what-the-hell-might-as-well-get-off-the-stoop-an'-check-this-shit* expressions lounge around. 'Al Green? He usedta be 'round here all day, ev'ry day,' says a man, blowing smoke through the gap where his front teeth once were. 'I remember the Cadillacs an' Lincolns they usta park out here. Good cars. American cars. Park right here outside Royal Studios.'

Royal Recording Studios, owned by producer Willie Mitchell (who cut Green's classic sides here), is the focus of this evening's celebrations. Where Sun Studios captured fifties electric blues/rockabilly and Stax birthed sixties Southern soul, Royal took

Memphis soul to its seventies zenith. City officials, finally realising how Memphis's musical history generates major tourist dollars, now pay attention: today they're honouring Mitchell's contributions to civic life by renaming the stretch of Lauderdale Street Royal Studios sits on 'Willie Mitchell Boulevard'. At least Willie's alive to enjoy the florid tributes they've been paying him; most other Memphis musical icons were in the cold, dark earth before the city noted their worth.

Soulsville (aka the Stax Museum of American Soul Music), located little more than five minutes' walk from Royal, stands as a monument to both Memphis neglect and an American beauty long vanquished. In Nashville the Country Music Hall of Fame may murmur with voices from the past but there still exists a market for hard country music; no matter how the likes of D'Angelo and Mary J. Blige are promoted as inheritors of the flame, their sound is simply too synthetic to suggest real engagement with the intense blend of sex and religion, black and white culture, that marked Southern soul music. Today soul music is relegated to the oldies arena or black Southern clubs. Wandering Soulsville before heading to the Royal Studios shindig got such thoughts flowing; the museum's exterior purposely resembles the old movie theatre at 926 E. McElmore Avenue that once housed pre-eminent Southern soul label Stax's offices and recording studio, while inside 17,000 square feet of exhibition space celebrate label, artists and black Southern culture. The likes of Otis Redding, Sam & Dave and Booker T & The MGs all cut deep Southern soul here, music thick with Hammond organ fugues straight out of black Baptist churches and gospel voices and guitars picking country melodies, community music, music that nourished black American pride and culture, deep Southern communion... *holy! holy!*... it felt like walking on sacred ground.

I ogled Al Jackson Jr's drum kit, set up in a recreation of what once was the studio – *the rhythms that kit delivered to the world!* – and checked Isaac Hayes's gold-trimmed, mink-lined Cadillac Eldorado pimpmobile: as with Elvis's gold Caddie in Nashville, only someone who grew up dirt poor could waste so much money on a blinged-out car. From 1960 Stax, with its interracial musicians and belief in developing local talent and the majestic, organic Southern sound that came to be associated with the label, represented Memphis at its most down-home yet visionary. That everything came crashing down in January 1976, bad business dealings and ego and graft rotting all, the entire dream ending sour and broken, is an American tragedy. The city demolished the original building in 1988 – *'Memphis has destroyed more history that it can ever remember'* runs a local saying – signalling that the dreams, pride and legacy of black Memphis's greatest achievement were consigned to the dumpster.

My 'London/journalist' front at the box office got me introduced to Soulsville's PR, Tim Sampson, a native Memphian who insisted I talk to Deanie Parker, Soulsville's founder and director. Deanie was initially reluctant to chat but mentioning I had met Mable John won an invitation to sit. 'Mable's organisation sent so many boxes of food and clothing down to us to help the Hurricane Katrina victims,' said Deanie. 'She's a Stax artist who ain't never forgotten her people.' Deanie, it turns out, started as a Stax artist, cutting a couple of 45s in the early sixties then set up the label's PR department, running it until those increasingly bitter days in 1975. The streets surrounding Soulsville are leafy and bleak – *stores bordered up, shanty houses, gangs in control, pure Southern ghetto* – a neighbourhood left to rot. Just as Memphis has never truly recovered from being the site of Martin Luther King's assassination, the city's also tainted by Stax's collapse: in 1973 Memphis was the fourth largest recording centre in the world, the music industry then the city's third largest business. But Stax's implosion levelled things; even Willie Mitchell's Hi Records felt reverberations with hits harder to score (Mitchell sold the label in the late seventies). Championing Stax as a hinge upon which Southern music, culture and race relations swung from one era into the next, Deanie convinced one of Memphis's richest citizens that the label's legacy needed to be honoured. Money in place, Soulsville opened in 2003.

'I had a great relationship with fabulous musicians, singers,

White hot: Linda Lyndell, Memphis, 1969

writers,' Parker noted of her Stax years. 'It was such an exciting time! I remember Otis Redding coming into the studio with all these ideas in his head. He'd pluck out the melody on his gee-tar – that's how he pronounced it! – and the musicians would pick up on it. He had the horn lines in his head and he'd give them to Wayne and company. He'd stomp around the studio until everyone got it out. It was painful the way we were recording – hot in the summer, freezing in winter – painful but it felt so good!' I asked whether it was the memories of Otis and co. which drove her to build Soulsville? 'It's more than just memories. In the early nineties I was approached by a local businessman who said, 'We're thinking of putting a Stax club and restaurant on Beale Street.' I said, 'Stax doesn't belong on Beale Street. Don't reduce it to a restaurant – the contribution is too significant.' So this eventually came to me putting a prototype and business plan together and working for five years to raise funds.'

Ironically, South Memphis is now the only part of Memphis producing contemporary music that sells strongly: *gangsta rap*.

'Rap is not music,' snapped Deanie when I mentioned this. 'We aim here to teach the neighbourhood kids how to play instruments, how to make music. There were once strong music programmes in local schools but they rarely have the funding to keep that going now. I get real sensitive when I think how the music industry has been victimised, lost any example to be creative, over the last twenty-five years.'

Surely, I reason, rappers sampling the Stax catalogue keeps the material fresh: I'm thinking of Salt-N-Pepa scoring a huge hit with their reinventing of Stax artist Linda Lyndell's 'What a Man'?

'OK, the funds provided from sampling are appreciated, always. But rap is rhythm and rhyme, not music, and its success has encouraged kids to forget about learning musical instruments. And don't get me started on rappers promoting violence and denigrating women.'

Yet rap's the pulse black America now moves to. Memphians Three 6 Mafia won the 2006 Oscar for Best Original Song with 'It's Hard Out Here for a Pimp' (from *Hustle & Flow*'s soundtrack), the biggest coup for any local artist since Al Green's early-seventies heyday. Rhyme pays and *Hustle & Flow*'s vivid depiction of hip-hop dreams bubbling in South Memphis offers a snapshot of a literal cottage industry: a modicum of rhyming and narrative talent paired with someone who can programme an electronic keyboard (and home studio recording skills) being all that's needed. Thing is, when Stax set up it wasn't so different: a disused movie theatre as a recording studio, the most basic one-track recording machine, reliant on a pool of poor black talent from the 'hood. But Stax required musicians who could play their instruments – 'everybody had to be in tune and on time,' recalled Deanie, 'sometimes you cut a song raggedy 'cos it had that groove. No way you can manufacture it' – while rap's largely devolved into selling badass persona or party songs: *who's the best liar? Who can market murder most effectively? Who's got a novelty dance?* Noting that Deanie isn't interested in debating rap aesthetics I ask after Linda Lyndell, the white soul singer who vanished after her first Stax hit, 'What a Man' – Lyndell sang soul so convincingly that the KKK started issuing her with death threats.

'From what I know she was mostly Cherokee Indian and had a very abusive father so she would run away and stay with her black neighbours and grew up singing in church with them. Then Otis Redding discovered her singing on the chitlin' circuit. He told her she had to get to Stax, made some phone calls, maybe was thinking of producing her. But then his plane went down. Anyway, I only knew her for one hot minute back in '69 and she was a lovely individual and great singer. When you heard her sing, man, it was hard not to believe she wasn't a soul sister that God took out of the oven a little too soon!' Deanie smiles and adds, 'Soulsville has made contact with her and she now performs at some of our events. She still sings great.'

Deanie witnessed Memphis throw off the shackles of segregation then implode as capital, citizens and musicians all fled a city spiralling into seemingly permanent decline. Today Memphis is the tenth poorest city in the USA. Does she see Soulsville's success as signalling the city's resurrection?

'The problems afflicting Memphis reflect on the wedge that greed is driving between people in the US,' she offered when I asked about Memphis's future. 'You can't eat but one forkful at a time, can't wear but one pair o' shoes at a time, but what's happening now is an American tragedy and the country is on a fast course to self-destruction. The masses are becoming very cynical, losing trust in everything, ruled by fear. What else can

Barber college, South Memphis

we expect when our leaders employ greed as policy and appear desensitised to the suffering of others? Stax was a finishing school for a lot of people like me and I'm hoping it can offer a similar kind of hope for the local children. This is the poorest zip code in all of Shelby County so we'll either rise with the community or be consumed by it.'

Outside Royal Studios the speeches continue with Mayor Willie Herenton – Memphis's long-reigning black mayor (he claims divine appointment) – praising Mitchell. I wander past the stage and down to where Willie Mitchell Boulevard again becomes Lauderdale Street and black Memphis slips into decay. Broken glass everywhere; weeds forcing their way through the sidewalk; a laundry and fried-chicken outlet, both look beat, dispirited – *if buildings could will themselves to collapse these two would be bricks and dust* – surrounding bungalows are small, weathered, many boarded up, overgrown; simple home-made signs advertise shoe repair ('*Best Shine Around*', says one next to a boot outline) or beauty services, and even though the sun's shining the feel here is ominous. A car crawls past, tyre flapping, chassis squeaking, driver scanning with dull, hungry eyes, me trying to look away – *so blatantly a tourist* – wishing to be invisib— *Someone's calling my name!* I turn to see Scott, a Memphis musician I'd met outside Royal Studios, signalling. 'C'mon,' he says, 'you don't want to be wandering 'round here by yourself. Bad things could happen.'

Back on Willie's Boulevard Al Green steps up to the mic, nervous in front of a small audience, no throngs of shrieking women to greet him. The band kicks into 'Let's Stay Together' and Al dishes out kisses and handshakes, swings hips, sylvan voice seducing all. Then the PA blows. Al continues a cappella for a minute, shrugs and vanishes behind muscle. While Mitchell's adult children attempt to salvage the situation Scott invites me into Royal Studios. Royal should look more impressive than it does: a boxy building with yellowing press cuttings and curling photos on the wall, cigarette burns in the carpet and insulation sticking out of the ceiling. I look across the recording space, a large sloping floor – like Stax, Royal was also once a neighbourhood cinema – with a grand piano among the amplifiers, and imagine the young Al listening to Willie issue instructions as to how he should phrase a vocal line. Syl Johnson. Ann Peebles. O. V. Wright. Otis Clay. All cut great material here. Al Jackson laying down the rhythm. Today the LBJ/Nixon era appears a high-water mark for black America, a time of immense social upheaval *and* musical creativity, soul-blues-jazz still made by African-Americans for their own community, those years before Ronald Reagan and cocaine levelled a culture built by America's poorest people into a twentieth-century Renaissance. A renaissance that conquered the world with good grooves and hot tunes. Will Memphis eventually turn Royal into a museum? More likely they'll knock it down first. Back on the street and there's no solution to the PA problems. 'This is so goddam Memphis,' says Scott.

Scott offers me a lift back to downtown; we first stop for gas on South 3rd Street. Most US gas stations resemble mini-malls, bright, spotless consumer temples offering everything from melted cheese Doritos to John Wayne DVD sets. Not this one. I step out of our vehicle and find myself confronted by a hunched and truly beat-looking black woman muttering some unintelligible mantra. Keep saying 'excuse me?' while trying to get around her as she hisses something that, after several attempts, I make out as 'gimmefiftycent'. Drop two quarters in her palm. 'Gimmedollar,' she says. Sidestep the crone and hike it into the gas station, a dark, dank box, the cash machine lacking a zero so the cashier, an incredibly cheery young Arab, is explaining, 'can you buy twenty-nine or thirty-one dollars gas as we can't do thirty?' Back outside a motley crew of black men, many in wheelchairs or on crutches, have joined the crone. They're malnourished, toothless, leftovers from an unmade George Romero black zombie movie. A chorus of 'hey fella'/'please, bossman'/'yo, white boy' greets me as I approach the car. Scott emerges, transaction finally processed, looking with increasing horror at the unfolding scenario, shooing the wretched away as he starts pumping gas, muttering, 'Never encourage these people by giving them money.' I've been to Calcutta, Cairo, Gypsy mahalas in Bulgaria, but the despair's worse here, Americans reduced to begging in the court of a dilapidated gas station. Scott replaces the pump, says, 'Get in' and we flee. 'Were they,' I ask, 'refugees from New Orleans?' 'I doubt it,' says Scott, 'just poor, fucked-up Memphians.' Memphians who look like they exist among Haiti's garbage dumps.

Back in central Memphis, Scott drops me at 2nd Street, shaking his head when I mention I'm heading to Beale Street. 'Beale Street's a farce,' he says, 'an affront to Memphis music.' *Absolutely.* This is why I'm interested in checking it. Beale Street was once among the most celebrated black American streets in the USA, the place every Southern blues musician headed to for bright lights/big city, home to black vaudeville theatres, cafés and bars. Back then it was called Beale Avenue, yet when Memphis composer W. C. Handy scored with 'Beale Street Blues' the city followed suit. To command such influence that Avenue gets flipped into Street only hints at Handy's early twentieth-century presence.

First stop on Beale is W. C. Handy's house. Information posted outside this tiny bungalow makes it clear Handy never actually lived on Beale; the city shifted the house here to capitalise on Beale Street's tourist trade. The house lacks historic material but Handy, self-proclaimed 'Father of the Blues', is the kind of self-made-man-with-a-vision Memphis once excelled at producing. Born in Alabama to freed slaves in 1873, Handy – *educated, focused, hard working* – led a black orchestra that hustled for coin at minstrel and tent shows, mixing ragtime, cakewalks and light classical pieces for their public, the mobile young William Christopher taking note of the jump-ups, spirituals, field hollers, work songs, country string bands, fife and drum and brass bands – the very origins of much popular American music – he heard on the road. One night in 1903, at a railway station in Tutwiler, Mississippi, he heard a ragged man sing *'Goin' where the Southern cross the Dog'*, each time he repeated the line sliding a knife along the guitar neck. *'Weirdest music I had ever heard,'* Handy later recalled. Not long after, his orchestra played in Cleveland, Mississippi, and at intermission allowed a local blues trio to take the stage. Dancers went wild and showered the musicians in a rain of silver dollars, more money than Handy's entire orchestra were receiving. He later wrote, '*Then I saw the beauty of primitive music.*'

Handy began noting these unsung singers' hooks and rhymes, incorporating such into his own 'blues'. Among his most famous compositions are 'St Louis Blues' and 'Memphis Blues' – songs that, by applying a pop aesthetic to a vernacular music, made Handy the template for everyone from Jimmie Rodgers, Bob Dylan and Berry Gordy Jr to Outkast. Handy wasn't 'authentic' but his ear for the everyday poetry of African-American speech and ability to write memorable songs, songs that still sound great today, helped popularise blues as an American musical genre. And he knew Beale Avenue well, claiming he wrote 'Beale Street Blues' after hearing a local barber say he was closing early as there hadn't been a murder on Beale that day: Memphis then having the highest murder rate of any US city.

Today Beale Street bars pump out generic blues-rock and serve margaritas and ribs. The street's prominence as part of black Memphis died in the 1960s when the city turned sour – this, the replica Beale Street, reinvented for conventioneers and Elvis tourists, is a nineties creation modelled on New Orleans' Bourbon Street. In between the bars are emporiums of crap memorabilia pouring scorn on a boulevard where a young Riley King earned his nickname 'the Beale Street Blues Boy', the teenage Elvis learned all he needed to know and countless performers squeezed out sparks that would later catch fire across the South, and farther afield.

The only business remaining from the street's golden era is Schwabs, a dusty department store that sells the same tourist tack as the other Beale Street stores alongside all kinds of everything (jams, work clothing, trinkets, toys) and the voodoo powders and candles ('Good Luck', 'Big Love', 'Make Money') produced in the Bronx by Haitians for suckers. Along Schwabs' staircase framed, faded publicity photos feature The Staple Singers and Little Milton in their Stax prime. And a photo of a man wearing shades, a sharkskin suit and a cocky, bemused look: *O. V. Wright.*

Little is known about Wright; I've never come across even

a quote from the man, while reference books state bald facts: born in Leno, Tennessee, in 1939, he worked the gospel circuit before breaking off to cut 'That's How Strong My Love is' for tiny Memphis label Goldwax in 1964. Turned out Wright remained under contract to Don Robey (a Houston-based black racketeer and record man). Robey made his feelings known, killing Wright's hit – Otis Redding got to recut 'That's How Strong' for Stax – yet leaving him in Memphis with Willie Mitchell in charge, and together they cut scorched gospel soul. Wright's voice – dense, tormented, a gravel road, a country church – suggests a soul on fire, and he served time in the early seventies for narcotics. Once freed, Mitchell signed him to Hi and they cut several fine albums. Publicity photos suggest Wright loved flashy diamond rings and, by all accounts, the high life, while his voice, a thick, rasping instrument that often drops into reflective oration (the way those of black preachers do during a sermon), hints at a warm, simple man. Wright was an immensely convincing singer and right now I think of him singing *every morning when I rise/I can see the heaven in your eyes* and believe O. V. meant every syllable. At his funeral in 1980 Mitchell and Al Green were among the pallbearers. *Wonder whether Wright spent much time on Beale Street?* Considering Beale's seventies rep it may have been here that O. V. scored the heroin that collapsed his veins and loosened his teeth.

On the sidewalk a plaque celebrates Ida B. Wells, a fearless anti-lynching campaigner, suffragette and journalist who ran a late-nineteenth-century paper called *Free Speech* from Beale Avenue. Wells's editorials so infuriated the local power elite that *Free Speech* was burnt out, forcing her to flee. Ida then set out on an international speaking tour, influenced the launch of the British Anti-Lynching Society, co-founded the NAACP and organised the first black women's political organisation. Ida very much fits Memphis's identity as a city shaped by visionary individuals.

Heading through downtown, I pass a marker stating how WDIA, the US's first station to pioneer an all-black music format in 1948, started here. Owned by whites yet failing, WDIA hired black DJs and programmers, so aiming itself directly at a black community until then almost totally ignored by US media. Calling itself 'the Mother Station of Negroes', WDIA acted as a major community voice and helped launch the musical revolutions Memphis would pioneer over the fifties and sixties. The building WDIA once occupied is now empty and a 'WE'RE MOVING' sign in the window confirms WDIA is now part of Clear Channel Corporation. A mall tempts me in by advertising Isaac Hayes's own soul food restaurant. Isaac, like Ida, W. C. and O. V., being a great Memphis character. Isaac's passion today is Scientology, he and Lisa Marie Presley having financed the construction of a Scientology centre in Memphis. I'm amazed Hayes would fall for Scientology's tosh but Memphis is celebrated as a renegades' city – Nashville being a company town – and renegades tend towards the eccentric. None more so than Harold von Braunhut, the late Memphis-born billionaire who amassed a fortune selling X-Ray Spex and Sea Monkeys in kids' comics then ploughed millions into funding the Ku Klux Klan and Aryan Nations. That von Braunhut was born to German Jewish immigrants makes him, like Elvis's manager Colonel Tom Parker, one of those American reinventions stranger than fiction.

Drifting through Memphis's unhurried streets, I pass the opulent Peabody Hotel and head towards America's most mighty mass of water, the Mississippi river. The Mississippi is muddy brown, the setting sun casting a scarlet wash across the water, its unhurried currents and rolling rhythm lending a sense of peace and grace to the City of Kings. I wander into Confederate Park, where a bronze marker, green with age, celebrates Nathan Bedford Forrest, the millionaire slave owner turned Confederate general whose tactical brilliance harassed Union forces during the war. Post-war, Forrest went on to found the Ku Klux Klan and memorials litter Tennessee. I almost trip on a plaque, which reads:

Palms For The Southern Soldier
Crowns For The Veteran's Head

And Loyal Love And Honour
For Our Confederate Dead

The sun winks its last, shadows extend across the fabled Confederate dead and, calm as the park is, my bones suggest it's time to leave. Wander down to Madison Avenue and wait for a Memphis Area Transit Authority bus.

'You came by bus?' asks Soulsville's Tim Sampson with a certain incredulity when we meet at Zinnie's, a fabled bar on Madison Avenue. Sure. I'm always interested in testing a city's public transport. Would have preferred to ride the tram but they don't stretch beyond downtown. 'You must have been something of a novelty,' continues Tim, 'as white people don't tend to ride buses. They're set up here so the poor black help – cleaners and maids – can get from their part of town to the Garden District and back.' Considering everyone else on the bus was black, mostly female, and the driver, a black woman, was the least hospitable Memphian I've so far encountered, this all sounds correct.

'Was I crossing the tracks in an unwelcome way?'

'I imagine they immediately recognised you as a crazy tourist. See, Memphis really is a city where you need a car to get around anywhere beyond downtown.'

This much I've grasped: the taxi driver who earlier drove me from the Greyhound station to Soulsville made it clear that walking into South Memphis is not only a helluva long journey but also unsafe. The ride revealed more than town planning: the driver and his companion, both black men, discussed a locked-up associate waiting for his family to raise bail bonds. 'They want a guarantee on property now,' said the driver, 'and no one's gonna put up property.' 'The system's set so you can't beat it. He's gonna have to take what they offer,' said his companion. 'I got a little brother serving ten years 'cos he believed innocent until proven guilty,' replied the driver. 'System don't let go of you. No way.'

Zinnie's is one of those fabled neighbourhood bars where everyone appears to know everyone else while the bartender,

Golden boy: Elvis's favourite Graceland portrait

Sandra Jackson, once sang in The Goodees, Stax's attempt at a girl group. The band scored one minor hit, 1968's 'Condition Red', the song's mix of pathos and innocence harking back to Shangri Las-era pop. That The Goodees were all white marked them as one of Stax's first post-soul experiments.

'We auditioned singing a Peter, Paul & Mary song and all the musicians burst into laughter,' says Jackson. 'We walked out shaking and crying, thinking they were laughing at us. But they came out and said, "We're not laughing at you, just your choice of song." We'd hardly ever been around black people before – I remember David Porter [Isaac Hayes's songwriting partner] putting his arms around me and saying, "Now, ain't I just like everyone else?" Stax was amazing 'cos it just got everyone together, workin' an' getting' along, lookin' out for one another. See, most of the time Memphis is divided by race an' money.

'Isaac named us. He wanted to turn us into a white Supremes. He really looked after us. We were arrested for hitchhiking after the assassination of Dr King – there was a curfew on – and Isaac paid out bail. He made us pay him back, though! We were so young it was a new world to us, only eighteen when "Condition

Red" was released. We got sent out on the road, did concerts, appeared on TV. One time I remember our plane landing and I saw all these kids surrounding the plane and screaming and I said, "There must be someone famous on this flight" and the chaperone said to me, "I think it's y'all"! We got off, were mobbed and then they put each of us in a limousine. Man, it was a crazy ride!'

Crazy but brief: The Goodees never sold enough records to make Stax continue its investment past their debut album, the trio disbanding back into Memphis life. 'There's a lot of people 'round Memphis who once were connected with Stax,' says Jackson, 'it gave the city such a focus. Memphis has never been the same since.' Indeed, without music Memphis would rarely attract attention; the local talent – and the money it generated – gave the city an international standing. But today? Does anything beyond gangsta rap thrive here? Tim suggests I go to Murphy's.

Murphy's is a dive bar in midtown and reportedly Memphis's premier rock venue for underground bands. Five dollars gains entry to a bar stocking the worst American beers and a tame psychedelic band. The last Memphis rockers of note were Big Star, the jangly, literate Anglophiles who continue to influence indie bands. Their lead singer, Alex Chilton, retains a cult but it's over thirty years since he recorded any music of note. Murphy's gets worse when the evening's headliners plug in and start playing at a volume more suitable to stadiums than bars so small they don't even have a stage. Their sound is a carbon of The New York Dolls. But the Dolls were teenagers and these guys all resemble Jack Black's *School of Rock* character, too tubby to be a day under thirty. After three songs I retire outside and watch young, white Memphis preen. Scott turns up and shakes his head when he sees me. 'Man, you are not having a good evening! The only place worse than this dump is Beale Street,' he says, adding, 'Memphis is full of crap like this. I hardly go out 'cos it's so awful.' A disgruntled musician then starts harassing him, something to do with an unfinished studio project, until Scott finally shouts, 'Fuck off!' Remarkably, the offender does. 'Jesus,' says Scott, 'this city is full of assholes.'

American heavyweights: Ali meets Furry

chapter 19

Memphis: Give Out But Don't Give Up

On a humid Memphis morning I hire a metallic-blue Pinto and
head south on Elvis Presley Boulevard, passing the Memphis
Union Mission (*'We Prepare People to Live in Graceland'*), passing
three white adults standing outside a Wal-Mart holding home-
made anti-death-penalty signs, passing two young black males
sitting in motorised wheelchairs (with US flags attached) outside
a liquor store, passing Battle Bonding Co., whose slogan is *'The
Battle Is Not Over Until You Are Free'* and features a silhouette
of a black soldier on horseback, passing Hernando's Hideaway,
a honky-tonk reputably so rough that older Memphis residents
recall the boarding up of HH's upstairs windows to stop patrons
being thrown through 'em. I surf the local radio stations,
skimming a pop station soaked with ads, a rap station blaring
aggressive bounce tunes and 103.5 Soul Classics which plays more
Al Green than is truly necessary.

Memphis quickly gets rural, and by the time I'm paying to
park it could almost be countryside. That is if it wasn't for the
industry set up to cash in on tourists visiting Graceland. Presley's
a long time dead but he remains profitable – $22 gets you into
Graceland, $28 gets you that and access to Elvis's planes and
automobiles while $55 gives 'VIP access'. Which, maybe, gets
you upstairs, where Elvis's bedroom had mirrors on the ceiling.
Though I doubt it. The prices are painful but in a metropolis
named after ancient Egypt's City of Kings, Graceland is the
equivalent to Tutankhamun's tomb. In Egypt I paid to visit King
Tut's tomb and in Memphis I pay ($28) to visit the mansion of a
man his fans often refer to as 'The King'.

A people carrier takes ticket-holders to Graceland, where we wander along an organised path offering select stations of the Presley cross: here's the kitchen where Elvis ate too many peanut butter and banana sandwiches, here's the TV room where Elvis shot out too many TVs, here's the police badge collection which made Elvis align himself with any law enforcement authority going… Elvis was dumb. Sweet but dumb, and Graceland reinforces this. Still, it is situated in rolling countryside and the Jungle Room's exotica ambience is superb; can just imagine Elvis kicking back here with a pharmaceutical cocktail, pondering on how a simple hillbilly cat could come to own such splendour.

The Graceland overload makes me ponder on how much Elvis I actually like. His 1954/55 Memphis sessions hot-wire blues tunes with a great hormonal roar. Teenage Elvis was what most Americans dismiss as 'white trash', a poor, gentle youth desperately seeking his identity through music, un-self-conscious enough at eighteen to be capable of channelling a blues/country hybrid. 'Rockabilly', they would eventually call Elvis's sound, and it set the South on fire; ever since Jimmie Rodgers' seminal 1920s recordings country singers have borrowed from blues, but Elvis was the first white singer to appear possessed by African spirit: the kid danced, he rocked! Much has been written on Elvis but little of interest, major biographies either damning Presley for the blank persona he wore through his adult life or offering tepid hagiography. Texan essayist Michael Ventura observed Elvis as *'A gash in the nature of Western things. Through him, or through his image, a whole culture started to pass from its most strictured, fearful years to our unpredictable fermentive age – a jangled, discordant feeling, at once ultramodern and primitive, modes which have blended to become the mood of our time.'* A gash in the nature of Western things… at once ultramodern and primitive… that sounds about right.

The Memphis Flash's inspiration was brief: leaving Sun for RCA in late 1955, Presley would find his fame mushroom on an atomic scale, yet his engagement with the music that shaped him would quickly fade. When he cut Big Mama Thornton's 'Hound Dog' for RCA in 1956 he's more blackface minstrel show than

Turban times: Sam & the Pharaohs

Beale Street blues boy. Occasional tunes engaged Elvis – Doc Pomus and Mort Shuman provided him with some great material ('Mess o' Blues', 'Viva Las Vegas', 'Little Sister') but the hunger was gone and he rarely sounds any more engaged in the music than he does in acting. His 1968 return-to-Memphis recordings find Presley's voice thick and mannered, only occasionally sparking: on 'Suspicious Minds' the beast in him, long sated by too much of everything, rises to roar one final time. Elvis never again engaged with a great tune – after 'Suspicious Minds' only extreme public decline would follow: that the man who had embodied sex-money-glamour more than anyone else on earth, an American god, would become obese, drug-saturated, a parody of his younger self, dying at forty-two, reflects on both the corrosive nature of fame and how a talent can be overwhelmed by the very revolution it set in motion.

Thing is, there're many Memphis musicians I rate above Elvis. Furry Lewis – the 1920s blues singer who lost a leg hoboing, spent decades sweeping the city streets then got rediscovered by white blues enthusiasts and went on to support The Rolling Stones and act in a Burt Reynolds movie – being one. Furry was a remarkable singer and guitarist as well as being one of the twentieth-century's masters of aphorism. Furry sang, *'give out but don't give up.'* Furry sang, *'if you cry 'bout a nickel yo'll die fo' a dime.'* Furry sang, *'follow me woman an' I will turn yo' money green.'* Furry sang, *'gonna buy me a grave yard all of my own/an' kill every one who done me wrong.'* Furry sang, *'they arrest Furry for forgery/ and I can't even sign my name,'* Furry sang, *'if I was a duck and the river was whiskey/I would dive down, oh Lord, and never come up.'* Furry sang, *'have you heard the news? Memphis women don't wear no shoes.'* Furry played shredding guitar, conveyed threat and laughter and, when introduced to Allen Ginsberg, sang, *'like the Chinaman say to the Jew/you no likee me, I no likee you.'* Ginsberg hailed Furry as 'King', and who would disagree? Furry never made much money but lived to be eighty-eight; that's more than double the time Elvis spent above ground. I'm thinking on Furry when I come across Elvis's grave with its bronze Taking Care of Business lightning-bolt insignia. The sad truth is, Elvis rarely took care of *anything*.

I aim the Pinto towards downtown, pondering on the link between this city and its Egyptian namesake, both once covered in glory and now adrift in the sands of time, ruins sifted by visitors sniffing after legend. Music lifted Memphis, Tennessee, very high, but as the music business became increasingly corporate little patience existed for the visionary, the eccentric, the offbeat. To many Memphians music remains a means of cultural survival and today music lends the city its identity – but what kind of identity exists in nostalgia? I slip through local radio and end up listening to HIP-HOP 107.1, checking to see what ultramodern/primitive Memphis modes are fermenting today. DJ Superman plays crunk, the Southern rap sound as unmusical as, I guess, many listeners once found the electric blues Sam Phillips produced. Superman's never less than entertaining and boasts he's the most knowledgeable Memphian in Memphis. In between ads for bail bonds and used-car dealers he fields calls about the probation service, wayward partners and refugees from New Orleans 'stinkin' up the crib'. A man on the run for outstanding child support warrants asks what to do? 'Go eat a steak, go to a titty bar and then turn yo'self in,' replies Superman. 'I don't have much money,' says the caller. 'Is it OK if I just eat a burger?' 'Brother,' says the most knowledgeable Memphian in Memphis, 'do what yo' gotta do.'

Back in central Memphis I stop at Gus's Fried Chicken. White soul man Dan Penn sang of Memphis being a town where the chicken's *'finger licking food and goes down greasy'* and Gus proves Dan right about the latter. Memphians boast of the city's fried chicken and BBQ pork, doughnuts and soul food; such a diet ensuring the city ranks as America's most obese and Gus's clientele are doing their best to keep Memphis No. 1. Customers and staff employ Southern manners – *'Yes, sir! No, ma'am! God bless! My Lord!'* – as they chew through plate after plate of fried bird, washed down with gallons of Pepsi and Dr Pepper. A towering redneck, noting my Graceland memorabilia, starts haranguing me about Elvis's majesty, beating out points with a chicken leg ('Elvis wuz King' – *thump!* – 'The colonel wuz a genius' – *thump!* – 'Priscilla wuz a ho' – *THUMP!*). If I voice any criticisms of El this hillbilly might assault me with his lunch (*Tourist Killed by Greasy Chicken* could be the headline). Nod ascent and recall a tall and true tale of Elvis turning up uninvited at Nixon's White House, flying on speed while swearing allegiance to the war on drugs. Not that Presley gave a damn about Nixon's policies, he was simply hustling for FBI badges.

Fleeing Gus's, I head up to 706 Union: Sun Studios. The small entrance area is stuffed full of memorabilia while a grand old Wurlitzer jukebox gives two spins for a quarter. Choose Elvis's 'Mystery Train' and Warren Smith's 'Ubangi Stomp' – both cut right in this building – Elvis transforming Junior Parker's spooky blues shuffle into a hillbilly hotrod, hear him *move*, no white singer tore it up quite like he did in the mid-fifties. Warren Smith never came close to tasting fame but as he roars about going to Africa and seeing *'those natives doing a crazy, crazy dance'* I can taste Sun Studios fifty years ago, skinny speed-freaks recording tales of hopped-up madness they spied in Beale Street bars, their sound raw and fresh, its furious pulse shocking even the musicians.

Lay down $8.50 and join a group of pensioners who 'ooohhh' and 'aaaahhh' over our guide's every mention of Elvis. The guide, sideburns impressively thick, is good on Sun's overall history, noting, much to the pensioners' surprise, that blues giant Howlin' Wolf was Sun founder Sam Phillips's personal favourite of all the artists he produced. The dusty relics here represent a past age very distant from our twenty-first-century existence: old recording gear, fan magazines, 78s – everything primitive, unfussy. Yet magic flowed through this basic technology between 1950 and 1958 (when Phillips lost Johnny Cash to Columbia and Jerry Lee Lewis self-destructed). Sideburns is telling the story of how Elvis paid to cut 'My Happiness' for his mama at Sun and Sam's secretary noted down how he might have 'something', which is how Phillips came into contact with him. A more enterprising story involves Elvis's mama's addiction to diet pills: Elvis would get Glady's prescriptions filled, giving Mama what she needed, then sell the rest to musicians. Follow this story and Elvis's 'something' at Sun was dealing speed. That's all right, Mama, indeed.

'You ever heard of a place called Jasper, Texas?' asks the man they call Sam the Sham.

Oh, yes, I certainly have. On 7 June 1998, Jasper natives Lawrence Brewer, John King and Shawn Berry picked up another local, forty-nine-year-old James Byrd Jr. Byrd was black and Brewer, King and Berry were white; King and Berry bearing tattoos pledging allegiance to prison gang the Aryan Nation. The trio beat Byrd unconscious before chaining him to their pick-up truck and dragging him to his death.

'Well, we got stuck there one night. Early sixties. There was a hill and a filling station halfway up it. Out car conked out going up that hill so we rolled back to the filling station – this was late at night – on our way to Dallas. I had a beard and an earring and David was part Native American with long black hair so we stood out but I was always courteous so I said to the man who

'I've just 'bout OD'd on character!': Sam The Sham, Memphis, TN, 2006

was minding the station, 'Pardon me, sir, I was wondering if we could get a jump start from you?' He was pretty old, one of those sanity markers along the road to life, a tar baby of sorts, and he said, 'We don't have no jumpers.' I said, 'You really don't have any?' and he just opened up his coat and pulled it back and he had a hog leg – that's an old .44 – strapped on. So I said 'thank you' and we got Vincent to drive while we pushed two or three feet at a time. We pushed that old van to the top, bit by bit, turned it around and it fired and we let out an Apache war cry as we turned around and took off.'

Domingo Zamudio, aka Sam the Sham, Memphis legend and Tex-Mex rock 'n' roll pioneer, reflects on a life mapped out by the road. Sam's seen worse and survived rougher than Jasper's bigots since he first landed on Earth in 1936. Born in dustbowl Texas, Sam grew up the hard way.

'My grandmother, they called her Apache, although she was only half Apache. Her mother was a full-blooded Apache. My grandfather was from Spain although he was really from Escudia, the Basque country. As you mentioned, I don't look like a Mexican because of my height but I never saw myself as a big person because growing up I was something of a runt. It wasn't till I joined the military that I began to grow. It shows what happens when you get three meals a day.'

Sam chuckles through a big white beard, adjusts his accordion, squeezes out a few notes and says, 'Living in Louisiana for all those years means I've got a good zydeco left hand.' At sixty-nine Sam's tall and dignified, biblical in stature and aphorism.

'West Dallas, that's where I'm from. My family used to know Clyde Barrow's family [Bonnie and Clyde]. That part of Texas had a way of marking its children as if vaccinating them. My father could not read or write. He knew how to write his name and that was it. When we were in the fourth grade we were helping him learn to read better and learn multiplication. We went to a great school in Dallas County. My brother blazed the way. He was very smart. At that time my father worked for Sherman concrete company. Hispanics and blacks lived there and down the road lived the Watsons, they were Anglos and friends of the family. So poverty knows no colour. We were latch-door kids after my mother died. We moved from the country after my grandmother died, to an area called Little Mexico Village. I guess my sister was about six and I might have been five. My dad would cook oatmeal and leave it on the stove for us and then leave for work at six-thirty a.m. and we'd eat it and go to school and when he got home around six-thirty p.m. he'd cook us sweet potatoes and wash us and do all that. He was a very strong man. He raised his brothers and sisters on an old plantation after their mother died and his father fell from a barn and suffered seizures. He fought for food, saw his best friend get dragged to his death by a spooked mule. That's grit.

'In Texas we lived in two worlds, studied in English and listened to Mexican radio. There was an African-American community in Trinity Gardens and on Friday night everyone would be playing music and having a good time. They'd have a house with gambling, prostitution in another, dancing in another. Many musicians came through. A man could get killed and by the time the constables turned up four days later he would be buried and people would say "he got kicked in the head by a mule" and that was all right with them. You know, during those times it was that kind of attitude, "don't let it spread, just keep it here". I grew up with that and Mexican films and *tejano* music: the accordion and how they sang from the throat.

'When I came out of the military I had my discharge papers on me and I headed to west Texas hitchhiking to find Omar. Omar is another story – he had part of his stomach blown away by a shotgun blast. Such craziness. Now Omar was sharecropping and I said, "man, let's get a band together." I called us The Pharaohs after seeing *The Ten Commandments*. We started off as strollers, playing Spanish songs. We were working this old beer joint in Fort Worth and I go in for our pay and say to this slob, "I've come for our money" and he says, "I've got a knife in one pocket and a gun in the other. There's a cemetery across the road. Which one you want to be paid with?" I thought, "I could take this guy but it ain't worth it" so I go out and Cat says "you got the money?" and I say "not worth it" and he says "let me show you how to collect money" so we go in and Cat says "we've come for our money" and the guy starts "I've got a gun" and Cat gets all steely-eyed, says "shut the fuck up" and the guy knows he wasn't joking. He counted out our five dollars. That was how I learned to collect money. I didn't want to work for five dollars a night all night so we'd make a deal with club owners saying "we'll work for a certain amount until we fill your club and then you pay us more." We played some real rough joints. Chicken-wire joints. Jack Ruby was one of the operators who employed us in Dallas. I spoke to Jack Ruby a few months before that thing went down with JFK. Jack had helped my schoolmate Trini Lopez get from Dallas to Las Vegas and at the time we had a hit in the South-west with "Haunted House" and Jack said, "I can get you a room in Vegas." But I didn't care to play Vegas. Him and his sister, they ran some burlesque clubs.

'We were playing Elmore James, John Lee Hooker, Jimmy Reed. One tough blues band. We got a residency at the Congo Club, Leesville, Louisiana, and people flocked to see us. They played rough down there, uncivilised, a real killing floor. A band had been playing, someone didn't like 'em so threw a dynamite cap under the end of the building where the bandstand was. Blew the Shure mic right through the ceiling. We came to Memphis in the spring of '63. Jerry Lee Lewis was playing at the Hi-Hat. Willie Mitchell at the Manhattan. Isaac Hayes at the American Legion. The Mar-Keys at Lil' Abners. Bill Black's all over. We got a residency at the Diplomat. It was half civilised here. I mean, at least the floor walker didn't have a .38 on his hip.'

Nicknamed 'The Sham' – 'because I could sing and I could sham' – Sam the Sham & The Pharaohs took shape. By 1964 these American pharaohs had established themselves as the hardest-rocking band in the City of Kings. A year later they had the biggest selling American song of the year, 'Wooly Bully': 3 million copies sold at the height of Beatlemania. 'Wooly Bully' could be dismissed as a nonsense song, it certainly doesn't 'mean' anything in the way objective song lyrics convey meaning, but from its distinctive intro, when Sam shouts *'Uno, dos... one, two, tres, quatro!'* through the pumping organ and jittery Tex-Mex groove, 'Wooly Bully' ranks among the greatest American rock 'n' roll ever waxed.

'People say "did you expect it?" and my reply is "of course I did". If you're not expecting to be successful then what are you hoping to do? I don't wish to sound arrogant but that was my philosophy. You can spend a lot of time in the studio and make a lot of money, but one day you will look in the mirror and you will be stale. Stale in your heart. You can play a thousand notes and feel nothing. Then someone can get up and field-holler a song and it moves the world.'

As 'Wooly Bully' moved the world Sam the Sham & The Pharaohs hit the road in a 1958 hearse. Tall and handsome, Sam wore a turban, pumping out roadhouse Tex-Mex/R & B to screaming teenagers.

'The moment I knew we'd really made it involved us appearing on *The Ed Sullivan Show*. There's fifty or sixty Fijian islanders backstage, all in grass skirts and with spears, and through their interpreter they asked what we were there to do. When we told them it was like a fire swept through them – they all went "wooly bully wooly bully wooly bully!" I said to David, "We're known in Fiji."'

The road ate The Pharaohs mark one up. Sam got a new band and scored again with 'Little Red Riding Hood', a leering slice of garage rock, in 1966. Minor hits followed but pop fashions changed fast in the sixties and the combined onslaught of British beat bands and San Francisco's psychedelic messiahs meant Sam ended up submerged. 'When people ask me what I thought of The Beatles I say "yeah, they were good" but I never tried to be The Beatles. With all due respect, we're from the Delta, we're different.' Sam played to US troops in Asia – 'Wooly Bully' remains a Vietnam war-era anthem – cut soul tunes at Stax and a 1970 solo album *Hard And Heavy* which won Sam a Grammy for Best Liner Notes. 'Miles Davis was also nominated. Now, I'm not fit to carry his trumpet but I always had a way with words.' *Hard and Heavy* sold poorly when issued and is unavailable today, so here's a sample of the liner notes that won Sam a Grammy.

I WANT TO THANK:
The people who mistreated me as a child; 'cause they made me strong.
A third grade teacher, who treated me like a leper and begrudged me not having lice; for she gave me pride.
The people who refused me service; for they made me save my money.
The people who rejected me because of the color of my skin and the texture of my hair; for they made me realise that I was different.
My friends the prostitutes for listening to me when no one else would; for I needed to speak.

The towns I was run out of; for they ran me to
better places.
　　Memphis for whippin' me down twice, which only made
me get up.
　　David, Jerry, Ray & Butch for sharing with me the
misery of the road; they too suffered the changes I went
through.
　　The women who loved me and ask their forgiveness;
lovin' the wind would have been easier.
　　And most of all, God, for letting me be a musician, in
doing so he's given me a taste of paradise.

'I was going through the rock 'n' roll meat grinder and every one of those dedications meant something to me. They say what I've been through builds character. Man, I've just 'bout OD'd on character!'

Sam lived in New York and studied acting, shifted to LA and put a new band together with members of Zappa's Mothers, lost his Atlantic deal and embraced the outlaw life: packing a pistol, running drugs, cutting across America on a huge motorbike. 'I used to believe I had to carry a piece,' says Sam, 'now I have peace in my heart.' Charlie Freeman, wild boy of Memphis guitar and Sam's best friend, went to a drug-induced grave in 1973.

'At first people were saying "oh, how sad, poor guy" and I said, "He was a no-account like the rest of us. If you really care for him, if you're really his friends, you'll look after his wife and daughter after he's put in the ground." I was a cautious drugger – oxymoron! How can you be a cautious drugger? – but after "Wooly Bully" and signing with Atlantic I decided to get into drugs, not marijuana, in Texas that was never anything. Quaaludes. Eating hash. Cocaine. And cocaine really put a dent in my style.'

Sam eventually fled the music industry, drugs and LA, resettling in Louisiana to work as a deckhand on Gulf of Mexico boats. 'I'd always liked the water and it's a haven for hiding. Good therapy as I needed to air out. Did a lot of writing out there. Met some great men and some dogs.'

Sam's return to making music involved Ry Cooder inviting him to contribute to the soundtrack of Tony Richardson's film *The Border*. The 1982 film, set on the Texas–Mexican border, is a static drama but the soundtrack is Cooder's finest, with Sam serving up two stomping slices of accordion-fuelled *tejano* music. A religious conversion happened around the same time and, for a while, Sam could be found street-preaching in Memphis's Court Square. When his marriage broke up Sam focused on raising his daughter. The rise in popularity of Vietnam-era films and TV shows found 'Wooly Bully' in demand; this allowed Sam to live comfortably, administering to prisoners in the South and the Caribbean, occasionally playing the oldies circuit, releasing new material, both gospel and secular, when he feels like it.

'I was on the water for five years, worked my way up to captain. Never let on I was Sam the Sham. Once one of my crew called me "Captain Sam the Sham". I said to him, "Whatever happened to that guy?" and he said, "Oh, he went down in the plane with Otis Redding."'

Before landing at Sam's country house I'd stopped in at Shangri-La Records, Memphis's finest record shop, purchasing for travelling music Andre Williams's *Bait and Switch* and Memphis Minnie's *Queen of the Blues*. Williams is a reactivated fifties pioneer while Minnie (1897–1973) remains the toughest woman to ever boss a guitar. Born Lizzie Douglas in Algiers, Louisiana, she ran away to Memphis aged thirteen and made a reputation as a street musician playing guitar and banjo. Aged fourteen she joined the Ringaling Brothers circus before returning to Memphis, where her Beale Street prowess won her and then husband Joe McCoy a recording deal in 1929. Minnie and Joe's recording debut, 'When the Levee Breaks' described 1927's Mississippi flood; almost eighty years on it provided the soundtrack to much Hurricane Katrina TV footage. A formidable musician, Minnie was a tough number. 'Any man fool with her, she'd go for them right away,' bluesman Johnny Shines recalled. 'She didn't take no foolishness off them. Guitar, pocketknife, pistol, anything she got her hand on she'd use it.' I slip Minnie into the Pinto's CD player and roll out of Memphis on Highway 61, the blues highway famed for carrying musicians from Mississippi to Memphis, Minnie roaring as she must have done along this same road almost a century ago. 'Often the blues musicians coming up the 61 didn't know where it went,' Sam had said, 'they just knew it went somewhere good.'

Many blues singers would enshrine the 61 in song, leading Bob Dylan to eulogise it as rock's most mythic road. There's little majestic now, Highway 61 cutting through South Memphis, the final traces of this City of Kings being Big Momma's Soul Food restaurant and a squall of liquor and loan stores. Then I'm crossing the state line, leaving Tennessee for Mississippi – such beautiful names, what fine poetry this region's Choctaw and Cherokee once possessed – cotton fields in bloom, stretching across the flat alluvial plain known as the Mississippi Delta. There's little sign of human habitation, small towns growing smaller, empty houses, ruined roadside churches claiming *'Salvation Cometh'*, populace having fled long ago. Nothing here to stop for, the atmosphere conjuring flight towards what William Faulkner called *'a terror in which you cannot believe towards a safety in which you have no faith.'* Yet across this awful landscape gigantic billboards advertise casinos; gambling having become the state's greatest revenue earner. Hurricane Katrina's destruction of the Biloxi casinos has made Tunica, a small settlement situated between Memphis and Clarksdale, the epicentre of Southern gambling. An evangelical church van overtakes wildly, driver hoping to meet Jesus in the near future. Honk hard and the jittery Jesus freak rips into the distance. Minnie's grinding out 'Me and My Chauffeur Blues':

Won't you be my chauffeur
Won't you be my chauffeur
I wants him to drive me
I wants him to drive me downtown
Yes he drives so easy I can't turn him down

But I don't want him
But I don't want him
To be ridin' his girls
To be ridin' his girls around
So I'm gonna steal me a pistol, shoot my chauffeur down.

Think about it: some South Memphis honey could rhyme those lines over a beat today and rewire Minnie for the twenty-first-century. But, *damn*, that woman could sing and shred a guitar. What did Minnie make of Tunica? I'll bet it hosted a juke joint she rocked.

Woman with guitar: Memphis Minnie

MISSISSIPPI STATE OF MIND

Tunica, Clarksdale, Greenville, River Valley, Oxford

All night now the jooks clanged and clamoured. Pianos living three lifetimes in one. Blues made and used right on the spot. Dancing, fighting, singing, crying, laughing, winning and losing love every hour. Work all day for money, fight all night for love. The rich black earth clinging to bodies and biting the skin like ants.

Zora Neale Hurston

Although this has been called the age of anxiety, it might better be termed the century of the blues, after the moody song style that was born sometime around 1900 in the Mississippi Delta. A hundred years ago only blacks in the Deep South were seized by the blues. Now the whole world begins to know them. In order to hear the blues, when I was very young, my girlfriend and I slipped into the black ghetto of my Southern hometown under the cover of darkness. If we'd been caught there, we would probably have been expelled from the university. Nowadays everyone sings and dances to bluesy music, and the mighty river of the blues uncoils in the ear of the planet. Indeed, the blues may have become the best-known tune humans have ever sung. At the same time, all of us are beginning to experience the melancholy dissatisfaction that weighed upon the hearts of the black people of the Mississippi Delta, the land where the blues began. Feelings of anomie and alienation, of orphaning and rootlessness – the sense of being a commodity rather than a person; the loss of love and of family and of place – this modern syndrome was the norm for the cotton farmers and the transient laborers of the Deep South a hundred years ago.

Alan Lomax

Out on the floor: juke joint, Clarksdale, MS, 1939

chapter 20

Tunica: Ghosts of Highway 61

Taking a right turn for Tunica Riverpark, an area developed solely for gambling, I drive through marshy rice fields, everything flat and humid, architectural spectacle hovering in the distance. Coming into sight, all bright colours and bizarre shapes, these nine casinos resemble Legoland and constitute the third largest gambling complex in the USA. Here is the golden goose at the heart of America's poorest, most neglected state.

The casinos are situated on the bluntly named Casino Strip Resort Boulevard and I cruise it until CSRB ends in front of Hollywood, Harrah's and Sam's Town. Which one to enter? Let's see how their Hollywood experience matches mine. Inside, the casino is full of machines designed to part money from fools alongside tame replica Bat Cars and Terminators. Like a hillbilly Vegas, Tunica is a dump. But Hollywood's buffet offers a superb spread of meats and salads, both more filling and nourishing than anything I ate in Memphis. The entertainment listings offers Nashville slop or faded pop-rock stars, acts dreaming of making it to Vegas while accepting bookings anywhere the oldies circuit cares to operate. Imagine still squeezing into spandex pants and saying to audiences 'you know this one'; concussed with memories of chart hits and media attention and groupies and applause… *everything rocks and nothing ever dies…* or so it seems in the wastelands of entertainment.

Drive down to the river, park and stretch my legs by thick, swirling Mississippi waters. An old white man, gummy and hunched, drives up in a trash-collection cart and suggests I take the river walk. 'Shure is preddy 'long da reevah,' he says. The turbulent Mississippi is not a river many would call 'pretty' but I attempt the walk. Within a couple of hundred metres I'm retreating, humidity and insects chasing this soft city boy inside the imposing River Museum. The River Museum offers catfish and eels swimming through murky aquariums, a diving bell recreating the experience of those who once worked submerged and footage of the infamous 1927 floods flickering on silvery screens. A wall of information on the region's first people, the Choctaws, and their hunter-gatherer life concludes with Spanish conquistadors arriving in search of El Dorado, fabled city of gold, murdering and murdering and murdering, malarial, rotting and psychotic, setting their greyhounds upon the Choctaws, dogs so vicious they could rip a child's face off in seconds, dogs fed upon Choctaw flesh, Europeans intent on exterminating pagans who had no gold to plunder. Mississippi would, across the centuries, be colonised with extreme brutality, the conquistadors setting a pattern, the state's rich soils soaked in human blood.

The museum avoids touching upon contemporary Tunica history: before gambling was legalised in the early nineties Tunica was infamous only for a black community who continued to endure poverty, discrimination and malnutrition on Third World levels. I wonder whether things are much better today? Let's employ that most facile of words: *hope*. Gambling created new roads and many jobs and casino work is infinitely preferable to the brutalities of picking cotton or industrial catfish plants; gutting and filleting catfish now the main form of employment for working-class black women in this non-union state, a job that mangles and ruins workers' hands after a few years on the production line. *Hope*. Yet this being Mississippi, a state once internationally infamous as a byword for racial hatred, I wonder.

A sign indicates I'm re-entering Highway 61. I punch Minnie out and slip on Bob Dylan's *Highway 61 Revisited*. The cult that surrounds Robert Zimmerman, obsessive fans poring over his every utterance, is reprehensible, the kind of idle idol worship we sneer at when exhibited by religious fanatics. But when 'Like a Rolling Stone' kicks off (exploding snare drum/overloaded organ) I chuckle

– *Yeah! Yeah!* – over how loud, obnoxious music can sound so *good*. After 'Like a Rolling Stone' finishes I quickly decide Dylan's not great road music (too many words, too many uneven songs) and, concentrating on changing songs, run a STOP sign, almost plough into a turning Cadillac, pulling wide with seconds to spare – Pinto sliding, the Cadillac's driver, a black woman, shrieking with wide-eyed horror – shooting across the hard shoulder, lurching right, regaining balance, cold sweat breaking out, aware I almost joined Highway 61's fabled list of road carnage. *'The highway is for gamblers/better use your sense,'* sang Dylan six months before *Highway 61 Revisited*. Good advice on the casino highway. Shut music off, slick with cold sweat, and focus on the road.

Soon signs indicate I'm entering Clarksdale. Here we are now, the heart of the Delta, a town where cotton was king and pretty much every major Mississippi blues/soul artist once spent some time. All appears ruined. Or if not ruined then run down, worn

The road most travelled: Highway 61

out, most commercial spaces vacant, trash cans limply hanging open, broken glass covering sidewalks, grass growing through railway tracks. I angle the Pinto towards Cat Head, an arts centre set up by Roger Stolle, the most effective promoter of Mississippi Delta blues today. Cat Head occupies an old, beat-up building surely chosen as it harks back to a simpler era, the antithesis of today's ersatz mall culture. Beyond CDs and books, T-shirts and magazines, Cat Head's stuffed with diddly bows, crucifixes, paintings, sculptures, primitive ceramics, painted plates, wall hangings, dioramas of Southern life, walking sticks, everything made out of recycled or reinvented materials, a treasure chest of Southern folk art. Roger speaks with the passion of a true believer. His accent has no Southern twang to it: he quit advertising in St Louis to set up Cat Head in this depressed Delta town.

'There's a lot of talent around this region, both musicians and outsider artists,' says Stolle, who first visited Mississippi for blues holidays, 'yet much of the talent was being taken advantage of by those only interested in personal profit. We try and work with the locals and make sure they get treated fair. Morgan Freeman's originally from here and he's recently set up a restaurant and the Ground Zero blues club so the town now has some focus. I've helped get a Juke Joint Blues Festival going so visitors will go to the little black bars where there's always been blues. Blues still exists in Mississippi because the situation remains rough for so many people here. Maybe the youth listen to rap but blues is black Mississippi culture and some eventually come back to it.'

A loud-talking local enters – Roger introduces him as Wild Bill Cooper – boasting how he's eliminated the local squirrel population. 'They make good bait for catching catfish. I filled my deep freeze. Seventy pounds o' dead squirrel!' Wild Bill exits and a beat-looking black man carrying an acoustic guitar enters and starts rapidly strumming while mumbling incoherently. Clarksdale's certainly not short of characters. The 'musician' suddenly loses interest and wanders out still mumbling.

'How difficult is adjusting to small-town Mississippi after life in St Louis?'

'Things can appear strange. I go to meet with local politicians and they start each meeting with a minute's silent prayer that ends with "Amen". Under US law the state and religion are clearly separated yet here they're intertwined. Also, there's centuries of racial injustice to be undone here, comparable to Zimbabwe, and still lots of extreme poverty and discrimination.'

The imagery Cat Head's artists employ varies from auto-biographical tales through biblical fable to musical iconography, the most popular of which involves Robert Johnson. Johnson lived fast, died young and made little impact within his lifetime (1911–38). A gifted synthesiser of country blues styles, he recorded twenty songs displaying debts to earlier bluesmen Son House and Lonnie Johnson alongside an individual artistry and intensity few before or since have matched. Dying young (and violently) has long made for good business in popular culture, and when the 1960s British blues boom stumbled upon an album of Johnson's recordings everything about him suggested 'doomed Romantic poet/nascent rock star'. Anointed 'King of the Delta Blues', he attracted disciples including Eric Clapton and The Rolling Stones; while they now wane in influence Johnson's star only continues to grow, his wild, swaggering persona making him a Tupac antecedent.

'It is kinda odd, the Robert Johnson fixation,' says Roger, 'but people appear to have latched on to him as the sole representative of Mississippi country blues. I try and direct them to his contemporaries – Son House, what a huge talent! – but he's the one they come through the door to buy day in, day out.'

There're three different headstones around Mississippi now claiming to represent Johnson's last resting place. A poor, black musician, almost unknown during his brief life, is now a sizeable local industry. And this in Mississippi, a state once so oppressive New Orleans banjoist Danny Barker suggested any black person who voluntarily entered 'must be insane'. Funny old world. What kept Johnson – who travelled widely – coming back here? Family? Lovers? Local-hero status? And why the ever-rising interest in a man whose music remains uneasy listening? Does his 'Me and the Devil' posturing really win over the latent Satanist in ageing rock fans? Or is his aura of mystery and lightning-flash creativity such that we latch on to him as a modern Icarus? Today, Johnson outsells the likes of Jimmie Rodgers, Louis Armstrong, Mahalia Jackson – hugely popular artists in their time and, to some degree, still influential. Observing Cat Head's bright paintings I imagine a Tragic Artists' Heaven where Johnson and Van Gogh gather to shake heads and moan at the fortunes their work now generates. Roger slips a Johnson CD on. Listen to his phrasing (tense, elliptical), alienation and dispossession, sex and violence, tenderness and brutality, all constants. There's little relief, even women are a source of constant sorrow:

> *Everything I do, you got yo' mouth stuck out*
> *And the hole where I used to fish, you got me posted out.*

Not that Johnson gave his lovers much levity; in song after song he threatens to beat or shoot them, Robert often having mean things on his mind. Maybe that's the key to Johnson's *fin de siècle* success, his anxieties reflecting our own increasing insecurities, the sense that hellhounds of all sorts dog our trails. Today, as Dale Watson noted, we've all got the blues. Roger offers directions to the Riverside Hotel along Sunflower Avenue. Cruising at twenty miles an hour I spot a wooden house with a sign out front. I park and bang on the door. A wiry black man opens it and looks me over cautiously. 'Yeah? Wha' choo want?' he asks. I feel about as welcome as the local Klan leader. Explain how Roger sent me and he nods, says, 'Can't give you Bessie's room but I got a nice one. Thirty-five dollars a night.' *Bessie's room?* Right: this used to be a black hospital and on 26 September 1937, pioneering 1920s blues singer Bessie Smith was brought here, arm severed, bleeding profusely, after crashing on Highway 61. *Got to stay.* Peel off $35 and we shake. He says, 'Call me Rat,' then suggests I clear everything out of the car or else 'the local kids will steal it'. My room has lacy curtains, tightly tucked bed, pictures of a blond, bathetic Jesus on the wall. The hallway's lumpy, subsidence evident, bathroom as basic as US bathrooms get, all old and worn and damp, reminiscent of Caribbean-coast accommodation.

Rat invites me to visit the master bedroom ('Bessie's Room'). A photo of Smith in all her finery hangs above the bed. 'She died righ' here,' says Rat. Recollect my own near-collision as I think of Bessie Smith, a woman with so much spirit, lying here as her life force leaked out. 'My mama loved Bessie,' says Rat, 'would travel 'cross Mississippi t' hear her sing.' Rick Danko sang about Bessie with the song's narrator going to see her in concert – Rick could have been imagining Rat's mom! Rat takes my silence for awe and chats on about his mama but I'm imagining Bessie, hard drinking, wild loving, brawling, squalling mess of a genius, wondering *was she friends with Memphis Minnie?*

Born in Chattanooga, Tennessee, in 1894, Smith established herself as *the* master female blues singer, her 78s selling strongly during the 1920s. Bessie was Billie Holiday's favourite singer and, like her charge, lived recklessly, fearless of white power structures – once attacking a KKK battalion – finger hovering over the self-destruct button, sassy foghorn of a voice carrying all before it. Bessie turned several W. C. Handy songs into standards, included a young Louis Armstrong among her sidemen, injected her '*Yeah!*' with more lusty panache than anyone before or since and has never lost her hold on the public imagination: plays and books were written about Bessie and a civil rights activist spread a story that she died owing to a white hospital refusing to treat her injuries. Myth surrounds Bessie but that story is fabricated: she died here attended by black medical staff, Clarksdale once an African-American epicentre.

I think of Bessie singing 'I Ain't Gonna Play No Second Fiddle', knowing she never did. Of Bessie singing 'Empty Bed Blues' and how that's my blues. Of Bessie singing 'Send Me to the 'Lectric Chair' which now sounds like a gangsta rap brag. Of how today's R & B divas fear the emotional forces Bessie explored in song: Beyoncé and co. are glamorous and wealthy but it is Diana Ross's thin spirit fuelling their ambition. *Oh, Bessie!* 'Some say they seen Bessie's ghost,' says Rat as we head into his cluttered living room.

He pulls out room-temperature tins of Dixie beer. I offer a toast to Bessie and he lights a Kool, nods, raises his Dixie. I start to recite:

Check all your razors and your guns
We gonna be arrested when the wagon comes
Do the Shim-Sham Shimmy till the rising sun
Gimme a pigfoot and a bottle of beer
Gimme a reefer and a gang of gin
Slay me 'cos I'm full of sin
Slay me 'cos I'm full of gin.

Rat looks at me, says, 'Yo' know yo' blues, boy.' Uh-huh, that's why I'm here. What, I ask, is your relationship to Clarksdale?

'I lived in Clarksdale since 1944. Not a house from the river t' the railroad track I ain't been in, ain't once ate in. Musicians use t' stay here 'cos it a black hotel, yo' unnerstan'? They playin' Clarksdale so they have t' stay in a black hotel. Robert Nighthawk. Sam Cooke. Ike Turner. Hooker. They all stay here.'

How's Clarksdale now blues tourism is attracting visitors?

'I ain't never seen it no worse than it is now. The sonuvabitch's dead. No jobs. People went from earnin' sixteen dollars an hour at the rubber factory to earnin' six dollars an hour at Wal-Mart when the rubber factory close. How's peoples goin' to cover a hole that big in their pay cheque? I worked for Wonderbread all my life. They left here. Budweiser left here. Streets raggedy here. Man, in Tunica the streets are smooth. Those casinos, they say they break this town. Man, they sure make Tunica sweet!'

How about Morgan Freeman's opening of a restaurant and Ground Zero blues club: surely that suggests Clarksdale's improving?

'Morgan Freeman... he got all that money but he ain't never gonna be a member of the country club. If I ever get in a conversation with him I'll tell him to come down here an' mingle with us 'cos all his riches ain't gonna get him into the Clarksdale Country Club.' Rat clears his throat, lights another Kool. 'I'm from here so I stays here. Wish I lived some other damn place, though.'

chapter 21

Clarksdale: No Time to Pray

Morning: Roger introduced me to Wesley 'Junebug' Jefferson, a local blues singer. Wesley, it turned out, works for Quapaw, a Mississippi river canoe company, and – fired with dreams of emulating Huck and Jim – I signed up for that afternoon's expedition. As we head off I listen to Wesley drawl, words slipping out and floating away before he's fully uttered them. 'Mmhhhmm,' he murmurs, the expression taking on definite meaning given how much emphasis he puts on the *hmm* sound. *'A Southerner talks music,'* wrote Mark Twain, *'their words may lack charm to the eye in print but they have it to the ear.'* And Wesley Jefferson – bluesman, sharecropper, canoeist, daddy to eight children – elicits a silvery quality as he abstracts spoken English in the manner descendants of West African slaves have done for centuries. Wesley propels his station wagon out of Clarksdale's environs, passing a well-kept Jewish cemetery (a Jewish community once lived in Mississippi, moving on when King Cotton lost its crown); his calm, reflective manner's similar to the way he drives. Attached to his station wagon is a large canoe, working for Quapaw Canoe Co. balancing out what he earns from playing blues in juke joints across Mississippi.

Wes, do you have to live a hard life to be able to sing the blues?

'I don't know 'bout that but ah can tell yo', honest t' God, mah life's been a long road, man. I come up sharecroppin' on a plantation. I was 'bout six years old an' just a shorty an' they'd be tellin' me wha' weed t' hit. I wuz ploughin' wit' mules age nine. Been doin' farm work most o' my life. Chopped cotton fo' three dollars a day, fifteen dollars a week. 'Til a few years ago I was getting' sixty-five cents an hour. Mr Joe Nowles Jr, dat was my bossman, he had a big farm, five hundred acres, an' I's his main worker. Mmhhhmm. I used t' be in the cotton fields an', man, I'd break down in tears. We didn't know much but dere had t' be sum'in' better dan dis. Work from sunrise to sunset.' Wesley pauses, purses lips, considers his lot, adds, 'Bossman, he didn't give us much but he take care o' us.'

'In what way, Wes? Money? Education? Healthcare?'

'Education? Huh-um. Bossman wouldn't let yo' go t' school. Said he needed yo' on the plantation. Wouldn't even lemme go int' the army. Got the call-up pushed. We'd work fo' bossman but we had an acre t' grow pinto beans, sweet potatoes, okra. We had a cow an' we'd churn the milk t' make buttermilk. Peas, beans, we wuz healthy. Greens, dey always good. We go huntin'. Get a couple o' rabbits. A 'coon. Dat wuz always the hardest t' get. Good meat. Boil it an' bake it wit' sweet potato. Mama always had a skillet ready. Caught lotsa catfish. Pull up a catfish sometime an' it jus' bone. Eel suck all da flesh off. Wolves an' bears 'round den, too. But it hard t' raise a family an' work an' feed 'em. Dey used t'

'Work from sunrise to sunset': Wesley Jefferson, Clarksdale, MS, 2006

give out tamales from a government buildin'. Food stamps came 'long an', man, dat really helped. Den mah first wife passed an' it kind o' tough so I got off the farm an' 'came a mechanic.'

The surrounding landscape is dead flat, baked dry by heat. Creamy-white cotton bolls dazzle in the sun, cruel beauty among dirt and shacks. These bleak acres, with their heat and cruelty, African sweat and blood, religious fervour and Jim Crow laws, shaped popular Western music like no other concentrated land mass anywhere. This unforgiving terrain's most gifted sons and daughters invented sounds that expressed the slaves' suffering, a music (for those with talent and ambition) capable of unlocking sharecropping's shackles, taking the beauty and torment of a people stolen from Africa worldwide. We cross the Helena Bridge, a formidable construction extending across a wide stretch of Mississippi water, and turn into Helena, Arkansas. Helena was once a major cotton port – Mark Twain waxed lyrically about its beauty in *Life on the Mississippi* – but the railway undermined the steamships and Helena's value, sending the town into a tailspin: down wide, empty streets stand large antebellum buildings, now tattered and faded, some boarded up, ghosts of the Civil War taking on the haunted visage of crack houses.

'Helena wuz a nice town,' says Wesley, 'long time gone. But West Helena in Mississippi, dey done got a casino an' a Wal-Mart an' dat just 'bout killed ole Helena.'

Helena was once home to Arkansas's most celebrated son, Rice Miller aka Sonny Boy Williamson II, the harmonica-blowing, cut-throat-razor-carrying, bowler-hat-wearing, diabolic bluesman. Miller's blues – full of threat and dark laughter – reveal a songwriter of genius (lyrics packed with bleak wit and absurdity; the music mercurial, jumping) while the man remained a mystery, famously suspicious of everyone. Understandably: on 11 August 1938, Miller and Robert Johnson were playing together at a juke joint in Three Forks, just outside of Greenwood, Mississippi, when a half-pint of whiskey with a broken seal was given to Johnson. Johnson, only twenty-seven but already a habitual alcoholic, grabbed for the whiskey. 'Man, don't *never* take a drink from an opened bottle,' warned Rice, a dozen years older and way less temperamental, knocking the bottle from Johnson's hand, 'yo' don't know *what* could be in it.'

'Man, don't never knock a bottle of whiskey outta my hand,' responded Robert, accepting the next open half-pint proffered, slugging what turned out to be an 'ice shot' (moonshine cut with strychnine, courtesy of a cuckold). Over the next forty-eight hours Johnson endured a terrible, drawn-out death.

Miller kept rambling through the South, so wary of Caucasians he delayed launching his recording career until the 1950s, living long enough to tour Britain as a hero of the sixties blues boom. 'They wants to play the blues so *bad*,' he told an acquaintance upon his return to the USA, 'and they plays it *so* bad.' As a tribute to the King Biscuit Show Miller once hosted on Helena radio, Sonny Boy continues to have a brand of white cornmeal named after him.

We exit the station wagon at Reach River Park, a development built upon a levee outside Helena. Lifejackets on, we're joined by John Ruskey, Quapaw's founder, an East Coast Jewish couple exploring the South and several Mississippi pensioners who've

On the road again: Sonny Boy Williamson and friends, Helena, AK

decided to enjoy a day out on the river. John and Wesley steady the canoe in the shallows while we pile in. I sit next to Wes, who smiles beatifically even if, deep inside, he's surely thinking, 'Oh no, *mo'* questions!'

We paddle out of the inlet and on to the river, sun high and heavy, a breeze encouraging some shoulder in our strokes. The Mississippi's choppy, tawny brown, the current picking us up, and we start rolling, rolling on the river; a thousand great songs sing through my skull. Soon we're sailing beneath the Helena Bridge's mighty metal spires, the thunder of trucks echoing down as we splash along. 'River can rise up forty feet,' says Wesley. 'Get yo' a lot closer t' the bridge.'

Around Helena factories and warehouses border the river and fishermen proudly yank a cluster of threshing catfish and striped bass from the water. Outside city limits the human presence disappears and thick floodplain forest covers both sides of the river's banks. Carp leap, water turkeys squawk, all else is silence. Such a rare opportunity: to be away from motorised vehicles, radio, TV. Concentrate on listening to the Mississippi as it's always sounded. A flock of Canada geese break from the riverbank, black wings and white bellies against blue sky.

'When I wuz a little boy my stepdaddy used to run a still,' offers Wes, 'make moonshine, an' I'd 'elp 'im. Man, the mosquitoes an' stuff... it wuz somethin'! I had t' keep the fire goin' t' get it steamed. We'd be in the middle o' the woods an' I'd be scared an' den he'd gimme a few tastes an' I weren't scared o' anythin'! I remember my stepdaddy takin' off runnin' 'cross the fields when dose federal guys came lookin' fo' him. They'd tear up yo' still. 'E'd be gone two, maybe t'ree, weeks den make a deal with 'nother farmer an' shift uz in the middle o' the night. Hogs an' chickens on the truck, me all sleepy, wake up next mornin' on a new farm. We wuz raisin' corn an' the plantation owner would take half an' den we'd take our half down to the mill an' dey'd charge uz half to mill our corn. Dat how it worked back den. I'd pick two o' t'ree hundred pound cotton a day. End up with five hundred dollars at end o' the year.'

'Sounds like a raw deal, Wes.'

'People like uz, we always gettin' a raw deal. I'd a bad accident comin' back from the Dew Drop Inn in Shelby: broken ribs, arms, hole in muh head. Then I'd fo' bypasses in muh heart. Everythin' got tough in one month. I got a son who went out fo' a swim, jumped in an' hit a rock an' knocked iz spine out. Been paralysed fo' eight year now.'

Wesley stares straight ahead. Let the river sing to us... *sing, river, sing that sweet, never-tiring river song...* Maybe it's the music of the river, those splish-splashes of watery rhythm against the canoe, but Wesley keeps talking, reflecting.

'I learn from muh granddaddy, Clark Jefferson, acoustic. He'd play when it rained. I'd sit beside him. I wuz so young an' I wanted to learn. He'd just play fo' a drink, people sit 'round... real nice an' easy.' Wesley's smiling, recalling a shotgun shack's porch as the rain beats against a tarpaper roof and Clark Jefferson plays songs about cruel bo-weevils and evil women, still hearing the music's beauty and mystery. He then looks at me quizzically.

'Yo' heard o' Emmett Till? Mmhhhmm. I wuz down farming when dat boy got killed. I knew the persons who did it. We were real scared of 'em. If we saw 'em comin' we'd run an' hide in the cottonfields. Dey had signs everywhere, "*colored don't go in*", "*colored go round*". Emmett, he came from Chicago, weren't used t' it.'

The Mississippi couples are chattering away, oblivious to our conversation. I'm guessing they were all about Emmett Till's age (fourteen) in 1955 when white thugs tortured and murdered him for whistling at a white woman. How different are things now, Wes?

'Dere's more opportunities but dere's also still some deep, dark corners. I still ain't got nothin'. An' neither have my people. I feel satisfied dat I made it dis far. A lot o' my friends didn't. I get my retirement pay ev'ry month an' I do simple t'ings.'

Simple things like rolling down the river and playing the blues in juke joints. There are worse ways to spend a life, for sure. John's now angling the canoe towards a large sandbar. 'Montezuma break,' he says as we enter a shallow inlet. Drag canoe on to sandbar then strip down and do something I've dreamed of since childhood: swim in the Mississippi. Wade in, feet sinking into sediment, water warm and mucky, my mind recalling that parts of the river are considered 'dead' owing to farm fertiliser run-off and factories dumping effluent. *Ugh!* Ask whether I'm going to turn into the Toxic Avenger but John dismisses such concerns. Next thought is of tales of Louisiana bayous full of alligators: anything going to bite me in here?

'Nothing you can't handle. Dig around and maybe you will find soft-shell turtles, leopard toad, bull frogs.'

A large industrial barge passes, its wake washing against the sandbar. The sun begins to slip through the sky. Wesley and the other canoeists are gathering driftwood for a fire. Twain's finest passages in *Life on the Mississippi* concern how a steamboat pilot learnt to read a constantly changing river; John mentioned when the river's high the sandbars and towheads are completely submerged yet when low form this island of sorts. John places catfish fillets on a steel tray, seasons with peppercorns and olive oil, then lowers the tray on to a solid section of burning log. Feeling like Huck Finn lighting out for the territory – *yee!* – I stand close to the fire, hair spiky with sediment, the smell of catfish frying as colours soak the sky (blue through khaki to a fabulous vermilion that drains into night) and then the stars come out to play, humidity and tranquillity making the Montezuma break an oasis of calm. The moon rises fat and silvery, laying a trail across the river. The pop and crackle of burning timber add texture to the primeval stillness surrounding us. Our ancestors once knew the night as ritual: moonlight and fire providing illumination, stories told and relations consummated. Can feel my consciousness slipping, a feeling of timelessness – *calm* – settling, imagination alive with all who have pulled up on a sandbar and fried catfish in the Mississippi night before us: boatmen and bluesmen, explorers and conquistadors, Choctaws and Chickasaws, fleeing slaves and runaway boys, all stretched out in the soft sand, staring at the universe above and wondering, surely, whether the stars could host any stranger and more magical wonderlands than this.

Red's Lounge, Clarksdale, a Mississippi juke joint best described as 'one cockroach away from condemnation'. The toilet's broken, windows boarded up and the band compete with a vintage air-conditioning unit and a TV playing endless loops of big men getting pulped over a pigskin. Red, grizzly and saturnine behind the bar, can only occasionally be bothered to serve. Customers wander in and out and shout and laugh and sing with the band or exhibit signs of chemical dementia, grinding teeth, howling, barking. Naked light bulbs and a spinning mirror ball add a tortuous glare and everything's ruined, busted chairs and rusty tables. Not that anyone cares, especially not the musicians, who play from the floor, playing whenever they want, often cranking out the same song maybe three or four times. This is it, blues in the Mississippi night.

Beer's limited to Budweiser and Colt 45. There's Coke, Pepsi, 7-Up. Maybe some bourbon if Red's remembered to stock a bottle. Juke joints like Red's are where blues – and the music forms that sprang from it – took shape. *Juke*: one of those intrinsically American words now known the world over, a word whose origins are suspected of being the Wolof word 'jug' (to lead a disorderly life) or the Bambara word 'jugu' (a wicked, violent person). *Juke*. In the twenty-first-century only a handful of such places still exist across Mississippi, Memphis, Arkansas, Louisiana, Alabama, most of them having fallen into disuse as the black community lost its taste for blues. Others burnt down or were condemned by local authorities owing to drug dealing and/or violence.

Wesley had mentioned there once were many more juke joints and they'd attract genuine crowds. In his *The Land Where the Blues Began* Alan Lomax describes a Clarksdale Friday night in 1941: thousands of sharecroppers, bars overflowing, music pumping. Not any more: those living here might drift in and nurse a beer but the youth go to Memphis for rap while others are moths to Tunica's casinos. If Lomax was the original blues tourist then I'm following in giant footsteps: where he risked imprisonment by crossing the tracks, jukes like Red's shrug and accept white blues fans. Maybe these last few juke joints can survive on what once would have seemed a joke – *tourism*. Big T caresses his guitar, pulling out hard electric-blue sparks. Wesley, who I'm again sitting beside, is dressed sharp, gold glinting, and proud: Big T is his son.

'He's good, Wes. Learned from the best, yeah?'

'Damn, Terry's a better guitar player dan his daddy ever wuz. Fo' a long time I tried t' convince Terry t' play the blues but he wanted to play dat disco stuff. But after he had some hard times he learnt t' play blues. Yo' got t' crawl befo' yo' walk.'

Big T, who's solidly built with cornrow hair and a wise, shrewd face, played tough roadhouse blues when I arrived but as Red's fills he drifts easily into Southern soul, the evening's most popular numbers being Tyrone Davis and ZZ Hill tunes that get one, two, even three vocalists rising to help out. A young black woman wanders over and sits by me. 'I hope y'all don't think I'm makin' a pass at yo',' she says, 'but I just wanna say y'all is so cute an' yo' momma an' daddy did a real fine job o' makin' yo'. That's it.' She smiles, gets up and walks away. Two minutes later she's back asking, 'Yo' ain't all offended by me, are ya?'

'Not at all. It was a sweet thing to say. I'm Garth. What's your name?'

'Kathleen. Nice to meet ya. Yo' sure are cute. Where yo' from with that funny accent?'

'I live in London.'

'London, England? Well, I never. How'd yo' get here? In a plane?'

'Yeah, I flew to San Francisco an' then drove here.'

'Yo' would never get me on no plane. Uh-uh. I would be too scared. What's it like?'

'Flying?'

'Uh-huh.'

'Not that different from Greyhound. You get on and hours later get off at a different destination.'

'Damn, yo' is a cute white boy. Tell me, do yo' date outside yo' race an' nationality?'

Race and nationality? The least of obstacles. Problem is, I'm heading to Greenville tomorrow. But, what the hell, it's not every day a Southern belle flatters me so I kick back and chat with Kathleen who, at twenty-seven, has two sets of twins and rarely travels outside of Clarksdale. 'Damn, I would like to see the world so bad,' she says. 'Ain't nothin' happ'nin' in sleepy ole Clarksdale.' Kathleen's tall, good-humoured, happy to chat about her kids, my rambling, the music (good, we both agree), what brings a white boy to Red's, her singing ('my daddy's a preacher so I learnt t' sing that gospel'). When the band unplug I take this as an excuse – admittedly lame – to leave; thoughts of Robert Johnson's juke-joint demise playing in my head.

Outside Red's I introduce myself to Big T. He shakes hands, mutters about being pleased to play for visitors. I mention spending the afternoon on the river with his father and he smiles, says, 'Pops is cool,' his attention distracted by friends who pass a spliff around while throwing gear into a pick-up truck. I ask whether we could talk a little about his blues. 'I get paid t' play an' I like t' get paid t' talk,' says Big T. With me, I offer, you get paid in ink. He shrugs and suggests I join them as they're heading back to his bar for an after-hours jam session. We get in the pick-up and T kicks the vehicle into reverse, talking at me.

'I'm from Clarksdale's South Side an' I always been there, on an' off. My pops played with Jack Johnson in the Mississippi Juke Boys an' not long after that Wesley quit an' Jack formed the Jelly Roll Kings an' they trained me up on bass. I was twelve o' thirteen. We played a lot o' shows an' they taught me the Delta blues style. I followed Big Jack into the Oilers an' we travelled all over the country. Even did a European tour as Jelly Roll Kings. My own band ended 'cos I did some criminal actions, became a bad boy, drinkin' an' drugs, ended up doin' six year on Parchman Farm. Parchman ain't designed t' rehabilitate anyone so I rehabilitated myself. During the time I was servin' I took it upon myself t' be free o' the things that robbed me o' my mind. Came out in 2000. Now I'm a club owner, known as a teacher an' band leader.'

Big T turns the corner, slams his truck right up on the sidewalk and everyone begins humping equipment into a bar with 'Big T's' written out front. Instruments are set up beneath a single light bulb. There's a pool table in the corner and a few tables. 'Big T's' is comparable to Red's if not so ruined. The cinder-block building's inky darkness gives all inhabitants a spectral presence. A silent black woman runs the bar and T asks whether I'm hungry. You bet. He instructs her to fry a burger. My stomach twinges when I see the greasy skillet she tosses patties on to; what the hell, when in a juke joint eat like a bluesman. A huge black man walks in and embraces Big T.

'This is Eddie, my little brother,' says Big T of the man mountain. Eddie mutters a pleasantry then wobbles off towards the bar. Another brother, Wesley Jr, whose smiling, shaven-headed presence I encountered at the last bar, plugs in an electric keyboard and starts singing lovely, high gospel-flavoured phrases. 'Yes, sir, God is great,' he says as Big T plugs in and strokes a chord, adding, 'You should come up to Memphis some time. We can check out some titty bars.' A small, beat-looking white guy arrives wearing a harmonica belt over a Hawaiian shirt. Obviously familiar with the bar and musicians, he plugs a microphone into a portable amplifier and begins to honk. 'That sounds cool,' says Big T, 'good groove.' He begins to dig deep Delta sounds out of his guitar. The silent woman running the bar serves the burger, mutters 'three dollar' and disappears back into shadows. Sound is building and Stan – that's what they're calling the harp player – blows hard, pulling out long fat notes, letting them echo and refract. Wesley Jr sings *'hound dog, hound dog, don't you run'* then hits the wrong note and Big T stops, shouts, 'This is a twelve-bar blues! Keep it on the one an' two!' Wesley Jr struggles to master a twelve-bar pattern and Big T glowers. Stan puts down his harp and says, 'I'll do some drinkin'.' 'That makes sense,' replies Big T, 'as all of us been drinkin'.'

Roger, from Cat Head, and his wife, Jennifer, arrive. We take a table, shadow dwellers in the bar's murkiness. Blues has existed in Clarksdale for more than a century, says Roger, and remains part of the community's DNA. To prove this a refreshed Stan starts playing long, mournful blue notes while Wesley Jr hits a minor chord and starts murmuring *'hard times, hard times... hard times on my mind'*. Big T picks out notes, slow, eloquent, midnight-hour blues. 'Hallelujah!' he shouts as the three musicians find common ground and roll forward. Wesley Jr sings *'somebody tole me 'bout Dr Jesus an' I was drinkin' my wine'*, digging deep into the keyboard, playing church chords. He then moans *'no time to pray, oh Lord, no time to pray'*. Stan blows a squall of blue notes and Big T nods and crouches low, unleashing a run of barbed-wire notes, peeling them off until they ring around the room. He straightens, chops a heavy chord in to signify 'job well done', and returns to playing rhythm. *'My woman done left me'*, sings Wesley Jr, *'don't know if it a good thing. Sometime it seem like a bad thing.'* The music's lovely, haunted, improvised in a loose, unhurried way, carrying across the bar and out into the night. The musicians jam, pushing and pulling at one another, Big T laughing then scowling when concentration fades and flubbed notes echo across the room. Enough, he finally says, and unplugs. Voices spark across the bar and a sense of the temporal returns. Jennifer's a teacher at Clarksdale's public school: what's Mississippi's school system like?

'Mississippi's the poorest state in the US and schools get their funding from the region's property tax base. That means a rich area will have a school with superb facilities while a poor area like Clarksdale will have schools desperate for funds. All the kids I'm teaching are black. We briefly had a white child enrolled and my pupils thought I'd greet this Caucasian arrival with great joy as they've grown up to see everything in racial terms. What appears to have happened with the ending of official school segregation in 1970 is that private schools were opened and Clarksdale's white families send their kids there.'

'We call them segregation academies,' says Roger. 'The school where most of Clarksdale's white kids go is probably no better than the school Jennifer works at but that's the way the parents want it. I think it's tragic, these kids growing up in the same town but living separate lives, yet that's how this place is run.'

I join Big T and Wesley Jr at the bar, where they're joking about Beale Street, bemused by its phoney blooze façade. 'Ain't no juke joints in Beale Street,' I offer as my opening tautology. Big T and Wesley Jr both nod but I can see they're looking at me as your typical blues tourist, the kind who hitches up in Beale Street then goes slumming in Mississippi. Opening gambit number two: 'Guys going to play some more?' 'Maybe later,' says Big T, who then reconsiders – 'I played my piece tonight, I reckon' – and courteously suggests I head down to Ground Zero, the blues club owned by actor Morgan Freeman. Although he doesn't say so, Big T's hinting it's time I get back to 'my people'. This makes me recall hearing about a wealthy Memphis photographer who parked his customised BMW convertible outside a Mississippi juke joint and went inside to snap the bar's inhabitants; exiting, he found the car keyed and *Go back to Beale Street white boy* scrawled in lipstick on the windscreen. 'Thanks,' I say, 'for the music.' 'Welcome,' says Big T, 'ya know the way back?' I reckon, Clarksdale's small. Back into the Mississippi night and outside Big T's several youths slouch against cars, listening to Dirty South hip-hop, near motionless in the midnight heat, exhaling whispers of reefer smoke, sipping syrup (cough mixture). The rapper spits and curses, referencing murdered New Orleans rapper Soulja Slim. One of the youths, red eyes, pipe-cleaner limbs and mashed Afro, clears his throat.

'Hey,' he says. 'Hey, *white* boy.'

Pick a bale of cotton:
Mississippi sharecropper

chapter 22

Greenville: King of the Chitlin' Circuit

Saturday morning and soft, moist heat hangs in the air. Fuel is coffee and pastries at a Mennonite bakery run by headscarf-wearing women, the shyest waitresses in America who make no eye contact, don't chat or attempt to flirt as they refill cups and serve sticky buns, women who appear to have stepped from Millet's *The Gleaners*, so lacking in bulk and noise it's difficult to recognise them as Southern white women. Jewish cemeteries... Mennonite bakeries... Clarksdale offers more surprises than its shanty surface suggests. Breakfast finished, I try to find my way on to Highway 1 and, predictably, get lost, driving through a tiny African-American hamlet of weatherboard houses. Young kids and old folk stare down from porches, faces set, giving off little expression. I imagine some of the older residents remember blues 78 collectors coming around in the sixties asking whether they had any old records they wished to sell. The tales told by collectors like Robert Crumb and Joe Bussard always make searching for 78s sound as enticing as hunting for pirate treasure, but I imagine Clarksdale turf has been truly well sifted. Crawl back towards the outskirts of Clarksdale, looking for the highway that will send me deep into the Delta.

Finally on Highway 1 and, typically, the gallon of coffee and ice water I've put away wants to get out. I stop on the side of the road and piss against a ruined billboard with VOTE BUSH painted in large letters across it. Well, those who bothered to vote did and the likes of the agribusiness who own this plantation surely enjoyed more corporate breaks. A hawk, all speckled beauty, cruises above, arcing across a blue sky as it rides the breeze, hungry for prey. I'm projecting, sure, but there remains an eerie, ominous flavour to Mississippi's highways and byways. Keep jamming through the radio stations, AM and FM, trying to find one that holds my attention. A country station openly advocates supporting Republican voting tactics in Congress. Another breaks from music to go into a long and gory anti-abortion advertisement. An R & B station features some Tupac wannabe crooning '*thugs have feelings too*'. Maybe, but not voices – damn, this cat sings flat. The road cuts through small towns with little more than a gas station and a general store, past trailer homes, imploding houses, windblown shacks and swampy bayous, water dark and brackish, finally snaking alongside the mighty Mississippi river, then back rolling through rural nothingness, wide open and seemingly uninhabited. Drive at cruising speed; there's nothing to rush for and I've been warned the local sheriffs love to whack hefty speeding fines on out-of-state visitors. *Think about it*: forty years ago strangers had much more to worry about than a speeding fine.

Hit Rosedale and – *doh!* – almost cause a wreck (again) by looking out for Joe's White Front Hot Tamale Café instead of watching turning traffic. This highway knows many ghosts but best I don't join them just yet. I find Joe's semi-legendary café and like so much of Mississippi it's a shack, weatherboard exterior peeling and warped. I enter, expecting a restaurant that resembles Red's but inside all is spick and span. Five dollars gets two tamales (cornmeal and minced beef wrapped in a corn husk and boiled for hours). I sit at a small table, unwrap the corn husks and pick at the reddish solution they hold inside. Tamales arrived in Mississippi when Mexican workers came through in the 1920s. The Mexicans moved on but the local sharecroppers adopted tamales as a regional delicacy – Robert Johnson celebrated them on 'It's Red Hot' – and while I eat locals wander in, glancing at me, ordering batches of tamales for Saturday family lunches. The tamales are oily and taste a little odd, meaty but fibrous. Not exactly food to savour.

Back outside little appears to occupy Rosedale's wide, leafy streets. There's a large Food Distribution Centre – last night

Jennifer mentioned how poor the quality of government food given to local schoolchildren for lunches is – and a small food stand serving chicken wings alongside a dozen boarded-up buildings. On the side of one building a Coca-Cola emblem has faded over the decades into near invisibility, symbolic surely of how small-town Mississippi has been left to die on the vine. A derelict shop is home to nothing more than a poster for the David Banner album *Mississippi: Screwed and Chopped*. Banner's the first Mississippi rapper to achieve any national prominence ('screwed and chopped' is hip-hop parlance for 'remixed'), conveying Dirty South ('Like a Pimp') raps alongside more reflective rhymes ('Cadillacs on 22s'). Thing is, he's a college graduate who sets aside royalties to send underprivileged Mississippi youth to college. A good man, then. But I find it hard to engage with much of his music, his tunes often employing the predictable tapestry of beats 'n' squeals that defines too much rap. I look at the poster – Banner glowering with menace – and wonder what happened to the Mississippi that seduced the world with its musical magic. This decline in the creativity of America's poorest citizens surely signals a psychic wound of sorts, cultural cancer.

At Chow's Super Market I purchase ice cream and bottled water, the ancient Chinese proprietors' low-level surveillance of customers lending them a phantom presence, Delta ghosts from an age when Chinese made up Mississippi's third largest ethnic group, thousands having been brought here to work on the railway in the 1870s. *'Where white men rent farms and live like niggers and niggers crop on shares and live like animals,'* wrote William Faulkner when considering his home state, *'where cotton is planted and grows man-tall in the very cracks of the sidewalks, and usury and mortgage and bankruptcy and measureless wealth, Chinese and African and Aryan and Jew, all breed and spawn together.'* Many of Mississippi's Chinese converted to Christianity and were allowed to operate as unofficial 'whites' during segregation; the state's lingering economic decline encouraging most to leave in search of better opportunities. Back in the car I find a radio station hosted by two lively locals who slip soul tunes on, name-check car

Play it sweet: Stavin' Chain
and friend, Mississippi, 1936

repair firms, joke about where the nearest bail bondsmen are and do shout-outs for the good people of Mississippi. 'Bobby "Blue" Bland and Bobby Rush gonna be singin' today in Greenville,' says one, 'ain't that amazin'?' His sidekick concurs and I can only agree, Rush and Bland being Mississippi legends.

Near Winterville, a site commemorates the Choctaw Indian Mounds. I pull into a neat area on the side of Highway 1, park and step out among a cluster of mounds. These smooth, rectangular structures curve on all four corners, trimmed grass providing fine cover. Hike up a mound and stand and stare towards where America's most powerful and ominous river runs: when the great flood of 1927 found the Mississippi bursting its banks and covering everything inland for many miles these mounds stood, ancient and imperious, above the flowing water. By then they were already a thousand years old and had borne witness to countless floods and hurricanes, watched kingdoms rise and fall, these cylindrical lumps from the civilisation that first settled and named Mississippi. '*The Delta. Five thousand square miles, without any hill save the bumps of dirt the Indians made to stand on when the River overflowed,'* wrote Faulkner. The 1927 floods were the Katrina of their day; the Tunica museum had silvery footage of families huddling on rooftops while waters raged, a sharecropper's defeated features linking this Mississippi turbulence with New Orleans' ordeal. Charley Patton, the pioneering Delta blues star, sang *'fifty men and women come to sink and drown/Oh Lordie, women and grown men down, oh women and children sinkin' down'* on 'High Water Everywhere', a blues almost cinematic in its account of the 1927 devastation. Wild Charley with his light skin and Choctaw features, processed hair and turbulent music, grew up on Dockery Plantation east of Rosedale. He knew this highway well.

I'm the only visitor at the mounds and silence surrounds me. I strain to hear gospel voices carried upon the breeze, a hint of human beauty and soul from one of the many tiny churches I've passed, but nothing comes my way. Thing is, I'm not alone... *can sense the dead veining this land, a mess of tongues, Choctaws fleeing Spanish hounds, African slaves bewailing the world they lost, Civil War carnage, soldier after soldier's blood fertilising the rich black soil, sharecroppers farming under the shadow of flaming crosses and Freedom Riders facing the boiling furies mobs generate...* I wobble, dizzy with heat and history. Stumble to the site's spotless restroom. Soak wrists, scrub face. My destination's the Mississippi Blues Festival, south of Greenville, and the Delta's turning the heat on in true Southern style.

'Somebody called me King of the Chitlin' Circuit an' they meant it to be less than a compliment but I figure, hell *no!* That a compliment, man. That my people. See, a one-eyed man's hell in a blind house!'

Bobby Rush has spent his entire adult working life playing juke joints, Chicago's South Side bars and the chitlin' circuit. For a man in his mid-sixties he's in good shape, slim, skin shining, eyes merry, a smile and a handshake for everyone. We're talking backstage at the Mississippi Blues Festival, a down-home event whose majority black audience munch their way through hot dogs and catfish while listening to artists who've been singing for them for several decades. No guitar heroes here, no acts trying to grab a rock audience, uh-uh, this is music made by people who, as Bobby noted, are proud to be part of the chitlin' circuit, that unofficial network of black clubs just up the ladder from juke joints. Rush's music – while often branded 'blues' – is Southern soul, a music left with an older, more rural audience when funk and disco won over black American tastes in the seventies. Compared to his most talented contemporaries – Al Green and O. V. Wright, Syl Johnson and Tyrone Davis – Rush is a journeyman, only occasionally scoring with an exceptional tune. Rush knows this and it makes him work harder than anyone else: Bobby's the King of the Chitlin' Circuit because he gets out there and entertains an audience who want – no, *demand* – a good time.

The chitlin' circuit was christened after chitterlings: fried pigs' intestines being one of the staples of 'soul food'. The unofficial nickname stuck just as soul food did to the cooking invented by African-American women who, in slavery days, made do with what the master decreed as 'leftovers'. Soul food has thrived into modern times, the inventiveness employed in African-American cooking making for some of the best eating in the USA. Likewise the chitlin' circuit – venues run by and for the black community – launched Ray Charles, Ike & Tina Turner, The Isley Brothers and many, many others; all built formidable reputations by criss-crossing the USA working the circuit throughout the fifties and sixties. The ending of segregation found many black business enterprises – especially sports teams and soul food restaurants – decimated by wealthier white competition. The chitlin' circuit thrived because black and white Americans largely listen to different music: beyond Bo, Chuck, Fats and Little Richard, Motown's superstars, Jimi Hendrix, Michael Jackson, Prince, Tina Turner and a handful of R & B and hip-hop artists, almost every black American popular musician has punched their weight harder on the R & B charts than pop. Or else found that when the black audience lost interest whites were getting attuned – as has

'Chitlin's always been loyal': Bobby Rush and friend, Greenville, MS, 2006

been the case with blues, soul and funk; even black-nationalist rappers Public Enemy play almost entirely to whites today. But for some chitlin's the only audience they know – Wynonie Harris, O. V. Wright and Tyrone Davis never won a white audience. Even Otis Redding, lionised Southern soul icon, scored only one Top 30 pop hit. And he had to fall out of the sky to achieve that.

'Chitlin's always been loyal. The kids don't know who Buddy Guy is, Robert Cray is. They crossed over but they can't go home again, y'hear me? They done left the black behind. *Not* Bobby Rush. I don' wanna go down in history as someone who left his people behind.'

Rush speaks with a certain intensity, never rhetorical but, as one of the hardest-working individuals in American music, he's aware who's paid for his sweat.

'I came up as a country boy on the farm. Ploughin' the mule, choppin' cotton, all fo' three dollars a day. I looked at a lot of black entertainers who worked hard but made no money. O' lost their money, gamblin' o' on drugs. I had two o' three beers in 1957 an' never touched anything since. I've been takin' care o' business an' that's why I'm still out there. I tell yo', I still work three hundred days a year. See, I think I can make it without owin' favours t' anyone.'

Rush lives in Jackson, Mississippi, as it places him within the vicinity of the chitlin' circuit's backbone. He's never had a breakout hit or been championed by rock bands and might have remained invisible to a wider audience if he hadn't appeared in *The Road to Memphis*, the standout feature among the seven-episode *Martin Scorsese Presents the Blues*. *The Road to Memphis*, directed by Richard Pearce, focuses on Rush and B. B. King, Roscoe Gordon and Ike Turner, as they moved towards the annual W. C. Handy Awards in Memphis. Rush, filmed working the chitlin' circuit, won viewers over through sheer force of personality.

'That documentary did more for me than anything in my life,' says Rush. 'Best thing that ever happened! I thank God for that documentary. Originally they wanted to film me playing B. B. King's club, bein' nice in front of a white audience. I said, "No. This is where I draw the line with Bobby Rush. You film me doin' it in front of my people." They did an', *man*, they got it.'

Back out front and the stage is being set up. Bobby 'Blue' Bland – one of the great interpreters of American song – performed earlier. Yet Bland, illiterate and shy, has never appeared willing to embrace an audience wider than the chitlin' circuit and this afternoon his people sang along to 'Members Only' and 'Cry Cry Cry'. Bland sang well but looked frail and, shorn of those long familiar Jheri curls, the blues Samson appears to be losing his strength. Not that I should be expecting his younger self at seventy-five. And it's hot. Wild, stinking, fluid-draining, brain-boiling Mississippi humidity. Rubbed a pack of ice cubes through my scalp while watching Bland. Twilight falls but the heat refuses to let up, heat that irritates like a loco mosquito, and when Shirley Brown takes the stage she appears mighty pissed off.

Shirley's huge, a whale of a woman, and her mouth's nasty, whether cursing the soundman or detailing sexual peccadilloes. The crowd hoot and holler at every innuendo, and when she demands to see some dick several men start shouting like they would willingly flash onstage. Shirley's greatest hit, 'Woman to

Woman' (Stax's last R & B No. 1 in 1974), becomes a filthy rap monologue and then suddenly she's stating how tomorrow's Sunday and *by Gawd on Sunday I'll be in church!* Talk about lift-off: Shirley's gospel breath sends the audience into a frenzy and the big black mama who's been insisting I bump and grind starts wailing about Jesus and – *goddam!* – the whole festival becomes a molten revival tent. Shirley struts and wobbles, sneers and sings, calling on Jesus while delivering an X-rated sermon, punching home how soul's the secular, sexualised bastard of gospel, her coarse Bible-bashing having fired something deep in the black Baptist psyche.

Bobby Rush's performance is delayed by technical problems: tonight he's being backed by a big band and his crew are having problems getting everything right. Eleven p.m. and the heat still oozes. Festival sites often bear a passing resemblance to battlefields, and among the mess and bodies collapsed across picnic blankets I can hear moans from those who overindulged during the day and are now felled by the fatal combination of food-booze-heat. The MC holding the stage is, I'm sure, the same DJ who praised Rush and Bland on the radio this morning. He brings his down-home manner to the job, addressing the audience as people who live 'cheque to cheque', and they respond in kind. Finally, Bobby's there, flanked by his big-ass dancers, who do nothing more than bounce their butts as he struts across the stage singing *'I got a little lady/who lives down the road/I go night fishin'/'cos she got a nice hole'*. Rush, like many chitlin' circuit artists, relies heavily on 'cheating' songs. I'm guessing the genre always existed – 'Dark End of the Street' being the *Citizen Kane* of cheating songs – and Clarence Carter and Millie Jackson both built large followings singing about little more than bed-hopping. Aids, STDs and unwanted pregnancies are never referenced; instead the act of getting off and away (or catching someone else out) is all that counts. Or maybe the cheating songs contain a code that, as an outsider, I simply can't comprehend. Never thought to ask Bobby why such songs dominate although I can guess his answer: *it's what the people want.*

As I leave the festival at midnight Greenville pulses with traffic, SUVs pumping beats, testosterone and exhaust fumes into the night. I toy with the idea of heading on to Nelson Street – home to Greenville's cluster of juke joints – but all I mentioned this to suggested Bad Idea: crack cocaine has scythed through Mississippi's poor, black communities and Nelson Street's Ghetto Central. 'Y'all find yo'self on Nelson Street an' some crazy nigga might just cut yo' o' shoot yo' fo' the change in yo' pocket,' said a paternal local, 'an' we don' want that happenin' to our guests, now.' Situated behind a levee on the Mississippi river, Greenville's home to 41,000 people, the majority black town cursed with low incomes and high violent crime rates. When I reach the intersection where I'd turn left to head towards Nelson Street police cars and ambulances cut up traffic, sirens piercing, searching out the madness at the town's heart. I pause, get honked by a jeep and decide – *fuck it!*, driving straight on. Call me chickenshit but those sirens don't need to be wailing my name.

On the outskirts of town I find a motel. The Asian woman at reception pulls a face, sweat and melted ice having reduced me to the Swamp Thing's Kiwi cousin. Images of Hindu gods, especially Ganesh, are pinned on walls while the smell of curry spices wafts through the air. *Oh, my beloved India!* Where, I enquire, is she from. 'Bangalore.' I recall visiting Bangalore but she displays no interest in furthering the conversation. Next question: anywhere open around here that I could eat at? 'I've no idea,' she replies, 'I've lived here nineteen years and never once eaten out. We are vegetarians. We cook for ourselves. The people here, all they eat is meat.' She shakes her head disapprovingly as a police siren fills the air. This kills my appetite and, realistically, I need a shower and a bed more than I need meat. I retire to a tidy room with creaky air conditioning to sleep the sleep of the truly drained.

chapter 23

River Valley: I Just Shot Him
in the Head

Greenville, Sunday morning. The moist climate and unhurried traffic suggest a good day for sitting on the porch, chewing the fat, sipping mint juleps. As ever, I've no time to hang about; instead I'm heading east on the 82, grateful that Hurricane Katrina made visiting New Orleans no longer necessary. A cynical thought, Louisiana being home to a wealth of regional music; rich music made by poor people, many of whom have been evicted from their homes and communities owing to vicious weather, poor investment in levees and a callous federal government. Katrina shouldn't have wrought such extreme damage yet decades of neglect are noticeable (run-down roads/public facilities) as I travel: Ronald Reagan's administration pioneered cutting taxes while pumping up military spending, heralding a reversal from what Roosevelt began with the New Deal. That the South should continue to suffer more severely than the rest of the USA is unfair but appropriate; extreme humidity and a sense of casual brutality mingle in the atmosphere like nowhere else in the USA. Time spent here is helping me appreciate why Memphis and Mississippi lend themselves to mania; blues and jazz, gospel and soul, country and rock 'n' roll, all arose from these hell-mouths. The east and west coasts (and Midwest) initially produced little original music of note, reliant on the South to provide American musical genius, which makes me recall *The Third Man* and Harry Lime's theory of Switzerland–peace–cuckoo-clocks versus Italy–war–Renaissance.

A car repair shop's sign reads '*Want Money? Try Working*'. A church advertises '*Tired of Church? Hell Has Lots of Space*'. I imagine Greenville citizen T-Model Ford could incorporate such slogans into his songs. T-Model is the most famous blues primitive working today, a man whose music and life combine in a harshness, a kind of brute ugliness, almost comical in its telling. Born James Lewis Carter Ford in the late 1920s, T-Model grew up illiterate ('can't read, can't write, ain't never been t' school a day in my life', he likes to boast), taking such beatings from his father he lost a testicle as a child. Working for a lumber company he continued to be embroiled in violence until he was sentenced to ten years on a chain gang for murder. When interviewers ask T-Model about this he typically states that it was good to be brought up the hard way because that meant he could handle anything. And murder? 'I could really stomp some ass back then, stomp it good. I was a-sure-enough dangerous man.' T-Model had never been outside of Mississippi until he hit his mid-seventies, was seventy-five when his first recordings were made, and makes a music so primitive even diehard Delta blues fans find it difficult to listen to. T-Model may appear a strange candidate for international cult stardom but the Mississippi label Fat Possum has proved brilliant at gifting the state's most ruined musicians with successful careers.

The most celebrated of Fat Possum's Delta primitives was the late R. L. Burnside. Burnside liked to boast that he shot a man who threatened him: when the judge asked him whether he intended to kill the man he replied, 'It was between him and the Lord, him dyin'. I just shot him in the head.' Convicted of murder, he served six months before being released through the influence of a white plantation foreman who requested the hard-working RL for the cotton harvest. Burnside spent the ensuing years doing farm work by day and playing juke joints and house parties at weekends. Occasionally recorded, Burnside rarely played outside Mississippi, driving a tractor for a day job, oblivious to the late-1980s blues boom kicked off by Robert Cray and John Lee Hooker. His fortunes began to change in 1991 when Mathew Johnson, then a student at Ole Miss University, befriended Robert Palmer (author of seminal text *Deep Blues*) and Palmer, intent on recording Burnside, encouraged Johnson to start a label. Fat Possum took the approach of marketing Burnside to an audience who generally favoured punk rock: Burnside's raw blues, bleak wit and nihilistic character won a wide youth audience. A surreal form of celebrity then enveloped R. L. – championed by the likes of The Beastie Boys and Bono, he became the most chic black man in North America: Richard Gere hired him to play his Manhattan parties, Uma Thurman attended his concerts, Jay McInerney wrote a profile for the *New Yorker*, Annie Leibovitz took photographs for *Vanity Fair* – all the while the Burnsides continued to live in a ramshackle, cockroach-infested Mississippi shack.

I shuffle Fat Possum CDs in and out of the car stereo. Some, like those of T-Model, spin for a few tunes before their sheer crudity becomes fingernails on an invisible blackboard and I throw 'em into the back seat. But when the late Junior Kimbrough starts moaning I relax; his shuffling trance-blues sound carries a drone reminiscent of West African griots and opens up space. Kimbrough's weird artistry possesses traces of what made the Delta blues recordings of the 1920s and '30s so majestic. On I drive with Junior moaning '*yo better run... don't let him catch yo... if he get yo... babe... he gonna rape yo...*', the threat implied made even more horrible by Kimbrough's shifting of narrative perspective, from first- to second- to third-person perspective, so seeming to have the victim forget the rapist and turn to Kimbrough and sing, '*Junior, I luuuuvvvvv youuuuu.*' Fucked up? This is Mississippi music and chaos is one of the few constants here. Not that conveying menace is Kimbrough's sole mania; on another song he sings '*I done got old/can't do what I used to*'. Then there's a tune called 'Most Things Haven't Worked Out'; Kimbrough's blues being those of despair, dysfunction, entropy, primal crunk.

Kimbrough and Burnside both played what's called 'Hill Country blues' and lived around the Holly Springs region of north-east Mississippi. To get to this region from Greenville I've headed east along the 82 into the Yazoo river delta, through Leland, where Jim Henson invented Kermit the Frog, that icon of the good-natured swamp-dwelling American; Indianola, birthplace of B. B. King and now home to the largest catfish

'Most things haven't worked out…': Junior Kimbrough

processing company in the world; and Greenwood, where the Yazoo river runs through a town whose nineteenth-century brownstones glint in the morning sun. Much of this terrain was covered in forest even while the Civil War raged, being cleared for cotton in the late nineteenth century, and a tough, stark environment surrounds a two-lane highway that stretches into the infinite. Sighting a gas station or a church – so many roadside churches, shanty churches with peeling paint and lopsided crosses and misspelled signs suggesting damnation lurks on the 82 – or a Wal-Mart or a burger shack gives me something to focus eyes on. '*Mississippi Goddam*', sang Nina Simone when things were very nasty down here. Yesterday's festival found me in agreement with Nina, 'cept it was only the climate which had me cursing the state. Lightweight? Featherweight, that's me.

Take the 1-55 north and then the 32. The landscape has lost its extreme flatness and is now slipping, curving, finding some freedom in undulating motion. Even the colours of the land, the greens and browns, appear a little softer, not so washed out. Notice thick tangles of kudzu weed growing on both sides of the road and think how kudzu, an unwanted Asian import growing feral, resembles crack cocaine, both spreading forth across Mississippi with a slow, coiled intensity that no authority can properly combat. I descend into Water Valley, a small, tidy town at the centre of the Mississippi Hill Country, where Fat Possum's based, and look up Mathew Johnson, who turns out to be very much the polite, middle-class Southerner. Over chicken steaks in a local diner he begins by announcing Fat Possum are now concentrating on recording punk rock, blues being dead and buried.

'The greater black community tends to think of blues as Uncle Tom shit and the white blues fans – if there's any left – are too set in their ways so I don't think there is any future for it. We got Junior out of such an awful landscape and we'd take him to a blues festival and he'd be on the same bill as horrible shit like Little Feat and Jimmy Buffett. See, when Johnny Vincent was running Ace in Jackson and the Chess brothers were doing Chess in Chicago they were cutting popular music for the black community. The Chess philosophy was "cut it on Tuesday, press it on Thursday, sell it on Friday/Saturday, get the leftovers on Monday, melt 'em down and start again". Today the independent labels don't count. We're irrelevant, boutique labels. I wish we weren't but that's the truth. The script is written and we're acting out the last scenes.' Johnson chuckles and adds, 'People have always been selling blues since the 1930s as "this is the last blues". I'd say this even if I didn't believe it.'

Johnson is talking a certain truth here: once blues musicians were found in every small Mississippi town; today few Mississippi musicians come up playing blues.

'We signed this new guy, Charles "Cadillac" Caldwell, and we were real excited about him,' says Johnson. 'Trouble is, he was diagnosed with pancreatic cancer and died within a year of signing. Paul "Wine" Jones died not long after RL. T-Model keeps on going. He's incredible. But he lives in Greenville, which is a fucking cesspit, and he's been robbed there. We've tried to get him out but he refuses to leave. Johnny Farmer won't cut any more blues for us. Says it's the Devil's music and whoever sings it will burn in hell. Blues is doomed. Who needs another version of "Sweet Home Chicago"? Music has to change. Fat Possum caught the last of what sprung from Mississippi a long time ago. It's all over now.

'I know a lot of people think I'm an asshole 'cos I market blues as rough music – B. B. King's always saying "I hate it that people think because I play the blues I beat my wife" – but, and I'm sorry, B. B., our guys are pretty crazy people!' Johnson laughs at this then adds, 'I mean, Junior and RL lived really rough lives. The Mississippi they inhabited is the worst, most deprived, most depressing region in the US. No wonder people go crazy, living in the conditions they did. See, T-Model might be a psycho but he's a very likeable psycho.' He laughs again then adds, 'The sense of humour has been taken out of this country. Look, when I was a kid people who rode Harley Davidsons were bad, scummy people. Now they're the Republicans' favourite form of transport. All the eccentric things have been cleaned up – Iggy's heroin songs are used to advertise banks. Ray Charles and Al Green are played to death as lifestyle muzak. Someone like Ol' Dirty Bastard, now, he was a genius, but there's hardly anyone like him in popular music any more. Did you see the Scorsese *Blues* series? Wasn't that the sorriest piece of shit? It just told viewers that blues was boring.'

Would Johnson consider shifting his label to LA or New York to be closer to the rock music industry?

'No. I don't like the South so much but the rest of the US is even worse to live in. Mississippi sucks in so many ways – schools and healthcare and infant mortality and all that broke-dick stuff – but I just don't see myself living somewhere like New York.'

What's Johnson's take on Hurricane Katrina and its aftermath? I'm surprised it's ceased to be a topical issue.

'It was so awful to watch on TV it felt like following a conceptual artwork. The government's response was exactly what you'd expect when it comes to dealing with poor people – they don't vote or contribute to Republican finances so leave 'em to rot. And a lot of Americans share that view, y'know, "poor blacks on welfare – got what they deserved!" This country's a mess.'

We rise to leave and Johnson starts on another story, this time about Booba Barnes, another deceased, minor Mississippi blues player.

'One time I was walking home at six a.m. and he came out wearing a shower cap, half dressed, one snakeskin boot in his hand. He says, "You seen anyone stolen my boot?" I said, "I don't think anyone would steal one boot, Bobba," and he said, "A one-legged muthafucker would!" He was looking down the street to see if someone with one leg had his boot! That's Mississippi for ya!'

Out of Water Valley and down the road to that lone beacon of Anglo culture in the deep South, Oxford. If much of Mississippi has the debilitated look found along the Caribbean coast, Oxford exists as a beacon of white wealth and sovereignty. Not too many black faces wandering central Oxford. Not that anyone in their right mind would be out in the mid-afternoon heat. There're plenty of cafés and bars and art galleries and boutiques, even a decent bookshop. Ole Miss University is based in Oxford and half the town's population are students. Posters and flyers stuck in every shop window solicit votes for such quaint emblems of the old South as Homecoming Queen, Colonel Reb and Miss Ole Miss. The candidates, groomed and toothy in the TV-presenter manner US politicians affect, are all white; this suggests James Meredith's incendiary 1962 enrolment at Ole Miss has not led to an influx of black students. I wander into the suburbs ($625,000 for a two-bedroom bungalow), searching for the Master's house. There're no signs offering directions; Oxford breathes such a superior atmosphere that the town doesn't even condescend to mark its monuments: William Faulkner spent a good part of his adult life living in Oxford, even apparently basing his fictional town of Jefferson on it, his house now preserved for the public.

For decades Faulkner was hailed as the greatest twentieth-century US novelist yet today he's largely unread while his contemporaries, Hemingway and Fitzgerald, tower above. For most readers Nick Carraway and Jake Barnes fit templates they themselves recognise: striving, frustrated, decent types who never achieve much but like to reflect and report on the world. Kerouac's Sal Paradise is cut from similar American cloth. Faulkner's dense treatises, jammed with faded gentry and Neanderthal white trash, appear almost medieval. Which isn't to decry his writing: *As I Lay Dying* remains a novel that invades the consciousness of those willing to tangle with the Bundrens' awful journey, a razor of Mississippi artistry comparable to the music of Skip James, Son House or Tommy Johnson. Wandering this perfect suburb, every house a dream home, I wonder whether Faulkner ever listened to blues? One can imagine him appreciating the bleak imagery, religious metaphors and desperate wish for salvation from temptation and oppression – '*to endure well grief and misfortune and injustice and then endure again*', he wrote of life: sounds like an apt description of Wesley Jefferson – but I've no recollection of music playing any role in his books.

Thinking about Faulkner's characters, all those Snopeses and Satoris and Bundrens and Compsons, and how deranged most were, I start wondering whether the heat drove them crazy: by the time I reach Rowan Oak, as Faulkner's home is known, I'm slick with sweat and more than a little flustered. On top of this the damn house happens to be closed. Not that I'm particularly enamoured of staring at rooms where celebrated writers once sat but Faulkner's gaff does hold a certain fascination, he being the original architect of Southern Gothic. Also, there's apparently one room where, when drunk (often), Bill would go and scribble on the walls. Rowan Oak is set in an acre decorated with oaks. The leafy grounds provide some temporary shade to sit and curse my folly: walking all the way to a monument the university can't see fit to keep open normal hours. Curse that I've now got to walk the same sweaty trail back. Curse even louder upon realising the rental car's due back by six and Memphis is still a good ninety minutes away.

Barrelling towards Memphis, aware the vehicle must be returned with a full tank of gas, I stop on the city's outskirts aiming to fill. It's a big gas station, yet a Pay Before You Pump. Thing is, I've no idea how much it costs to fill the goddam tank and when I enter the emporium I'm overpowered by the smell of fried chicken: mountains of dead bird rest on hot plates without any effective ventilation system. The woman working the till is having problems and as the crowd grows she gets only more flustered and I'm just wanting to throw $$$ at her but this chook abattoir appears near meltdown and a guy who looks like he survived the plane crash that totalled Lynryd Skynyrd wanders unnaturally close and the combined stench of him and chicken sends me fleeing back to the car and once again on to the 55. Traffic's early-evening dense and I'm fretting about petrol and returning the car until I see a tiny gas station tucked off the highway. Man, the station's so old and run-down I have trouble figuring how to pump. As I pay, the man behind the counter says '*Parlez vous français?*'

'No, I'm from New Zealand. And you?'

'Palestine.'

'Palestine? *Damn*. Well, your people have really suffered. I hope one day they can live in a free and peaceful Palestine.'

He smiles, a sad, gentle smile, and starts talking; imagine it's not every year he gets to talk about 'home' with a customer. I'd love to stay and chat about Middle East peace but there's a $70 fine if I'm not at that airport in twenty minutes. 'Sorry,' I say, 'gotta run. Just tell me, what's the quickest way to the airport?'

'Three sets of lights then you exit following the airport signs.'

What would Faulkner, not known for his love of change but never immune to Biblical metaphor, make of Palestinians in Mississippi?

I make it to Memphis airport with three minutes to spare. The cheapest way into town is the Downtown Airport Shuffle, costing $7 to ride a shuttle bus for twenty minutes. The bus driver's accommodating, dropping me close to the train station. 'I ain't been here long,' says Bill, who sells me a train ticket to Chicago, 'just twenty years. I work thirty hours' overtime a week so my wife can go out and spend it all. I take home thirteen hundred dollars after tax and she can blow five, six hundred of that at the casinos, easy. She pays all the bills, don't get me wrong, but she loves to spend my money. We live cheque to cheque. I ain't been married long, just twenty-eight years.'

Bill details his existence while I repack. He asks nothing of my experiences, simply happy to have an audience to listen to his Memphis blues. The heat's gone out of the day, air less solid. Good weather for a stroll. The railway station's centred downtown, the mighty Mississippi river to one side and what once was urban squalor on the other. This area's been cleaned up considerably, designer bars and art galleries lining the main street, all gentrification relating to the National Civil Rights Museum. I wander along a quiet boulevard, trams shuttling past, everything appearing normal, almost quaint. Never thought I'd describe Memphis as quaint. Chuckle at the thoug— OK, there *it* is: the Lorraine Motel, now home to the Civil Rights Museum and surely the saddest building in all the Americas.

Nothing about the Lorraine's appearance suggests tragedy; instead everything, from the bright, decorative neon motel sign to the large American cars parked out front, speaks of sixties zest and optimism. There is one odd thing, a metal wreath welded on to the first-floor balcony rail outside room 306. Odd only, of course, if you don't know the building's history: in April 1968 Dr Martin Luther King was in town to lend support to the sanitation workers' strike (against low wages and racial discrimination in the workplace). King had recently founded the Poor People's Campaign to address issues of economic justice and spoke with an increasingly militant consciousness, calling for a massive government jobs programme to rebuild inner cities and decrying Congress's willingness to boost military spending while refusing to spend funds fighting poverty. On 3 April King took the podium at Memphis's Mason Temple and addressed an audience largely made up of striking sanitation workers with a speech containing the following:

'*It really doesn't matter what happens now... some began to... talk about the threats that were out what would happen to me from some of our sick white brothers... Like anybody, I would like to live a long life. Longevity has its place, but I'm not concerned about that now. I just want to do God's will. And He's allowed me to go up to the mountain. And I've looked over, and I've seen the Promised Land. I may not get there with you. But I want you to know tonight, that we, as a people, will get to the Promised Land.*'

King and entourage stayed in the Lorraine Motel; it was then among the best accommodation available to blacks in this still-segregated city. On 4 April, a fine spring evening, King was on the motel's balcony talking with friends about their planned meal. A shot rang out and King went down. Riots broke out from coast to coast. The Memphis music scene's magical bond of interracial brotherhood began to crumble while the city went into severe decline. And the USA, with its most eloquent and visionary oracle murdered... The Promised Land King spoke of with such conviction is nowhere in sight. Walk towards the motel, crisp and peaceful in the sunshine, and note a plaque which reads:

They said one to another, Behold, here cometh the dreamer... Let us slay him... And we shall see what will become of his dreams. Genesis 37: 19–20

Dust to dust: ghost town

CHICAGO BREAKDOWN

Chicago North and South, East and West

If heartache were a city it would be Chicago.

Luis Rodriguez

We live in a *community*, understand? Not the *projects* – I hate that word. We live in a *community*. We need a helping hand now and then, but who doesn't? Everyone in this building helps as much as they can. We share our food, just like I'm doing with you. My son says you're writing about his life – well, you may want to write about this community, and how we help each other. You'll cook for me if I'm hungry. But when you're here, you're in my home and my community. And we'll take care of you.

Ms Mae in conversation with Sudhir Venkatesh

You aint nothin' but a...: Hound Dog Taylor

chapter 24

Oh, We Had a Good Time

The *City of New Orleans* leaves Memphis at ten-forty p.m. and rolls north through the night. My first train ride this entire journey and it's on a locomotive immortalised in song: Arlo Guthrie scored with 'City of New Orleans' in 1972, the infectiously optimistic chorus of

> *Good morning, America, how are you?*
> *Don't you know me? I'm your native son.*
> *I'm the train they call the City of New Orleans.*
> *I'll be gone five hundred miles when the day is done*

establishing a contemporary standard. We roll out of Memphis, crossing the Mississippi's dark, shimmering waters, and I'm revelling in the sheer luxury of train travel. The near-extinction of the locomotive as a form of public transport is poignant – '*the disappearing railroad blues*', goes Guthrie's song – there's a dignity to train travel, a human scale, and no other mode matches the rhythm of trains: you can feel their chug-chug-chug in early blues and country recordings.

Millions have made this same journey over the decades with nearly every great Chicago blues, jazz and soul musician either born in the South or to parents who were. Post-slavery, when Southern racism was at its worst – the Jim Crow Laws enforcing discrimination existed 1876–1965 – Chicago appeared the Promised Land, home to factories and slaughterhouses that paid a living wage, home to Jack Johnson and Joe Louis, Louis Armstrong and Memphis Minnie, black newspapers and political figures. The reality of Chicago – more poverty and discrimination combined with a ferocious winter – allowed much blues, jazz and soul to germinate. But, for most, any alternative to sharecropping appealed and what's now known as the Northern Migration saw seven million black Americans leave the South: Texans headed west, those from the Carolinas fled east, while citizens from the Deep South went directly north: Detroit and Chicago. Today, over one third of Chicago's population is black, second only to that of New York.

The train crawls into darkness, picking up speed outside Memphis, rocking and rolling. Most everyone is attempting to sleep. Insomnia forces me to consider Chicago's musical heritage. In the 1920s musicians from New Orleans arrived to play Al Capone's clubs, turning jazz into an American, then international, phenomenon while composer Thomas Dorsey and singer Mahalia Jackson developed gospel's sonic structure and social power. Bluebird began recording blues in the 1920s, electric blues taking ferocious shape in 1940s Chicago speakeasies. A decade later aspirant bluesmen Chuck Berry and Bo Diddley would inadvertently invent much of what's now known as rock 'n' roll. Curtis Mayfield and The Dells established the city as a soul music powerhouse. Steve Goodman, composer of 'City of New Orleans', was a local. Admittedly, that's the only song of his I know. Still, one great song is worth noting. John Prine, master songwriter of early 1970s ennui, is a local boy. I rate Prine's wry, lyrical songs higher than the efforts of, say, Warren Zevon and Leonard Cohen, but that's me, always championing the underdog. Early blues-rockers Paul Butterfield and Mike Bloomfield both learned their chops on the South Side. Alt.country label Bloodshot are based in Chicago and they issued Alejandro Escovedo's finest albums. Jeff Tweedy's Wilco occasionally cut a striking song. Impossibly bland soft-rock outfit Chicago sold millions during the seventies. They really should have called themselves Boise, Idaho or something and left Chicago's rep intact. What else? House music sprang from the city's gay discos in the mid-eighties but beyond early efforts by Ten City and Inner City I never embraced the high-energy groove. There's also a large alt.rock scene dominated by The Smashing

Pumpkins, Steve Albini and Al Jourgensen... the whitest music you will ever hear, rock bleached of all but its narcissism. Post-rock dullards Tortoise are also locals. R. Kelly sings beautifully but an emotional and sonic flatness levels his material. Even the hip-hop scene, dominated by Common and Kanye West, rarely inspires. Chi-town, they call it, with gruff affection. But Chi-town, once home to America's toughest sounds, has faded as a musical powerhouse. Just thinking about it depresses me.

Appropriate, then, that Chi-town's my last stop: I've covered too many miles with too little money. Time to wind up this American journey, yet there's entire US regions I'm yet to explore: Louisiana and the Appalachians maintain regional music traditions; Detroit may be a shell of its former self yet Eminem, The Gories, White Stripes and Detroit Cobras all rose from its ruined streets; the outer boroughs of New York still produce the occasional rapper of note; Washington, DC maintains a go-go scene; maybe St Louis and Louisville host pockets of creativity? And Portland, Oregon, is now the epicentre of American alt.rock. But I'm tired of rock – alt. or not – those three thrashed chords and shouted vocals have become a carbon of a carbon of a carbon, more pose than endeavour. 'I Want My MTV', went an advertising slogan for the cancerous cable channel, and today so much of what is offered up as American popular music appears to be shaped by a desperate desire to conform, MTV slaves, fast-food-nation muzak.

What thoughts to pass a night on, exhausted and sweaty, beat from constant motion and an inability to relax a little, to stop asking questions and just feel my way into a place, a community. But where, if I had time and funds, would I choose to stop? San Francisco is gorgeous but little more than a boutique city. LA's an interesting confusion yet it's hard to imagine living there. Nashville's grim. Memphis and Clarksdale cling to dreams of a bygone age. New Orleans is ruined. Miami could be interesting – lots of Haitians and Cubans – but the city's dominated by salsa, crunk and jam bands; all exhaust my ears. Seattle? Vancouver's preferable. Austin, admittedly, is lively. San Antonio and Tucson are both fragrant with the scent of Mexico. Maybe set up a shack next to Kell's chicken coop and from there explore the South-west. Not a bad idea. Get a horse, learn how to talk from Cormac McCarthy novels, pretend to be a cowboy... such thoughts that circle a tired traveller's mind.

Unable to sleep, I gaze into darkness, electric light illuminating the occasional town or farmhouse. Think of Jack and Neal, tearing across the Midwest in a gigantic Cadillac, always on the verge of totally losing control, then rushing around Chicago searching for *kickskickskicks*. Chicago back then – late-1940s – one hot place for music, raucous jazz and blues blasting out of speakeasies, wide open. Dig *On the Road* out of backpack and find Kerouac reporting of bebop clubs that go all night until everyone staggers out *'into the great roar of Chicago to sleep'*. Hard to imagine anywhere in the USA today where jazz clubs are anything but solemn places, mania free, not what the Beats were looking for. That was a different America, the post-WW2 winner-take-all nation, brimming with confidence and boiling with industry, its music adolescent, hormonal, growing rapidly, the dream seemingly wide open. Not that Chicago was ever easy: RL Burnside's father and two brothers were murdered here while John Lee 'Sonny Boy' Williamson succumbed to an assailant with an ice pick one warm Saturday night. More recently crack cocaine cut a swathe through black Chicago, street gangs becoming increasingly wealthy and psychotic: throughout the 1990s the city often posted the highest US homicide rates.

Dull dawn light reveals a Midwest flat and opaque, wheat fields burnished gold against the grey sky. Churches, trucks, houses, telegraph poles, factories, clusters of woods, wreckers' yards, red-brick buildings, shops offering 'Antiques & Curios', farm supply outlets and gas stations stake out what once were prairies where buffalo roamed. Dawn breaks and bright orange school buses chug across the land. In the distance loom spectral outlines of what I guess to be grain silos; my imagination assumes they're missile depots, each farm home to a neutron bomb. Sun sweeps over the prairies, illuminating green and blond and blond and green. Across lakes, through thickets, on we roll. Passengers are

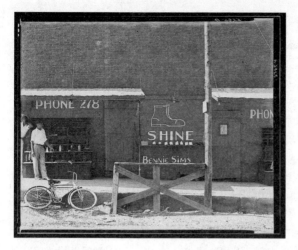

Shine: South Side
Chicago

waking now, starting to move around. There's a nervously polite
Amish couple, an obese black woman who loudly discusses her
family's medical history, a Willie Nelson lookalike wearing a
Willie Nelson T-shirt. At every stop an assortment of neatly
dressed workers board, ready for offices and boardrooms. *Good
morning, America, how are you?* A little stiff, cold and grumpy by
the look of this carriage.

Union Station, Chicago, *wey-hey!* Brisk gusts of wind whip up
a welcome, all Southern humidity banished. I wander on to West
Adams Street, overwhelmed by traffic, pedestrians and the Sears
Tower, Chi-town being an epic city such as I've not seen since LA.
Yet where LA sprawls Chicago bristles, city of skyscrapers and
above-ground El trains that rattle and grind past. People stride
– jaw clenched/shoulder forward – determined to get somewhere,
anywhere, out of the wind. What a fine city this was. Or is.
For little ever changes in Chicago. Always Democrat. Always
unionised. Always run by a mayor named Daley. Every little detail
evokes a cultural pride, a sense that this city, more than any other
in the USA, knows its worth and isn't about to let the lunatics in
DC trash its state of grace.

My previous Chicago experience in 1990 proved this city offers
no cheap motels. Back then I was travelling with Karl, another
Kiwi music nut, and after finding nothing affordable in central or

outer Chicago we went to the South Side. The hotels weren't too different from the surrounding liquor stores – reception tucked behind steel and mesh, urban decay shadowing all – yet none would receive us: room rates were by the hour and the looks we got suggested even if we'd wanted to test the bedsprings with local whores a room might be refused. Back on the street a friendly black guy approached us and enquired, 'You boys want some drugs?' No thanks, we need a cheap hotel. 'Man, that's a first! Only time we ever normally see white people here is when they wanna buy crack!' It's understood: I'll stay at a youth hostel. Step into the wind. Imagine if all you had ever known was Louisiana heat…

I arrive at the hostel to find a Latina beauty on reception. In Nashville-Memphis-Mississippi I rarely saw an attractive woman, most being swollen from a diet where everything's fried and supersized. But this one, all curves and angles, blonde rinse not detracting from a Mayan mouth and sloe eyes… *Albaesque*… is that a new noun? Take the reception process slow and easy, just enjoying her presence. Luis Rodriguez mentioned Chi-town had a strong Latino presence and here is my initial evidence. I enquire as to where she's from – the accent isn't Americanised enough to be native – and she says, 'Guatemala. I came here with my folks when I was four but we still speak Spanish at home.' With sheet and pillowcase I search out my bed. *A youth hostel.* A man my age having to stay in one. *Pathetic.* Then again, why pay downtown hotel rates when you have no Jessica to share the room with? Shower, shave, sleep: engaging with the city can wait until later.

'Chicago's like everywhere else in the US in the sense it's become a lot more homogenised as a city. TV really was a killer of neighbourhood music. And they built an expressway through the South Side and West Side and that knocked a lot of the heart out of the old neighbourhoods. Another change involves the black professional classes moving into the suburbs from the South and West Side where, traditionally, blacks had to live. This has left a hole where the professional organisations used to be. As for blues… it's an old music now. You won't find many clubs today.

When I arrived in town there were forty clubs. Now there's four or five.'

Bruce Iglauer, founder of Alligator Records – Chicago's pre-eminent blues label since the demise of Chess Records in 1975 – is musing on his city. Alligator's served as home to Hound Dog Taylor, Albert Collins, Charlie Musselwhite, Son Seals and Koko Taylor, capturing post-civil-rights blues like no one else, music rural in origin but blunted, pessimistic, from decades in the urban ghetto. The rise of Fat Possum, with its punk-rock ethos, made Alligator look old fashioned – a paradox of sorts when considering the likes of Hound Dog Taylor and Son Seals made music tougher, more dissonant, than Iggy and Black Flag. But understandable: where Fat Possum sells to youths who rate NOFX, Alligator's audience is their fathers, Stones fans. What Alligator shares with Fat Possum is a high mortality rate and few new artists worth investing in.

'Way I see it there's been three waves of blues recording in Chicago,' continues Iglauer. 'Pre-World-War-II 78s were issued for a black audience by Bluebird Records. This was the era of Tampa Red, Big Bill Broonzy, Sonny Boy Williamson. After World War II Bluebird shifted to the coast and the indie labels took over and sold blues 45s to the black audience. Chess lead there. The third wave was led by Bob Koester of Delmark Records and then myself with Alligator. We were about albums, not trying to get airplay on black radio stations, selling primarily to white audiences. This involves a very different mentality to Chess and their competitors. Those guys had to play a very dirty game, handing out cash to DJs and that kind of thing. Back then a song had, at most, a couple of months' life and then it was dead.

'With Alligator the whole idea was that if you bought one album and liked it you could buy another comfortably. I worked so you trusted the label, saw Alligator as a brand. From day one I tried to get the artists airplay on rock and jazz radio stations. I started the label with an inheritance of $2500 in 1971, using my one-room apartment as the office. I've built it up since then but I still work a seventy-hour week. I've got good people working for me but I can't pay great so I offer healthcare and profit sharing. But it's tougher right now than it ever has been – we lost a thousand record shops in the US last year. Admittedly, not all were friends of Alligator, but for an independent label it's hard to get your product into Wal-Mart and the chain stores. OK, we sell over the Internet but nothing near what we lose from people downloading and burning CDs. I also have to recognise the ageing of the blues audience and the artists. Where blues was once a folk culture, black learning from black, a lot of the younger musicians are learning from records. That makes a difference. There's lots of good young players out there but I don't know if anyone is going to make a major statement. Also, the blues audience tends to back away from anything new.'

Iglauer's dedicated his life to Chicago blues (label owner, producer, manager, promoter) yet never come near the kind of money common in the rock and rap industry. The Alligator offices are sparse, furniture and fittings resembling those of a thrift shop. Only a few posters and a framed *Chicago Sun Times* feature celebrating the label's thirtieth anniversary decorate walls.

'I only came to Chicago originally for a year,' he says with a resigned chuckle, 'didn't realise I was going to set about capturing the last great flowering of Chicago blues. It's been a great ride but I've grave concerns about the future. My biggest fear about blues is that it could become the new Dixieland... audiences not allowing artists to develop... music petrifying... awful.'

Architecturally, Chi-town's the opposite aesthetic of Nashville, real thought behind much of what got built. The human architecture is also worth noting with lots of fine-looking women striding around. Chicago is home to huge Serbian, Polish, Romanian and Lithuanian communities; this surely explaining things. There's an odd flavour to the city, not unpleasant, just a vibe I can't quite work out. It's different to the South and the South-west. Comparable to San Francisco but rougher, tougher, less navel-gazing. While New York is faster, more shrill, edged with narcissistic hysteria. Chicago, then, might just be the most balanced American city going. Appropriate for the capital of the Midwest. I think of Kerouac musing, '*Old brown Chicago with the semi-Eastern semi-Western types going to work and spitting*' and guess Jack nailed it again. Not that I notice much spitting.

One thing Chi-town shares with both Los Angeles and New York is a history of extreme segregation. Alligator Records is based in north Chicago; Iglauer explained that the neighbourhood – Edgewater – was primarily Italian. Other parts of the city are German and Irish – these two groups dominating Chicago politics – while the Chinese, Romanians, Poles, Serbs, Mexicans and African-Americans have all marked out their communities, street by street, 'hood by 'hood. Not that the ethnic divide is immovable; downtown neighbourhoods, once emptied by the 1950s flight to the suburbs, are today where the young and restless wish to live. Even the city's northern suburbs, suburbs that came out en masse in 1966 to jeer, spit and throw bricks at Martin Luther King and his civil rights marchers as they protested against a policy of local government segregation ensuring black citizens had access only to the worst housing and facilities, have progressed. Now those suburbs are called 'cosmopolitan'. Then there's the South Side.

Shit-coloured buildings, interminable liquor stores, crazy winos… little hints that the South Side was once home to a twentieth-century renaissance but, having clocked where Chess Records stood, Muddy Waters lived, the Chicago Defender monument, sites of clubs that once hosted Louis Armstrong and Dinah Washington, I'm now certain this area – named Bronzeville but widely known as 'the Black Belt'- is akin to Florence in the traces of creative genius that once sparked here. And I'm on my way to meet a Chicago renaissance veteran, a man familiar with the Black Belt for the last sixty years, one in whom much American musical history flows. So many things I want to ask him. Imagine myself like Caine in *Kung Fu*, bowing before the Master. Excited? I'm damn near levitating.

As we roll down Martin Luther King Drive I notice a U-shaped tower block, monolithic, grey and crumbling. 'That's the last of the Robert Taylor Homes buildings,' says the driver. 'They've been knocking them down one by one. There used to be a couple dozen of 'em housing over thirty thousand people. America's largest housing projects. They were built in the late 1950s and have been falling apart ever since. Obviously, bad things happen in that kind of environment but what you've got to remember is most of the people who live there are ordinary people trying to get by on not much money.' Agreed but, in the early nineties, weren't there a huge number of murders in the Chicago projects? 'Crack was the worst thing that ever happened to this community,' says the driver. 'But violent crime's been declining in Chicago for a long time. This area's still a rough neighbourhood but nothing compared to what it once was.'

The driver is Michael Frank, musician and manager of David 'Honeyboy' Edwards, the Mississippi bluesman who has lived in Chicago since he gave up rambling in the 1950s. Honey isn't, by all accounts, too keen on interviews, but Frank understands that with an annual European tour booked the occasional visiting hack should be accommodated. Today manager and artist have agreed to meet at a South Side pawnshop where Honeyboy gets his equipment. Having parked, we enter a veritable fortress filled with tatty furnishings, jewellery, guns, electrical equipment and battered musical gear. Outside, the sun is shining but inside, beneath fluorescent light, the air's stale. An old black man is opening and shutting guitar cases. He's small, slightly hunched, his skin inky black, face severe and totemic. Frank approaches and Honeyboy – for it is him, the last country bluesman standing – glances over then returns to this routine task with a veteran's eye: 'Nuh... nuh... nuh' – he pushes past many proffered. He's ancient yet his presence is formidable, a deity of sorts, skin taut over Indian cheekbones. I start to approach and he looks at me sideways, battered features creasing when he's told I want to ask questions. He then emits something between a growl and a chuckle. 'Go on,' says Frank, 'ask.' *Where to start when facing a blues oracle?* Ummm... something simple: is he surprised to still be playing the blues aged ninety?

'I've had my fun!':
Honeyboy Edwards,
Chicago, IL

'I shoulda been dead fifty, sixty year ago,' he says, voice a raspy Southern drawl. 'God jus' wuzn't ready fo' me. Because I usedta raise hell an' drink. I've had mah fun!'

Born to sharecroppers in Shaw, Mississippi, Honeyboy – a childhood nickname – describes his early years with a relish worthy of Mark Twain. He grew up on a plantation where panthers and bears roamed, picking cotton, catching catfish, hunting raccoons and possums. His parents instilled in him both literacy and racial pride while his maternal grandmother recalled slavery days. Sharecropping was, in many ways, legitimised slavery with plantation owners ensuring their black farmers remained trapped by debt and fear. Honeyboy, seeing the plantation consume his parents, looked to escape. A guitar was his ticket to freedom.

'My father, he play violin and guitar. A pretty good musician. He play "Staggerlee", songs like that, in a ragtime style. I first heard blues in 1929 when Tommy Johnson [author "Canned Heat Blues"] came, him and iz brother Clarence, in an old T-Model Ford to pick cotton wit' us. We be playin' the blues on cotton sacks an' drinkin' white whiskey. Play the blues all night an' go pick cotton the next mornin'.'

In 1931 the restless sixteen-year-old began hoboing around the South, begging and doing casual labour, jumping on trains whenever he felt restless. 'Sometimes I'd ride the rods, too, underneath the train, cuz the cops would never look down there for ya. The rods are kinda rough, tho'. The train be runnin' so fast it throw rocks up an' they hit yo'.'

Arrested for 'trespassing' on a freight train, Honeyboy got put to work on a prison farm. Here he witnessed fellow prisoners being flogged to death while 'they worked the rest of us to death. The boss always said, "When a nigger dies, hire a nigger. If a mule dies, buy a nigger." Tha's right!' Malarial, he was released after four months and returned to sharecropping. Plantation life held little appeal and an encounter with Big Joe Williams a year later introduced Honeyboy to the itinerant bluesman's life, hitching and hoboing, playing on streets and at parties. Williams took Honeyboy to New Orleans – 'it wuz something to see them bright lights' – then the youth set out on his own.

Subsequent adventures as bluesman and gambler are documented in his autobiography *The World Don't Owe Me Nothing*, a remarkable oral history that reads like a mix of *Huckleberry Finn* and *On the Road*, if considerably wilder and funnier ('*I had every kind of women but a blue one!*'). As Honeyboy recorded rarely – preferring to hobo and play wherever he landed (recordings for Chess and Sun weren't issued until decades later) – *The World Don't Owe Me Nothing* stands as his major artistic statement, an alternative history of the United States. Beyond describing Honeyboy's life, the text illuminates a master storyteller, Uncle Remus as two-fisted bluesman who flees racist plantation owners, outwits brutal cops and juke-joint thugs, meets Mississippi's master griots and never quits. On building levees alongside pianist Sunnyland Slim he saves his greatest descriptive skills for the weekend:

> *On Friday and Saturday nights they set aside a big tent, like a revival tent, and had a wooden floor inside and a platform*

for the piano. They'd barbecue hogs and all that stuff, and
people come from all around to drink white whiskey and
have a good time. It was beautiful. They'd make a whole
barrel of lemonade and drop a big block of ice down in there.
Get a ice stick and bust it all up. Have that hog all mopped
with that good sauce, cooking slow all day. Take a nice slice
off and make sandwiches, barbecue sandwiches. Eat, drink,
and gamble all night. Oh, we had a good time.

Wang dang doodle! Honey's a Mississippi Zelig, associating
or playing with almost all the major figures in twentieth-century
American blues: he witnessed Charley Patton and Tommy
Johnson, the musicians regarded as Delta blues founders, play.
Big Joe Williams tutored him in hoboing mythic blues trains the
Pea Vine, the Southern and the Yellow Dog. He busked with the
Memphis Jug Band, befriended Howlin' Wolf when both were
teenage farmhands, Alan Lomax recorded him for the Library of
Congress in 1942 and teenage harmonica prodigy Little Walter
trekked with Honeyboy to Chicago. 'I was lucky to come up in the
middle of all those musicians,' he says. Edwards lived an itinerant
life for decades, finally settling with wife and child in the South
Side in 1951. He was signed to Chess Records, but Muddy Waters,
the label's star performer, sabotaged his contract ('felt threatened,
I guess'). Memphis Minnie, Elmore James, Rice Miller – Honeyboy
encountered them all. Most notable was a mid-1930s friendship
he formed with a youth four years his senior, both of them crazy
about playing blues and having a good time.

'He wuz a nice person,' says Honeyboy quietly of his now
mythic friend Robert Johnson. 'I knowed him pretty good. He
usedta go wit' my cousin in Tunica, Mississippi, Willie Mae.
Robert wuz about the quietest musician I ever did come across.
He liked to drink whiskey an' play the blues lonesome an' sad.
He wuz never a hellraiser, never cussed an' fought. But he played
blues good. Played 'em *hard* an' *good*. He'd take his time to put a
lot of things together, put the notes together like drops o' water.
An' the people liked what he wuz doing.'

Honeyboy witnessed Johnson's agonising death and speaks of his friend with quiet reverence.

'Now, when he died, 16 August 1938, that wuz on a Wednesday, I come over there and I wuz twenty-two years old. Twenty-two? Twenty-three? Yeah. Robert wuz twenty-eight then. He got poisoned out there, a little place called Three Forks. He'd been playin' out there fo' pretty close to a year. They had a roadhouse out there called Juke House – white whiskey, gamblin' – Robert start goin' with the man's wife an' she a good lookin' woman. An' the man, he *got* him.'

Honeyboy lived in constant motion, rarely staying anywhere longer than a week, playing music, hustling with loaded dice and living off accommodating women. The American outlaw life kept him free but rarely out of trouble: he's been jailed for vagrancy (several times) and assault (once), stabbed, shot at, beaten with rocks and a hammer, somehow, some way, defying death, too much joy in Honeyboy to allow him to stumble. He acquired a wife and child, and the family settled in Chicago in 1951. Edwards cut back on making music in the 1960s when the city's black community embraced soul music. European enthusiasm for blues got him touring internationally in the 1970s. Surely travelling city to city, gig to gig, must make a man born in 1915 feel, well, shattered?

'When I was comin' up runnin' 'round I'd travel wherever I had t' go t' chase some money. Just me an' mah guitar. Down t' New Orleans. 'Cross t' Texas. Up t' Missouri. Same today. I go to Tok-y-o. Bra-zil. What that place next to Bra-zil? Chilll-ehh? Chil-eh! Now Eu-rope.'

I'm impressed, I say, by how physically and mentally tough he remains after a life lived the hard way.

'Tourin' can be hard. It don' get no easier, that's fo' sure. My knees got arthritis but I still can walk without a cane. Gettin' upstairs is difficult. I just have t' walk slow.'

Walking slow must seem an anomaly for a man who likes to describe his early decades as 'always runnin''. Having outlived his contemporaries, wife, girlfriends, brothers, sisters and a son,

Honeyboy believes he's blessed. His face carries scars marking many scrapes but creases with gold-toothed merriment as he recounts a life lived on the margins of American society. Carjacked in 1996, he boasts of stabbing the thief ('I cut him good!') and carrying a pistol ('crack makes them boys go crazy'). Which is surely why he remains such a convincing blues singer. Being the last of the original Mississippi blues men standing, Honeyboy's now in more demand than ever and Frank regularly fends off interviews. '*Vanity Fair* rang today. Wanting to ask Honey about Robert Johnson,' he mentioned earlier.

Honeyboy insists his appetite's strong. Ask the secret of such longevity and he replies, 'I'm wonderin'! Got to take it easy, that's it.' Unlike many of his contemporaries he never allowed drugs or alcohol to take over. 'I used to be a pretty heavy drinker when I was young but I found out how bad it was and I let it alone.' And of a USA so radically altered during the course of his lifetime he notes, 'I seen a lot of changes. You got to make changes. I even make changes in my blues.'

And Chicago, you've sure seen this city change a lot?

'I livin' here when the old man put the towers up an' I'm still here when the kid pulls 'em down,' he says, referring to Mayors Daley Sr and Jr. 'When I first arrive Chicago wuz just a big country town. Gravel roads come to Chicago then, wuzn't no toll roads or nothin' like that. Just two lanes from St Louis, Route 66, blacktop roads. People makin' whiskey, just like they do in the country, white whiskey. It wuz a big country town!' He laughs. 'Chicago wuz wide open then. Us musicians could work every day.'

Honeyboy places his guitar in the chosen case and snaps it shut. Interview, I understand, is over. On the sidewalk Honeyboy and Frank discuss upcoming concerts. The South Side is bathed in sun and locals wander past, paying no attention to an ancient black man who looks to be carved from granite and a tall white man with long, grey curls. Business concluded, Honeyboy shakes my hand, flashes that great gold-toothed smile, leans forward, the oracle's final advice: 'Preachers and musicians are just alike. They ain't *no* good!'

'Played 'em hard an' good': hot band, 1938

chapter 25

Crazy Mixed-up World

From Chicago Millennium Station I take a Metra train towards University Park. The train crosses the South Side, chugs through gloomy industrial landscapes, clips Mexican barrios (*El Ranchita Lounge*) and then snakes across suburb after suburb. A grey sky covers Chi-town and wind tosses leaves across the horizon, sour weather breeding ominous thoughts. Detroit and Memphis are celebrated as soul music cities owing to Motown and Stax once being operational within their city limits, while Chicago, for almost two decades the centre of mercurial, cerebral soul music, is largely omitted from American music history as a rhythm and blues city. Ignored even by those who aim to promote Chicago music: the city annually hosts free three-day festivals of gospel, blues and jazz but soul music gets no look-in. A cynic might argue that Detroit and Memphis, ruined cities, only have their legacies as manufacturers of foot-stompin', hip-shakin' music to boast of. And Chicago's found the blues tourists make for big business. What we're really dealing with, then, is a failure of marketing.

Motown's creative genius means the Motor City's imprinted in generations of music fans' consciousness. Stax's finger-popping logo keeps the Memphis brand burning brightly. Chicago soul lacks a distinct label focus, instead offering an array of individual talents: Curtis Mayfield, Jerry Butler, Betty Everett, Gene Chandler, Jackie Wilson, Etta James, Marlena Shaw, Tyrone Davis and The Dells found their way quite separately. And where Motown and Stax dominated Detroit and Memphis, Chicago became home to several competing labels: Mayfield's Impressions were on ABC-Paramount, Butler and Everett on Vee-Jay, Davis on Dakar, Wilson on Brunswick, James and Shaw on Chess and

The Dells alternating between Vee-Jay and Chess. The city's two most prominent labels, Vee-Jay and Chess, never attract the attention or affection surrounding Motown and Stax: Vee-Jay, a pioneering black-owned label, collapsed in 1965, its catalogue remains neglected. Chess imploded in 1975 and is celebrated today as a pioneering blues/rock 'n' roll label, yet from the late 1950s onwards soul and jazz releases were Chess's strongest sellers. Such neglect hurts: much great American music is known via brilliant packaging – mythic location/label/studio/graphics all creating identity. Thus Curtis Mayfield (brilliantly intuitive guitarist/singer-songwriter) receives far less attention than Otis Redding or Marvin Gaye (superb singers but lesser talents). And then there're The Dells.

I descend from the train at Olympia Fields, a wealthy suburb approximately twenty-five miles south-west of Chicago's Loop, and am collected by the smiling figure of Rose McGill. A short drive away is the home she shares with her husband Mickey McGill, The Dells' baritone. The McGills' residence is a spacious two-storey house. Like The Dells' music the property is immaculate. Hard work and fine singing bought this property and love and pride inform it. Entering, I'm greeted by Mickey. He introduces me to Chuck Barksdale (bass vocal) and tells me lead vocalist Marvin Junior is outside enjoying a pre-interview cigarette. I mention I've been exploring Chicago, including the South Side.

'Chuck and I grew up in Chicago, on the South Side, both single-parent families,' says Mickey. 'Our mothers got us out of there to Harvey [a factory town on the outskirts of Chicago] because they knew it wasn't no place for children to grow up in. Back then the South Side could be rough but nothing like it is today. Today it's dangerous. Very dangerous. There's a drug culture and kids with no hope, no belief in anything, so they don't care who they hurt.'

'If you were here for longer I'd take you to where I used to live on the South Side,' offers Chuck. 'Man, I still know most of the people living around there. But it's not good now. Not good at all.'

Mickey and Chuck explain that Harvey, now scalped of industry, has become a violent, rust-belt town. The Dells all live within Chicago city limits, except for Marvin Junior. 'Marvin lives in the same street as Harvey's chief of police so he's OK,' says Chuck, 'but, man, a lot of what's going down there is awful. Our lovely little town overrun by gangbangers with machine guns.' Marvin enters moving at a slow, limping pace. 'Marvin's had both hips replaced,' says Mickey, 'which makes walking difficult for him. But his singing's as great as ever.' Marvin's built out of tough, solid matter and speaks in a thick, rasping voice. No surprise he was once a steel worker. There's an easy interaction between the three as they chat about grandchildren while coffee is served. Who would believe it – I'm sitting with the Mighty Dells?

The veteran group, formed in 1952, boast only one line-up change. More importantly, they possess the richest, most distinctive vocal blend in American music history. The drama of The Dells' sound involves a gospel force field matched with the emotional engagements of a keen and loving heart. In song their voices weave and climb – a vocal basketball team of sorts, lots of deft passing and rim shots – gathering around Marvin Junior, who charges things home. Detroit's The Temptations (who studied

'She took us to school': Dinah Washington and The Dells

The Dells closely) scored a phenomenal string of hits but for dramatic, complex, emotionally drenched harmonies The Dells remain twentieth-century masters.

The Dells took form among a group of teenage friends attending Thornton Township High School.

'No one ever came to Harvey so we used to go to Chicago for the shows,' says Marvin of the group's origins, 'and we'd go five or six of us 'cos if we went alone we'd get jumped by these Chicago guys. We were hanging out together before we were The Dells.'

'We hung out together,' adds Mickey, 'and it just so happens that one was a tenor, one was a bass, one was a baritone, Marvin was a lead singer… You can call it magic, call it fate, but we had no control over it. We couldn't've of scripted it any better.'

'Everyone in Harvey thought they were a singer,' says Marvin. 'Go to the basketball court and twenty, thirty guys be there singing.'

Did they, I enquire, start out singing doo-wop?

'We were five guys who didn't even understand some of the notes we were singing but the sound was so great,' says Chuck. 'Doo-wop was what they named a certain style of group on the East Coast but we didn't do that style. We did a closed-mouth harmony style.'

'On the East Coast you had the doo-wop groups and on the West Coast the novelty-type groups, The Coasters and bands like that,' clarifies Marvin. 'We came out of a Midwestern singing style. A more pure, intense style.'

Scoring their first R & B hit with 'Oh, What a Night' in 1956 on Vee-Jay, The Dells began working the chitlin' circuit. Debuting at Harlem's Apollo Theatre in 1956, they found themselves at the bottom rung of the showbiz ladder.

'We were at the Grampian Hotel and it was fourteen dollars a week each and we had trouble paying that,' adds Mickey. 'The Apollo wised us up on how to survive.'

'We'd drive from New York to Atlanta, Georgia to play for $175,' says Chuck. 'We worked one-nighters across the US for $150 to $200 a night, driving everywhere.'

On the road from Cleveland to the Apollo in 1958 one of the axles on the band's station wagon snapped. The resulting accident crushed Marvin's throat against the steering wheel, threw Chuck through the windscreen and almost cost Mickey his leg.

'The car flipped three times,' recalls Marvin. 'I remember looking out and seeing Chuck stand up in the road and dust himself off.' Disbanding while McGill healed, The Dells reformed in 1960 with their lead tenor, Johnny Funches, replaced by Johnny Carter. Dinah Washington, the singer who blended blues and jazz like no other, hired The Dells as her harmony singers. 'She took us into places where we would have never gone. Taught us choreography. Taught us performance skills. Took us to school,' says Chuck. 'But she was tough. She'd cuss us out. Tell us "you're fired, get your asses out". The next day she'd say "why weren't y'all at rehearsal?" "Well, Dinah, you just fired us." "Well, you're hired again."' After two years with Washington, The Dells went out alone. One memorable tour found them opening for Ray Charles. 'Singing with Ray's seventeen-piece orchestra, that was another experience,' continues Chuck. 'Then we played Carnegie Hall and got like five standing ovations. So Ray's manager came round to our dressing room and said, "Listen, there's only room for one star in this show and that's Ray Charles. Where you want us to drop you off at?"'

Back in Chicago The Dells provided vocals for sessions: that's them whooping it up behind Chuck Berry ('an arrogant guy') on 'Back in the USA' and driving Andre Williams home on 'Cadillac Jack'; the foot-stomps on Betty Everett's smouldering 'You're No Good' are theirs while the gorgeous harmonies carrying Barbara Lewis's 'Hello Stranger' are also these Chicago soul brothers. Remarkable, I say. Yeah, they offer, those were the days. Chicago was a music town then.

Recording again for the now faltering Vee-Jay ('they tried to go pop. Go white. Assholes,' says Mickey), they returned to the charts with 1965's 'Stay in My Corner'. Chess signed the band, pairing them with producer Bill Miller and Charles Stepney, a brilliant arranger steeped in jazz, and The Dells rose to the challenge. Their greatest hit was a 1968 reworking of 'Stay in My Corner' that topped the US R & B charts (and went Top 10 pop).

'After we had a hit with "Stay" on Vee-Jay it became one of the most popular songs in our live set,' says Mickey, 'and Marvin had the idea to re-record it when we were back on Chess. Leonard Chess didn't believe anyone would play it on radio [at six minutes ten seconds] and wanted to cut it in half – you know, A-side and B-side – and they originally issued it that way. But the DJs went "No, no, no, we want to hear the long note!" so they issued it at full length. And it became a phenomenon.'

'We'd been playing the bases in Germany,' adds Chuck, 'and when we came to get off the plane in the US it was like we were The Beatles, reporters everywhere wanting to know about "Stay In My Corner", and we didn't know what they were going on about. Chess hadn't told us and we were not sure what all the fuss was about. We played the Regal in Chicago and then we went to Washington, DC and then to the Apollo Theatre on a Monday or Tuesday and the place was packed and going crazy! That's when we knew we'd really hit the big time. Everyone related to that record. Girls were sending it to their boyfriends serving in Vietnam. That was their way of saying they were staying true.'

'We've always sung love songs and that's why our audience has always remained loyal,' says Marvin. 'We've done our part in populating the world – a lot of people were conceived to Dells records!'

The Dells increased Chess's fortunes – 'from '67 to '75 we carried that label' – yet today much written on Chess focuses on blues and ignores The Dells.

'You gotta understand this,' says Mickey, 'when we came up that kind of blues, we called it gutbucket – Muddy Waters, Little Walter, Howlin' Wolf… we looked at them as some kind of country thing. We looked at them like the hip-hoppers look at us today! We were into vocal groups, the smooth singers, not that old Southern music.'

'But they were all friends of ours,' adds Marvin. 'We were all using the same studios and playing on the same shows because a black variety show would feature all the talent.'

'Let me say,' adds Mickey, 'Muddy Waters was a sharp man. He sang gutbucket but he was a classy man. Always had a fine process, dressed in sharp suits, drove a Cadillac and made a lot of money.'

After Leonard Chess's death (1968) the label faltered, both mismanaged and battered by the increasingly corporate nature of the American music industry. The Dells moved to Mercury in the mid-seventies and kept scoring hits.

'If the disco era hadn't come along we would all probably be dead,' says Chuck. 'We were partying so much.'

'If you think about it,' adds Marvin, 'what other entertainer has had hits in the fifties, the sixties, the seventies, the eighties and nineties? Us and The Isley Brothers, we're the only two acts.'

Today The Dells remain in demand. Something that fascinates me is their loyal Mexican-American following – both Luis Rodriguez and Lydia's daughter Yolanda spoke appreciatively of them.

'They love The Dells!' roars Marvin when I mention this. 'We got class. That's something all the old groups had. Not like today where they can't play an instrument, have to use a sampler. A lot of groups have the hottest record of this year and are forgotten next year. Not us. We just kept makin' it.'

The Dells are happy men, satisfied with their achievements if frustrated that The Beatles and Stones get considerably more attention and money. 'If The Dells were white we'd be billionaires,' says Chuck. Marvin and Mickey voice agreement. Still, The Dells have endured both musically and physically, unlike many of soul music's pioneers: Curtis Mayfield's spine crushed by a lighting rig, James Brown insane on angel dust, Jackie Wilson dying a comatose pauper.

'Curtis was a great man and Jackie was one of our best friends,' says Mickey, offering a photo of The Dells with Wilson. 'Look at the scars Jackie had. He's been shot and stabbed, through hell and back. He was quite the lover man.' The band chuckle and Marvin recalls meeting his old friend James Brown. 'We were sharing a show with him one time when he was smokin' that dust and he calls me to his hotel room and starts goin' on 'bout "they watchin' me". "Who, James?" "All of them. They spyin' on me. They out to get me." Man, he was fried!'

I mention the evident decline of American music and society and they all sigh. 'We were in Buffalo when Dr King was murdered,' says Mickey. 'Everyone believed in the dream he talked about and we always sang about love – we came up in a time when people loved one another. But now… the politicians… the gangs… what's it all about?'

'We all need to sit back, take a deep breath and learn to love one another,' adds Chuck. 'You cut me and I cut you and it's the same red blood that rolls out. It's time for the healing to begin.'

My flight back to San Francisco's booked for tomorrow; the quest's almost over. Chi-town, beyond its bad weather and overpriced hotels, is the bit of America I feel most at ease in. Segregated as the city remains, it's still possible to sense all kinds of everyone rubbing up against one another and – for the most part – getting on. And it's a city that sizzles with creativity, lots of live music venues and museums, potent architecture and civic pride. Chicago's also allowed for closure of sorts: here I found a marker for where Route 66 began, forgave Frank Gehry's LA atrocity on accountant of his engaging Grant Park pavilion, visited the Biograph Theatre, where the FBI executed John Dillinger, and the house Ida B. Wells settled into after fleeing Memphis mobs. Even got to kneel before Jack Johnson's grave in Graceland Cemetery: Elvis is buried at his Graceland so suggesting some odd shared state of grace for these revolutionary American icons. I tried, unsuccessfully, to find 1950s proto-rap pioneer Andre Williams – Bruce Iglauer, bless him, rang 'round South Side bars to no avail – but Andre's laying very low. Another time, another book.

Most importantly, I heard a lot of music. Say what you like about Chicago, and the weather's varied between luscious and dreadful, but you can still hear good blues and jazz here. Initially, being downtown, I visited the clubs aimed at people like me: white out-of-towners staying in well-lit neighbourhoods free of gangs. In Buddy Guy's Legends and Kingston Mines, Blues Chicago and B.L.U.E.S., I caught a variety of local artists, all having put in decades playing the sound that once came from the South and here took on electric muscle. Lindsey Alexander and Larry McRae both played tough electric blues-rock, Willie Kent & The Gents shuffled through standards, Bonnie Lee and Patricia Scott provided bawdy boasts of female sexual prowess. But I rarely felt the music catch fire; instead, for the most part, I saw black musicians playing the same set they perform night after night to white audiences, all of us out for the Chicago Blues Experience. No disrespect intended but the overall feel kept recalling Bruce Iglauer's fear that blues was becoming the new Dixieland, nostalgia music, Americana safe and tucked in. So I called Bruce, hustling him to take me to the South and West Side clubs.

Downtown after dark: corporate America has succeeded in creating a space devoid of human activity, Dunkin' Donuts blinking blankly on every street corner. During daylight hours the Loop offers the contrast of American success in Brooks Brothers suits alongside homeless black men hovering on every street corner, begging or holding 'Will Work for Food' signs, a Third World life in a First World city. At nine p.m. there's only the wind and me. Iglauer arrives in a rusted Honda Civic, berates me for standing in the wrong place, and then we're under way. Our first stop, he says, is Rosa's, a West Side club, and as we roll across the city Bruce reminisces on the countless nights he's spent in black Chicago blues bars.

'The thing that's so wonderful is how the people on the bandstand and those in the audience were the same people. Neighbourhood, y'know? Locals would get up, sit in for a song, sometimes they were as good as the paid musicians. When Magic Slim asked, "Are there any single women out there?" what he meant was "Are there any women in the club I haven't slept with yet?" Slim fucked a lot of women! And everyone would be having a great time, celebrating that they didn't have to walk behind a farting mule till it got dark, day after day.'

Did his adventures in black clubs ever attract any ill will?

'I've never felt threatened in the clubs. Ran into a tiny bit of anti-white racism but for every person who was unpleasant forty or fifty were really nice. Things could've got nasty once. I was standing outside of Pepper's and Left Hand Frank came up to me and shouted "you recorded me", "yes", "you paid me", "yes", "you got me gigs", "yes", "but you didn't do as much for me as you did those other niggers!" and came at me with a knife.'

C'mon, what happened?

'Oh, one of Hound Dog Taylor's musicians grabbed his arm.' Iglauer laughs, puffs on a cigar and starts pointing out where neighbourhood borders begin and end. 'See there's lots of vacant lots around? That's from property burnt out in the '67 riots.' This signals we're entering the West Side. As we drive on the ghetto manifests: *One Stop Liquor & Food*, *Edna's Soul Food Kitchen*, *Cheques Cashed*, *Friendly Laundrette*, boarded-up houses, the projects looming in the dark. Bruce points out where Silvio's – a once legendary blues club – stood. Howlin' Wolf and Elmore James, he says, both played there. Today it's a vacant lot where even the weeds look lank, their stubborn attempts at growth defeated by such an environment. Saturday night but few people are on the street. CCTV cameras are perched on every street corner, youths hidden beneath hoodies make uneasy eye contact with passing traffic, on the lookout for clients, cops, gangs. Yesterday's *Chicago Tribune* carried a report documenting the escalating number of drive-by shootings in The Dells' home town of Harvey. I recall how Luis Rodriguez's son is serving life for a Chi-town drive-by and ponder on the wretchedness of it all. *Snap out of it*: Rosa's Lounge looms from the gloom.

Rosa's is a narrow joint decorated with handprints, polystyrene stars and oriental carpets. On a tiny stage at the far end Billy Branch honks on a harmonica while his band lock in behind him. Branch is light-skinned, green-eyed, plays with an eloquent beauty reminiscent of the late Junior Wells. Appropriately, a poster-sized photo of Wells and Branch hangs on a wall. The audience is largely black and Bruce knows many of them. He then introduces me to a ragged-looking old white man, Bob Koester, founder of both the sprawling JazzMart record store downtown and Delmark Records, the label that inspired Alligator and unleashed Junior Wells on the planet with 1966's superb *Hoodoo Man Blues* album. Koester's recorded some of the finest blues and jazz of the last fifty years and I'm hungry to hear his stories.

'I started up the label in St Louis in 1953 to record Dixieland jazz and first cut Big Joe Williams in 1955. I came to Chicago in 1958 and went around listening to a lot of blues. Back then there was no album market for blues. OK, Chess had just done *Best of* on Muddy and Wolf but no one was recording actual albums. I cut an album on Big Joe Williams in 1961 and figured I'd sell maybe one hundred copies. Sold seven hundred straight off. Then I knew something was happening. Not too long after Paul Butterfield and Mike Bloomfield started appearing at South Side clubs. Once they got successful I never saw them there again. Charlie Musselwhite came up from the South around the same time and he could play and sing. He was a hillbilly intellectual – you'd find him in the

Cigarettes and alcohol blues: Big Joe Williams

bath with a pint of cheap wine and a book. Nice guy, Charlie, never stopped playing the blues.'

Big Joe Williams composed 'Baby Please Don't Go' and remains a seminal figure in blues lore: what was he like?

'Big Joe… he made me understand the problems of illiterate people. What the hell can you do with your free time? Joe liked women, alcohol, cowboy movies and to travel – he'd hit the road at a moment's notice, wandering America, staying with relatives. He'd get drunk and nasty, they'd throw him out, so he'd wander some more.'

And the great Junior Wells?

'Junior was a beautiful guy and *Hoodoo Man* went on to be Delmark's best ever seller. Done six figures and even today keeps selling. He told me "that record got me out of Chicago!" Junior dressed beautifully and always looked out for his friends. He had a gun he called Big Charlie and one time in Theresa's a gang attacked the bandstand so Junior pulls out Big Charlie and shoots the ceiling. People flew out of there! The gang made it clear that Junior would be killed if he returned to the street so he comes down in a borrowed limo, gets out with a shotgun and says, "Where are these motherfuckers who are looking for me?" He never had a problem after that!'

Billy Branch is shaking juice out of 'Who's Making Love' and I notice for the first time that his four-piece band is half black/half Japanese. Branch teaches blues in Chicago schools and never stops attempting to develop his music, adding Latin funk flavours on one tune, favouring an Eastern scale on another. Plunging into 'Crazy Mixed Up World' he moves offstage, blowing for a table of black women who roar approval, sweet 'n' nasty notes rolling forth, juke notes, Billy holding and caressing the music, sound seducing the women, the club, then drifting out to melt cold October air.

Next stop is Bossman Blues Centre, a bar long famous as Mister Tee's, buried deep in the West Side. As we head down Lake Street, a major thoroughfare divided by concrete pillars supporting the El train line, urban Chicago feels ominous, bleak, unforgiving. Trains rattle and shriek overhead while burnt-out cars rust outside wrecked tenements... not a neighbourhood to be stranded in. We park right out front of Bossman's and, upon entering, attract bemused glances, obviously not locals but quickly made welcome. There's no stage, the three-piece band are tucked in a corner, while Joanne Graham moves among tables, wailing soul-blues to a well-dressed, middle-aged crowd who dance and whoop and sing along. 'I can be a lady on the street and freaky in the bedroom,' sings Joanne. Women roar approval and Joanne shakes her hips, teases the fellas: *wouldn't you like some o' this?* She launches into 'Feel Like Breaking Up Somebody's Home' – a cheating standard – her voice throaty and full of threat. Her three-piece band are crisp, fluid, chewing the groove. Joanne takes a break and an older man gets up and starts singing Temptations hits, carrying the crowd. Bossman's feels like a party, everyone knowing everyone, having a fine Saturday night. Except Larry Taylor, a soul-blues singer who introduces himself and declares, 'It's all them white guys running blues now. Us African-Americans should be in control. Europeans understand but Americans don't.'

Back in the chill midnight air a train thunders above, vibrations pulsating through me. Imagine living here... a life measured in train tremors. We drive on and note a carload of white youths pulled over by police. 'They don't live here so the cops figure they're here to buy drugs,' says the driver. Onwards through the night, past comfortable bungalows, past acres of public housing, past mixed-income development housing built where tower blocks once stood, down streets as inky as the night, no street lamps, everything seemingly shut down, not even a liquor store, and at the darkest end of a dark street we find... nothing. The bar we were looking for having somehow been swallowed by the city. On to the freeway and I feel relieved as cars rush around us after so much ghetto emptiness. Deep in the South Side rests Lee's Unleaded, a bar so dark its velvet furnishings glow. Johnny Drummer is working the stage, soul-blues again the evening's currency, and we are welcomed. Mention our expedition and someone whistles and says, 'You boys are crazy – driving around the West Side!'

Whiskey flows like water and at some point Lee's is closing. I decide there's no point in returning to a youth hostel for a few hours' snatched sleep before heading to the airport. Instead, the whiskey determines that I'm going to Maxwell Street Market. Maxwell Street Market's where Honeyboy and Little Walter (and most everyone else) would gather on Sundays to busk, a truly legendary musical street. Problem is: Maxwell Street was demolished in October 1994 to make way for the expansion of the University of Illinois. Did the UOI really need the land? Doubtful. Many observers suggest the demolition was part of the ongoing gentrification of Chicago. Chicago, the most proudly working class of American cities, is being turned into a metropolis for the comfortably off. Comfort's nice but comfort's not what made this city great. Or so I try to convince myself as I shiver in a freezing El station, waiting and waiting for a train. *Comfort's nice... right.*

The brutal climate sobers me, encouraging reflection on all the territory I covered, people I met. From wise old prophets to pouting indie-rock icons and Rez shepherds, all singing their American songs, helping me make sense of this vast land little by little. Finally it comes, a ghost train, the El empty this early. When I dismount I'm lost, finding only huge university grounds, all hidden behind pastel-coloured walls. Did the area many referred to for decades as 'Jewtown' really once exist here? No trace, no legacy, just roads, walls and empty wasteland. Eventually there's someone else on the street and they listen, nod, point east. I next come across an orange-and-red building, Jim's Original, a Polish sausage stand founded by a Macedonian immigrant in 1939, which once stood on Maxwell Street. *God, I'm hungry.* Order a pork chop. It comes slathered in caramelised onions and yellow mustard, all stuffed into a bread roll, and I eat like it's the finest food known to man. Cross Dan Ryan Expressway, morning unfolding bleak and damp, a winter missive. City gristle all around, downtown's skyscrapers looming through mist, railway tracks weaving towards Union Station, an old smokestack from the days when Chicago was the planet's pre-eminent industrial city and then, well, here it is!

Nu-Maxwell Street Market runs along a street next to a huge Wal-Mart and even at this ungodly hour on Sunday it's heaving. *Maxwell Street Market...* here Jewish traders, black musicians and Gypsy fortune-tellers once gathered and interacted, collectively shaping Chicago blues. And today, well, *I can hear music*. But it's not blues, no, it's the sound of an accordion playing a Mexican ballad. Yes, a man dressed in all his finery, white Stetson proudly atop a broad brown face. He's singing something in Spanish about... *concentrate...* about missing those back home. The blues are still alive on Maxwell Street. Drop him a dollar and look around: street's crowded with blacks, whites, Koreans and many, many Mexicans. And the vendors, beyond selling fruit, vegetables, household appliances and trainers, they sell Mexican DVDs, CDs, T-shirts, religious icons and food. I purchase two $1 tacos from a makeshift canvas kitchen. *Tastes good!* Maxwell Street Market's not what it once was but the USA's not what it once was. Wind buffets the canvas kitchen, spilling napkins and salsa. Step back on to a street that's turned from Jewish to black to brown... *Albaesque...* America remains a chrysalis, worth believing in. Now I need a cup of strong coffee and two new feet. They're hurting from standing all night. From being on them constantly. Chewed at by Burning Man's toxic sands and worn out by walking, sticky and sore, in threadbare socks. What's Spanish for socks? *Los calcetines.* Notice a stand selling all kinds of clothing. 'How much?' I start to ask, then correct myself. '*Cuantos por los calcetines?*'

After five days travel, Mexican field workers ('braceros') arriving in
Sacramento, California, October 6 1942

If of No Account Go Away from Home…

Huck and Jim lit out for the territory and I aimed to do the same, riding as long and far as possible. *Too many miles, too little money*: by the time I hit Chicago, aware that this journey through American music must remain unfinished, I was finished off. One day, maybe, I'll pick up the trail and continue down through the Appalachians and into Louisiana. Or head out east, see what's worth picking over in New York, then carry on to Philadelphia and look up Lee, see whether he knows a bar equal to the Esquire. But right now, back in South London, I'm content to consume the USA via TV, radio, movies, CDs, newspapers, books, magazines, Internet sites, noting how it continues to produce the West's dominant popular culture icons. Most salient of the new icons is Barack Obama. While I doubt Obama's victory will set in motion a process of repairing the deep flaws evident in US society, Barack does offer similar qualities to those supposedly found in Las Vegas: *genuine, justifiable hope*. Americans tend to be optimists, but the Bush–Cheney administration has corroded national self-belief and the sense of the USA being the good guys. Obama's public looks to him as capable of restoring a sense of decency. This may be naive but it is understandable: after eight years ruled by men who blatantly emphasise America at its ugliest, purveyors of smooth hypocrisies and brutal cruelties – 'All', as Fat Possum's Mathew Johnson would say, 'that broke-dick stuff' – there is a sense of the USA on its knees, searching for someone to sing a redemption song.

Will Obama's presidency produce such troubadours? Doubtful. The removal of American music from its community has led to many things, including the loss of what I like to call *a sense of wonder.* Every art form has an epoch: just as no one expects contemporary Italy to produce painters and sculptors capable of matching their Renaissance forefathers, it would be naive to expect American music to recapture lost form. The practice of making and sharing music within a community is now largely removed from American life. With access to instant entertainment at fingertips, few Western citizens feel the need to create their own, and Americans are no different here from the British, Australians or Scandinavians. Which means American music becomes Fergie and Mariah Carey and endless rock and rap and hot new country automatons all hooked on the same fame fixation. Since the 1970s an increasingly corporate music industry – one embodied in MTV's employment of music as a soundtrack to shrill youth glamour – has reaped huge profits from peddling endless pap. American music, once so regional and creative and strong and proud, is reduced to just another franchise: McMusic. Alan Lomax, who recorded so much great American and

American music gets hot, 1921

European vernacular music throughout the twentieth century, wrote towards the end of his life, '*our descendants will despise us for having thrown away the best of our culture.*' Some will question whether anyone really cares. I would ask, if a nation loses its music, what else dies with it?

Making music is a gift, one allowing the marginalised, those lacking access to the dominant media, to express themselves. For some musicians music provides an escape from poverty and drudgery, yet music remains hard, demanding work, work that can cost you everything – relationships, security, health: all will be tested and possibly broken. Those I met on the road understood such, and as I write this is how things stand: Lydia Mendoza suffered a hernia, recovered, then fell and broke a leg. Her spirit faded and she died aged ninety-one on 20 December 2007. Obituaries followed in every leading US newspaper (not counting all the regional and Mexican papers) and several UK broadsheets. Alejandro healed, won a recording contract with Backporch (a subsidiary of EMI) and got his hero John Cale in to produce *The Boxing Mirror* – a static mess of an album; 2008's *Real Animal* found AE produced by Tony Visconti and delivering a solid rock album reflecting on his musical history: Alejandro's albums on the Bloodshot label remain the ones to start with.

Charles Wright attended South By Southwest 2007 and delivered a powerful polemic on the music industry fleecing African-American artists. Jimmy Castor remains in Las Vegas – sample Jimmy without consent and you will meet him in court. Mable John acted in John Sayles's nostalgic 2008 film *The Honeydripper*. Kell Robertson continues to live in his chicken coop and write fine poems (his 1989 poetry collection *Bear Crossings* was reprinted by Pathwise Press in 2007). In July 2008 he sang at a memorial to his old friend, the songwriter, hobo and activist Utah Phillips. Stax Records was relaunched by its new owners Concord Records – a Californian label wealthy from purveying smooth jazz. Nu-Stax is unlikely to engage with those who continue the Southern soul tradition yet Soulsville's success sees it sending South Memphis's musical children as far as Sydney to spread the sound. Luis

Rodriguez remains extremely busy, publishing poetry, fiction and journalism. Radmilla Cody took Navajo culture to Russia as a representative of the US government. Howie Gelb's *Sno Angel Like You*, a CD collaboration with a black gospel choir, won him the best notices of his career and found him headlining Howiefest at London's Barbican Centre – he invited a variety of friends and collaborators along for a rambling, rocking gig.

Diana Jones's stature continues to grow in the USA and Europe. Billy Joe Shaver shot Billy Bryant Coker in the face after an argument in Papa Joe's Texas Saloon in Lorena, Texas, on 31 March 2007. Coker survived and Shaver pleaded self-defence, refusing to cut down on his touring or praying. LA *narcocorrido* icon Lupillo Rivera's SUV was shot seven times while leaving a restaurant in Guadalajara, Mexico. He survived to sing about it but many others didn't, Mexico's internecine drug wars (cartels fighting over who gets to supply the US with cocaine and methamphetamine) slaughtering tens of thousands annually. Honeyboy Edwards continues to wow adoring audiences internationally and plays out in the USA most weekends. Bobby Rush entertained the troops in Iraq, his big-ass dancers driving the grunts crazy, then found himself honoured by the Mississippi legislature. Dale Watson plays out night after night, keeping the honky-tonk flame burning. Big T continues to rock Clarksdale juke joints while Wesley Jefferson fights lung cancer, the cost of medical treatment hampering this good man's recovery. Chicago blues veterans Willie Kent and Bonnie Lee both died, as did Memphis icon Isaac Hayes and Grand Ole Opry stalwart Porter Wagoner. On occasion The Dells go out to sing beautifully. Sam the Sham releases home-made country and zydeco albums, delivers a mean 'Wooly Bully' and preaches to prisoners. Speaking of preaching, St John's got a new home in the Fillmore. Cat Head and Canyon, Earwig and Fat Possum, Delmark, Arhoolie and Alligator all struggle on, times tougher than ever. Without the likes of these labels there is little chance the artists they represent will get to be heard: buy music, don't burn or illegally download it. Rising petrol prices mean the miles cost much more to cover than they once did for these musicians, many having never made much money.

'*Nothing in rambling*', sang Memphis Minnie, who won her wisdom the hard way. But she kept rambling, and so did I, our journeys separated by almost a century and more differences than one can begin to consider. We both got to sing of our rambling; she played guitar, I play an iBook. As I'm sure Minnie knew, there is some good in rambling, it just tends to cost the rambler more than they envisage. For *Roughing It*'s coda Mark Twain wrote, '*if you are of any account, stay at home and make your way by faithful diligence; but if you are of "no account", go away from home, and then you will have to work, whether you want to or not.*' Good advice to dreamers who go searching for the musical key to American highways. Time for me now to stay at home and practise faithful diligence.

Masters at work: Armstrong and Handy

Select Bibliography

Innumerable books have been written on American music and society. Those listed below are the ones I've found myself continually returning to and would recommend for anyone wishing to read further. The Internet allows for much greater access to American newspapers/magazines – Michael Ventura has his own website (www.michaelventura.org) while his regular 'Letters at 3AM' column can be read at the *Austin Chronicle* (www.austinchronicle.com), the finest weekly newspaper I can think of anywhere. Gary Younge's reports in the *Guardian* provide a black British overview of the USA. *Harper's* magazine provides superb essays on American life and politics (www.harpers.org). *No Depression* magazine is no longer printed but its website (www.nodepression.net) maintains both a huge repository of good writing on country music and up-to-date reports and reviews. The UK's *fRoots* magazine covers roots music internationally and this includes US features/reviews (www.frootsmag.com). *Living Blues* (www.livingblues.com) magazine contains the foremost reportage on US blues. For informed debate on music from across the planet check out Charlie Gillett's website (www.thesoundoftheworld.com). US magazines *Sing Out* (www.singout.org) and *Dirty Linen* (www.dirtylinen.com) and UK magazines *Maverick* (www.maverick-country.com) and *Juke Blues* (www.bluesworld.com/JukeBlues.html) all contain excellent reportage. Roger Stolle regularly updates Mississippi blues gigs and info (www.cathead.biz). Memphis journalist Andria Lisle runs a fine blog at www.memphismc.com/. French Stax fan Patrick Montier runs a wonderful online photo history of Stax (http://staxrecords.free.fr/museum). Veteran rock journalist Dave Marsh's Rockrap.com (www.rockrap.com) contains interesting reports on American music and society, while author and musician Ned Sublette covers New Orleans, Cuba and all things Latin with regular e-mail reports: people are free to join nedslist by e-mailing ned@qbadisc.com and saying 'subscribe'. Elijah Wald is one of the foremost writers anywhere on roots music – US and international – check his files at www.elijahwald.com.

Acosta, Oscar, *The Revolt of the Cockroach People*, Vintage, 1989

Alexi, Sherman, *Reservation Blues*, Minerva, 1996

Booth, Stanley, *Rythm Oil*, Jonathan Cape, 1991

Bowman, Rob, *Soulsville USA*, Books with Attitude, 1997

Brothers, Thomas, *Louis Armstrong's New Orleans*, W. W. Norton & Company, 2006

Burr, Ramiro, *Tejano and Regional Mexican Music*, Billboard Books, 1999

Davis, Mike, *City of Quartz*, Verso 1990

Davis, Mike, *Magical Urbanism*, Verso, 2000

Dawidoff, Nicholas, *In the Country of Country*, Faber and Faber, 1997

Diaz, Junot, *Drown*, Faber and Faber, 1996

Edwards, Honeyboy, *The World Don't Owe Me Nothing*, Chicago Review Press, 1997

Escott, Colin, *Tattooed on Their Tongues*, Schirmer Books, 1996

Escott, Colin, *Hank Williams: The Biography*, Little, Brown, 1996

Escott, Colin, *Good Rockin' Tonight*, St Martin's Press, 1998

Fowler, Gene and Bill Crawford, *Border Radio*, Texas Monthly Press, 1987

Grant, Richard, *Ghost Riders*, Abacus, 2003

Guralnick, Peter, *Feel Like Going Home*, Penguin, 1970

Guralnick, Peter, *Lost Highway*, Random House, 1979

Hernandez, Jaime, Locas, 2004

Hickey, Dave, *Air Guitar*, Art Issues Press, 1997

Hildebrand, Lee, *Stars of Soul and Rhythm & Blues*, Billboard Books, 1994

Hirshey, Gerri, *Nowhere to Run*, Pan, 1984

Hoskyns, Barney, *Waiting for the Sun*, Viking, 1996

Larkin, Colin, *The Virgin Encyclopedia of Blues/R&B and Soul/Dance Music and Rap*, Virgin

LaVere, Stephen, Robert Johnson: *The Complete Recordings*, Sony, 1990

Lomax, Alan, *The Land Where the Blues Began*, Minerva, 1993

Momaday, N. Scott, *The Man Made of Words*, St Martin's Griffin, 1997

Neihardt, John, *Black Elk Speaks*, University of Nebraska Press, 1988

Palmer, Robert, *Deep Blues*, Penguin, 1981

PoKemper, Marc, *Chicago Blues*, Prestel, 2000

Quinones, Sam, *True Tales from Another Mexico*, University of New
    Mexico Press, 2001

Robertson, Brian, *Little Blues Book*, Algonquin Books, 1996

Rodriguez, Gregory, *Mongrels, Vagabonds, Orphans and Vagabonds:
    Mexican Immigration and the Future of Race in America*,
    Pantheon, 2007

Rodriguez, Luis, *Always Running*, Touchstone, 1993

Rodriguez, Luis, *The Republic of East LA*, HarperCollins, 2002

Rodriguez, Luis, *My Nature is Hunger*, Curbstone Press, 2005

Rodriquez, Richard, *Days of Obligation*, Penguin, 1992

Russell, Tony, *Country Music Originals*, Oxford University Press, 2007

Santelli, Robert (ed.), *American Roots Music*, Abrams, 2001

Shaver, Billy Joe, *Honky Tonk Hero*, University of Texas Press, 2005

Stecyk, Craig and Glen Friedman, *Dogtown – The Legend of the Z-Boys*,
    Burning Flags Press, 2002

Thompson, Hunter, *The Great Shark Hunt*, Picador, 1979

Unterberger, Richie, *Music USA: The Rough Guide*, 1999

Ventura, Michael, *Shadow Dancing in the USA*, Jeremy P. Tarcher,
    Inc., 1986

Venkatesh, Sudhir, *Gang Leader for a Day*, Penguin, 2008

Vincent, Rickey, *Funk*, St Martin's Griffin, 1996

Wald, Elijah, *Narcocorrido*, Rayo, 2001

Whiteis, David, *Chicago Blues*, University of Illinois Press, 2006

Wondrich, David, *Stomp and Swerve*, Chicago Review Press, 2003

Younge, Gary, *No Place Like Home*, Picador, 1999

Zinn, Howard, *A People's History of the United States*, Perennial, 2003

Guidebooks

USA: The Rough Guide, 2004

Cummings, Joe, *Texas Handbook*, Moon, 1998

Hard work and trouble: Mexican field workers in California

Discography

More Miles Than Money (Ace). Forthcoming CD compilation of the music covered in this book. Deep blues, Southern soul, Native chants, mariachi magic and more!

As the CD market shrinks and albums are deleted (or reissued with new packaging and perhaps a new title) I've listed albums I enjoy by the artists in this book; whether or not most of them are widely available right now I'm unsure. But eBay and other Internet sites can help in the tracking down of most things – or going to the label website. For blues go to www.cathead.biz and Roger will personally search out your requests. I've compiled two budget three-CD sets for London's Union Square Records – *The Essential Guide to American Roots* and *Native American* – both of which provide the novice listener with a decent enough introduction to the respective genres. Beyond that, keep your ears open and enjoy the ride.

Louis Armstrong – *Plays WC Handy* (Columbia)
John Coltrane – *A Love Supreme* (Impulse)
Alejandro Escovedo – *Bourbonitis Blues* (Bloodshot)
Alejandro Escovedo – *More Miles Than Money: Live 1994–96* (Bloodshot)
Alejandro Escovedo – *A Man Under the Influence* (Bloodshot)
Giant Sand – *Selections circa 1990–2000* (Loose)
Giant Sand – *Chore of Enchantment* (Loose)
The Gun Club – *Fire of Love* (Slash)
Diana Jones – *My Remembrance of You* (New Song Recordings)

Diana Jones – *Better Times Will Come* (Proper)
Los Super Seven – *Los Super Seven* (RCA)
Los Super Seven – *Heard it on the X* (Telarc)
Bobby Rush – *Absolutely the Best* (Fuel)
Bobby Rush – *Live at Ground Zero* (Deep Rush)
Isidro Lopez – *15 Original Hits* (Arhoolie)
El Movimento de Hip Hop en Español Vols 1 & 2 (Univision)
Jae-P – *Esperanza* (Univision)
Lydia Mendoza – *Mal Hombre* (Arhoolie)
Lydia Mendoza – *La Alondra de la Frontera* (Arhoolie)
Lydia Mendoza – *Live* (Arhoolie)
Lydia Mendoza – *La Gloria de Texas* (Arhoolie)
Lydia Mendoza – *The Best of* (Arhoolie)
Flaco Jimenez – *Flaco's Amigos* (Arhoolie)
Brennen Leigh – *Too Thin to Plough* (Downtime)
Jimmy Castor – *16 Stabs of Funk* (RCA)
Jimmy Castor – *The Everything Man: The Best of* (Rhino)
Charles Wright – *Express Yourself: The Best of* (Warner Archives)
Charles Wright – *Love and Poetry* (Warner Brothers)

Support your local gospel record store

Charles Wright – *Doing What Comes Naturally* (ABC)
Charles Wright – *High Maintenance Woman* (M&WM)
War – *All Day Music* (United Artists)
War – *The World is a Ghetto* (United Artists)
War – *Why Can't We Be Friends* (United Artists)
War – *Live* (United Artists)
Sly & The Family Stone – *Greatest Hits* (Epic)
Luis Rodriguez – *My Name's Not Rodriquez* (Dos Manos)
The Watts Prophets – *Things Gonna Get Greater: 1969–71* (Water)
Various Artists – *Straight To Watts: The Central Avenue Scene* 1951–57
              Vols 1–3 (Ace)
NWA – *Straight Outta Compton* (Ruthless)
Goodie Mob – *Dirty South Classics* (Arista)
Chalino Sanchez – *Nieves de Enero* (Musart)
Chalino Sanchez – *Historia y Música de* (Musart)
Various Artists – *Corridos & Narcocorridos* (Fonovisa)
Various Artists – *Todo Banda* (RCA)
Various Artists – *The Soulful Women Duets of South Texas* (Arhoolie)
Various Artists – *The Roots of the Narcocorrido* (Arhoolie)
Lupillo Rivera – *Despreciado* (Univision)
Lupillo Rivera – *El Rey de las Cantinas* (Univision)
Selena – *12 Super Exitos* (EMI Latin)
Radmilla Cody – *Seed of Life* (Canyon)
R. Carlos Nakai – *Canyon Trilogy* (Canyon)
Ed Lee Natay – *Navajo Singer* (Canyon)
Billy Joe Shaver – *Old Five and Dimers Like Me* (Monument)
Billy Joe Shaver – *I'm Just an Old Chunk of Coal* (Koch)
Billy Joe Shaver – *Salt of the Earth* (Lucky Dog)
Billy Joe Shaver – *The Real Deal* (Compadre)
Billy Joe Shaver – *Everybody's Brother* (Compadre)
Gillian Welch – *Time (The Revelator)* (WEA)
Doug Sahm – *The Best of Doug Sahm & The Sir Douglas Quintet*
              (Mercury)
Various Artists – *When the Sun Goes Down: The Secret History of Rock
              & Roll vols 1–11* (Bluebird)
Various Artists – *The Legendary Story of Sun Records* (Metro Doubles)

Kell Robertson – *When You Come Down Off the Mountain* (Desp)

Dale Watson & His Lone Stars – *Live at Newland* (Me & My)

Stevie Ray Vaughan – *Texas Flood* (Epic)

Sonny Boy Williamson – *King Biscuit Time* (Arhoolie)

Sonny Boy Williamson – *The Chess Years Box Set* (Chess)

Various Artists – *Earwig Music: 20th Anniversary Collection* (Earwig)

Junior Wells – *Hoodoo Man Blues* (Delmark)

Little Walter – *Stray Dog Blues* (Rev-Ola)

Al Green – *Hi and Mighty* (Hi)

O. V. Wright – *The Complete O. V. Wright on Hi Records* (Hi)

O. V. Wright – *The Soul of O. V. Wright* (Duke)

Merle Haggard – *For the Record* (BMG)

JJ Grey & Mofro – *Country Ghetto* (Alligator)

Joe Ely – *Honky Tonk Masquerade* (MCA)

Guy Clark – *Old No. 1* (Camden)

Hazeldine – *How Bees Fly* (Glitterhouse)

Townes Van Zandt – *The Very Best of* (Union Square)

Various Artists – *Country Outlaws* (Metro)

George Jones – *The Essential* (Sony)

Hank Williams – *The Essential* (Metro)

Lefty Frizzell – *Give Me More, More, More* (Proper)

Jimmie Rodgers – *The Essential* (RCA)

Gram Parsons – *GP/Grevious Angel* (Warner)

Terry Allen – *Lubbock* (On Everything) (Sugar Hill)

Robert Johnson – *Complete Recordings* (Sony)

Various Artists – *Robert Johnson & The Old School Blues* (Metro
        Doubles)

Charley Patton – *Pony Blues* (Orbis)

Big George Brock – *Hard Times* (Cat Head)

Andre Williams – *Bait & Switch* (Norton)

Sam the Sham & The Pharaohs – *20th Century Masters* (Mercury)

Sam the Sham & The Pharaohs – *Wooly Bully/Little Red Riding Hood*
        (Collectables)

Various Artists – *The Stax Story* (Stax)

Various Artists – *It Came from Memphis* (Union Square)

Mable John – *My Name is Mable* (Motown)

Mable John – *Stay Out of the Kitchen* (Stax)
Rufus Thomas – *Walking the Dog* (Stax)
Booker T & The MGs – *The Best of* (Stax)
Otis Redding – *The Definite Collection* (Warner)
Sam & Dave – *The Best of* (Atlantic)
Isaac Hayes – *The Man! The Ultimate Isaac Hayes 1969–1977* (Stax)
Elvis Presley – *The 50 Greatest Hits* (RCA)
Ray Charles – *The Definitive* (Rhino)
Big Joe Williams – *Shake Your Boogie* (Arhoolie)
Memphis Minnie – *The Essential* (Classic Blues)
Memphis Minnie – *Queen of the Blues* (Sony)
Bessie Smith – *The Essence of* (Delta Music)
James Carr – *The Complete Goldwax Singles* (Kent)
Honeyboy Edwards – *White Windows* (Evidence)
Honeyboy Edwards – *Blues, Blues* (Document)
Honeyboy Edwards – *Roamin' & Ramblin'* (Earwig)
Bill Withers – *The Best of* (Sony)
Bill Withers – *Live at Carnegie Hall* (Columbia)
Bobby 'Blue' Bland – *The Voice: Duke Recordings 1959–69* (Ace)
Furry Lewis – *Shake 'Em On Down* (Ace)
Furry Lewis and Frank Stokes – *Beale Street Blues* (Orbis)
Furry Lewis – *Furry's Blues* (Going For A Song)
Elmore James – *The Complete Trumpet, Chief & Fire Sessions* (Snapper)
Junior Kimbrough – *All Night Long* (Fat Possum)
Junior Kimbrough – *You Better Run: The Best of* (Fat Possum)
R. L. Burnside – *Mr Wizard* (Fat Possum)
T-Model Ford – *You Better Keep Still* (Fat Possum)
Johnny Farmer – *Wrong Doers Respect Me* (Fat Possum)
Various Artists – *New Beats From The Delta* (Fat Possum)
Jelly Roll Kings – *Off Yonder Wall* (Fat Possum)
Wesley Jefferson Band – *Sings The Blues* (Rerap)
R. L. Burnside – *First Recordings* (Fat Possum)
R. L. Burnside – *A Ass Pocket of Whiskey* (Fat Possum)
T-Model Ford – *Bad Man* (Fat Possum)
Johnny Drummer – *Unleaded Blues* (Earwig)
Hound Dog Taylor – *And His Houserockers* (Alligator)

Hound Dog Taylor – *Beware of the Dog* (Alligator)
Koko Taylor – *Old School* (Alligator)
Various Artists – *35 Years of Houserockin' Music* (Alligator)
Various Artists – *Crucial Rockin' Blues 3 Pack* (Alligator)
Howlin' Wolf – *Sings the Blues* (Ace)
Howlin' Wolf – *The Genuine Article* (Chess)
Various Artists – *The Chess Story* (Chess)
Bo Diddley – *Chess Masters* (Chess)
Muddy Waters – *His Best 1947–1955* (Chess)
Chuck Berry – *His Best* (Chess)
The Dells – *The Great Ballads* (Chess)
Various Artists – *Vee-Jay Records: Chicago Hit Factory* (Charly)
The Impressions – *Definite Impressions vols 1 & 2* (Kent)
Curtis Mayfield – *Superfly* (Charly)
Curtis Mayfield – *Move On Up: The Singles Anthology 1970–90* (Castle)
Various Artists – *The Anthology of American Folk Music* (Folkways)
Willy DeVille – *Pistola* (Eagle Records)
The Ramones – *Anthology* (Sire)

Special mention: *The Arhoolie 40th Anniversary Collection 1960–2000*, five CDs celebrating Chris Strachwitz's journeys and recordings in American roots music. Essential!

Road: more miles than…

Photograph credits

Index

Bold page numbers refer to photographs; *italic* page numbers indicate entries in the Discography